Study Guide

Financial Accounting

NINTH EDITION

Belverd E. Needles, Jr.

DePaul University

Marian Powers

Northwestern University

Edward H. Julius

California Lutheran University

Houghton Mifflin Company   BOSTON   NEW YORK

Publisher: *George T. Hoffman*
Senior Sponsoring Editor: *Ann West*
Senior Development Editor: *Chere Bemelmans*
Editorial Assistant: *Brett Pasinella*
Senior Manufacturing Coordinator: *Renee Ostrowski*
Marketing Manager: *Mike Schenk*

Printed in the U.S.A.

ISBN 10: 0-618-62677-8

ISBN 13: 978-0-618-62677-9

123456789-CRS-10 09 08 07 06

Contents

To the Student V

CHAPTER 1 - Uses of Accounting Information and the Financial Statements 1

SUPPLEMENT TO CHAPTER 1 - How to Read an Annual Report 17

CHAPTER 2 - Analyzing Business Transactions 19

CHAPTER 3 - Measuring Business Income 34

SUPPLEMENT TO CHAPTER 3 - Closing Entries and the Work Sheet 54

CHAPTER 4 - Financial Reporting and Analysis 57

CHAPTER 5 - The Operating Cycle and Merchandising Operations 70

CHAPTER 6 - Inventories 88

CHAPTER 7 - Cash and Receivables 99

CHAPTER 8 - Current Liabilities and the Time Value of Money 112

CHAPTER 9 - Long-Term Assets 126

CHAPTER 10 - Long-Term Liabilities 141

CHAPTER 11 - Contributed Capital 156

CHAPTER 12 - The Corporate Income Statement and the Statement of
Stockholders' Equity 170

CHAPTER 13 - The Statement of Cash Flows 183

CHAPTER 14 - Financial Performance Measurement 193

CHAPTER 15 - Investments 204

Answers 218

To the Student

This study guide is designed to help you improve your performance in your first accounting course. It is designed for use with *Financial Accounting,* Ninth Edition, by Bel Needles and Marian Powers. The features that appear in each chapter of the guide are described below.

Reviewing the Chapter

This section provides a concise but thorough summary of the essential points covered by the learning objectives in each corresponding chapter of the text. It also provides a review of key terms and, when appropriate, a summary of journal entries introduced in the text.

Self-Test

The self-test reviews the basic concepts introduced in the text chapter and helps you prepare for examinations based on the chapter's learning objectives.

Testing Your Knowledge

This section provides matching, short-answer, true-false, and multiple-choice questions to test your understanding of the concepts and vocabulary introduced in the text.

Applying Your Knowledge

Developing the ability to work problems is an essential part of learning accounting. In this section, you can exercise your ability to apply principles introduced in the text to "real-life" accounting situations. A number of these sections are followed by crossword puzzles that test your knowledge of key terms.

Answers

The study guide concludes with answers to all the questions, exercises, and puzzles that follow the chapter review. Answers are cross-referenced to the learning objectives in the text chapters.

CHAPTER 1

Uses of Accounting Information and the Financial Statements

REVIEWING THE CHAPTER

Objective 1: Define *accounting* **and describe its role in making informed decisions, identify business goals and activities, and explain the importance of ethics in accounting.**

1. **Accounting** is an information system that measures, processes, and communicates financial information about an identifiable economic entity. It provides information that is essential for decision making.

2. A **business** is an economic unit that sells goods and services at prices that will provide an adequate return to its owners. To survive, a business must meet two goals: **profitability,** which means earning enough income to attract and hold investment capital, and **liquidity,** which means keeping sufficient cash on hand to pay debts as they fall due.

3. Businesses pursue their goals by engaging in financing, investing, and operating activities.

    a. **Financing activities** are needed to obtain funding for the business. They include such activities as obtaining capital from owners and creditors, paying a return to owners, and repaying creditors.

    b. **Investing activities** spend the funds raised. They include such activities as buying and selling land, buildings, and equipment.

    c. **Operating activities** are the everyday activities needed to run the business, such as hiring personnel; buying, producing, and selling goods or services; and paying taxes.

4. **Performance measures** indicate the extent to which managers are meeting their business goals and whether the business activities are well managed. Performance measures thus often serve as the basis for evaluating managers. Examples of performance measures include cash flow (for liquidity), net income or loss (for profitability), and the ratio of expenses to revenue (for operating activities).

5. A distinction is usually made between **management accounting,** which focuses on information for internal users, and **financial accounting,** which involves generating and communicating accounting information in the form of **financial statements** to persons outside the organization.

6. Accounting information is processed by bookkeeping, computers, and management information systems.

    a. A small but important part of accounting, **bookkeeping** is the mechanical and repetitive process of recording financial transactions and keeping financial records.

    b. The **computer** is an electronic tool that rapidly collects, organizes, and communicates vast amounts of information. The computer does not take the place of the accountant, but the accountant must understand how the computer operates because it is an integral part of the accounting information system.

    c.   A **management information system (MIS)** is an information network of all major functions (called *subsystems*) of a business. The accounting information system is the financial hub of the management information system.

7.   **Ethics** is a code of conduct that addresses the question of whether an individual's actions are right or wrong. Users depend on management and its accountants to act ethically and with good judgment in the preparation of financial statements. This responsibility is often expressed in the report of management that accompanies financial statements.

8.   The intentional preparation of misleading financial statements is called **fraudulent financial reporting.** It can result from the distortion of records, falsified transactions, or the misapplication of accounting principles. Individuals who perpetrate fraudulent financial reporting are subject to criminal and financial penalties.

9.   In 2002, Congress passed the **Sarbanes-Oxley Act** to regulate financial reporting and the accounting profession. A key provision of this legislation requires chief executives and chief financial officers of all publicly traded U.S. companies to swear (based on their knowledge) that the quarterly statements and annual reports filed with the SEC are accurate and complete.

Objective 2: Identify the users of accounting information.

10.   The users of accounting information basically fall into three groups: management, outsiders with a direct financial interest in the business, and outsiders with an indirect financial interest.

    a.   **Management** steers a business toward its goals by making the business's important decisions. Specifically, management must ensure that the business is adequately financed; that it invests in productive assets; that it develops, produces, and markets goods or services; that its employees are well managed; and that pertinent information is provided to decision makers.

    b.   Present or potential investors and creditors are considered outside users with a direct financial interest in a business. Most businesses publish financial statements that report on their profitability and financial position. Investors use these statements to assess the business's strength or weakness; creditors use them to determine the business's ability to repay debts on time.

    c.   Society as a whole, through government officials and public groups, can be viewed as an accounting information user with an indirect financial interest in a business. Such users include tax authorities, regulatory agencies, and other groups, such as labor unions, economic planners, and financial analysts. Among the regulatory agencies is the **Securities and Exchange Commission (SEC),** an agency of the federal government set up by Congress to protect the investing public by regulating the issuing, buying, and selling of stocks in the United States.

11.   Managers in government and not-for-profit organizations (hospitals, universities, professional organizations, and charities) also make extensive use of financial information.

Objective 3: Explain the importance of business transactions, money measure, and separate entity.

12.   To make an accounting measurement, the accountant must answer the following basic questions:

    a.   What is measured?

    b.   When should the measurement be made?

    c.   What value should be placed on the item being measured?

    d.   How should what is measured be classified?

13. Financial accounting uses money measures to gauge the impact of business transactions on specific business entities.

   a. **Business transactions** are economic events that affect a business's financial position. They can involve an exchange of value (e.g., a purchase, sale, payment, collection, or loan) or a "nonexchange" (e.g., the physical wear and tear on machinery, and losses due to fire or theft).

   b. The **money measure** concept states that business transactions should be measured in terms of money. Financial statements are normally prepared in terms of the monetary unit of the country in which the business resides (i.e., in dollars, euros, etc.). When transactions occur between countries that have different monetary units, the appropriate **exchange rate,** or the value of one currency in terms of another, must be used to translate amounts from one currency to another.

   c. For accounting purposes, a business is treated as a **separate entity,** distinct from its owner or owners, creditors, and customers—that is, the business owner's personal bank account, resources, debts, and financial records should be kept separate from those of the business.

Objective 4: Describe the characteristics of a corporation.

14. The three basic forms of business organization are sole proprietorships, partnerships, and corporations. Accountants recognize each form as an economic unit separate from its owners. A **sole proprietorship** is an unincorporated business owned by one person. A **partnership** is much like a sole proprietorship, except that it is owned by two or more persons. A **corporation,** unlike a sole proprietorship or partnership, is a business unit chartered by the state and legally separate from its owners (the stockholders).

15. The corporation is the dominant form of American business because it enables companies to amass large amounts of capital. The stockholders of a corporation are at risk of loss only to the extent of their investment, and ownership (evidenced by **shares of stock**) can be transferred without affecting operations. The most universal form of stock is called **common stock,** and the number of shares held by stockholders is called *outstanding stock.*

   a. Before a corporation may do business, it must apply for and obtain a charter from the state. The state must approve the **articles of incorporation** included in the application, which describe the basic purpose and structure of the proposed corporation. Included in the articles of incorporation is the number of shares of stock the corporation is authorized to issue.

   b. The stockholders elect a board of directors, which sets corporate policy and appoints managers to oversee the daily operations. Some of the board's specific duties are to declare **dividends** (distributions of earnings to stockholders), authorize contracts, determine executive salaries, and arrange major loans with banks.

   c. Management consists of the operating officers, such as the president and vice presidents. In addition to carrying out the policies set by the board and running the business, a corporation's management is responsible for issuing at least one comprehensive annual report on the corporation's financial performance.

   d. The much-publicized financial scandals of some major U.S. corporations have highlighted the importance of **corporate governance,** or the oversight of a corporation's management and ethics by its board of directors. To strengthen corporate governance, the Sarbanes-Oxley Act requires all public corporations to establish an **audit committee,** which is the front line of defense against fraudulent financial reporting. One of the audit committee's functions is to engage independent auditors and review their work.

Objective 5: Define *financial position*, and state the accounting equation.

16. Every business transaction affects a firm's financial position. **Financial position** (a company's economic resources and the claims against those resources) is shown by a balance sheet, so called because the two sides of the balance sheet must always equal each other. In a sense, the balance sheet presents two ways of viewing the same business: the left side shows the assets (resources) of the business, whereas the right side shows who provided the assets. Providers consist of owners (listed under "stockholders' equity") and creditors (represented by the listing of "liabilities"). Therefore, it is logical that the total dollar amount of assets must equal the total dollar amount of liabilities and stockholders' equity. This is the **accounting equation,** which is formally stated as

$$\text{Assets} = \text{Liabilities} + \text{Stockholders' Equity}$$

Another correct form is

$$\text{Assets} - \text{Liabilities} = \text{Stockholders' Equity}$$

17. **Assets** are the economic resources of a business that are expected to benefit future operations. Examples of assets are cash, accounts receivable, inventory, buildings, equipment, patents, and copyrights.

18. **Liabilities** are a business's present obligations to pay cash, transfer assets, or provide services to other entities in the future. Examples of such debts are money owed to banks, amounts owed to creditors for goods bought on credit, and taxes owed to the government.

19. **Stockholders' equity** (also called *shareholders' equity* and *owner's equity*) represents the claims by the owners of a corporation to the assets of the business. It equals the residual interest in assets after deducting the liabilities. Because it is equal to assets minus liabilities, stockholders' equity is said to equal the **net assets** of the business.

20. Stockholders' equity consists of contributed capital and retained earnings. **Contributed capital** represents the amount invested by the stockholders. It consists of the **par value** amount and the amount the exceeds par value, called **additional paid-in capital. Retained earnings,** on the other hand, represents the accumulation of the profits and losses of a company since its inception, less total dividends declared.

21. Retained earnings are affected not only by dividends, but also by revenues and expenses. **Revenues,** which result from selling goods or services, increase retained earnings. **Expenses,** which represent the costs of doing business, decrease retained earnings. When its revenues exceed its expenses, a company has a **net income.** When its expenses exceed its revenues, a company has a **net loss.**

Objective 6: Identify the four basic financial statements.

22. Accountants communicate information through financial statements. The four principal statements are the income statement, statement of retained earnings, balance sheet, and statement of cash flows.

23. Every financial statement has a three-line heading. The first line gives the name of the company. The second line gives the name of the statement. The third line gives the relevant dates (the date of the balance sheet or the period of time covered by the other three statements).

24. The **income statement,** whose components are revenues and expenses, is perhaps the most important financial statement. Its purpose is to measure the business's success or failure in achieving its goal of profitability.

25. The **statement of retained earnings** is a labeled calculation of the changes in retained earnings during an accounting period. Retained earnings at the beginning of the period is the first item on the statement, followed by an addition for net income or a deduction for net loss and a deduction for dividends declared. The ending retained earnings figure that results is transferred to the stockholders' equity section of the balance sheet.

26. The **balance sheet** shows the financial position of a business as of a certain date. The resources owned by the business are called assets; debts of the business are called liabilities; and the owners' financial interest in the business is called stockholders' equity. The balance sheet is also known as the *statement of financial position.*

27. The **statement of cash flows** focuses on the business's goal of liquidity and contains much information not found in the other three financial statements. It discloses the cash flows that result from the business's operating, investing, and financing activities during the accounting period. **Cash flows** refer to the business's cash inflows and cash outflows. *Net cash flows* represent the difference between these inflows and outflows. The statement of cash flows indicates the net increase or decrease in cash produced during the period.

Objective 7: Explain how generally accepted accounting principles (GAAP) relate to financial statements and the independent CPA's report, and identify the organizations that influence GAAP.

28. **Generally accepted accounting principles (GAAP)** are the set of conventions, rules, and procedures that constitute acceptable accounting practice at a given time. The set of GAAP changes continually as business conditions change and practices improve.

29. The financial statements of publicly held corporations are audited (examined) by licensed professionals, called **certified public accountants (CPAs),** to ensure the quality of the statements. CPAs must be independent of their audit clients (without financial or other ties). On completing the **audit,** the CPA reports on whether the audited statements "present fairly, in all material respects" and are "in conformity with generally accepted accounting principles."

30. The **Public Company Accounting Oversight Board (PCAOB)** is a governmental body created by the Sarbanes-Oxley Act to regulate the accounting profession.

31. The **Financial Accounting Standards Board (FASB)** is the authoritative body for development of GAAP. This group is separate from the AICPA and issues *Statements of Financial Accounting Standards.*

32. The **American Institute of Certified Public Accountants (AICPA)** is the professional association of CPAs. Its senior technical committees help influence accounting practice.

33. The **Securities and Exchange Commission (SEC)** is an agency of the federal government. It has the legal power to set and enforce accounting practices for companies whose securities are traded by the general public.

34. The **Governmental Accounting Standards Board (GASB)** was established in 1984 and is responsible for issuing accounting standards for state and local governments.

35. The **International Accounting Standards Board (IASB)** is responsible for developing worldwide accounting standards. To date, it has approved more than 40 international standards.

36. The **Internal Revenue Service (IRS)** enforces and interprets the set of rules governing the assessment and collection of federal income taxes.

37. **Ethics** is a code of conduct that applies to everyday life. **Professional ethics** is the application of a code of conduct to the practice of a profession. The accounting profession has developed such a code, intended to guide the accountant in carrying out his or her responsibilities to the public. In short, the accountant must act with integrity, objectivity, independence, and due care.

    a.   **Integrity** means that the accountant is honest, regardless of consequences.

    b.   **Objectivity** means that the accountant is impartial in performing his or her job.

    c.   **Independence** is the avoidance of all relationships that impair or appear to impair the objectivity of the accountant, such as owning stock in a company he or she is auditing.

    d.   **Due care** means carrying out one's responsibilities with competence and diligence.

38. The **Institute of Management Accountants (IMA)** has adopted a code of professional conduct for management accountants. This code emphasizes that management accountants have responsibilities in the areas of competence, confidentiality, integrity, and objectivity.

39. Ratios are used to compare a company's financial performance from one year to the next and to make comparisons among companies. One such ratio is the **return on assets,** which shows how efficiently a company is using its assets to produce income. Expressed as a percentage, it equals net income divided by average total assets.

SELF-TEST

Test your knowledge of the chapter by choosing the best answer for each item below.

1.   Which of the following is an example of an exchange of value?

     a.   Collection from a customer
     b.   Loss from fire
     c.   Accumulation of interest
     d.   Loss from theft

2.   Which of the following groups uses accounting information for planning a company's profitability and liquidity?

     a.   Management
     b.   Investors
     c.   Creditors
     d.   Economic planners

3.   Economic events that affect the financial position of a business are called

     a.   separate entities.
     b.   business transactions.
     c.   money measures.
     d.   financial actions.

4.   For legal purposes, which of the following forms of business organization is (are) treated as a separate economic unit from its owner(s)?

     a.   Sole proprietorship
     b.   Corporation
     c.   Partnership
     d.   All of the above

5. If a company has liabilities of $20,000 and stockholders' equity of $37,000, its assets are
    a. $38,000.
    b. $76,000.
    c. $57,000.
    d. $19,000.
6. Revenues and dividends appear, respectively, on the
    a. balance sheet and income statement.
    b. income statement and balance sheet.
    c. statement of retained earnings and balance sheet.
    d. income statement and statement of retained earnings.
7. Generally accepted accounting principles
    a. define accounting practice at a point in time.
    b. are similar in nature to the principles of chemistry or physics.
    c. rarely change.
    d. are not affected by changes in the ways businesses operate.
8. Independence is an important characteristic of which of the following in performing audits of financial statements?
    a. Governmental accountants
    b. Certified management accountants
    c. Certified public accountants
    d. Accounting educators
9. All of the following are considered basic management functions *except*
    a. Producing goods and services
    b. Financing the business
    c. Managing employees
    d. Electing the board of directors
10. The purchase of land would appear within which section, if any, of the statement of cash flows?
    a. Operating activities
    b. Investing activities
    c. Financing activities
    d. It would not appear in the statement of cash flows.

TESTING YOUR KNOWLEDGE

Matching*
Match each term with its definition by writing the appropriate letter in the blank.

1. _____Accounting

2. _____Bookkeeping

3. _____Computer

4. _____Management information system (MIS)

5. _____Management accounting

6. _____Financial accounting

7. _____Accounting equation

a. The value of one currency in terms of another

b. A business owned by stockholders but managed by a board of directors

c. A distribution of earnings to stockholders

d. The concept that all business transactions should be measured in terms of money

8.   _____Dividend

9.   _____Certified public accountant (CPA)

10.   _____Sole proprietorship

11.   _____Partnership

12.   _____Corporation

13.   _____Generally accepted accounting principles (GAAP)

14.   _____Balance sheet

15.   _____Income statement

16.   _____Statement of retained earnings

17.   _____Statement of cash flows

18.   _____Separate entity

19.   _____Money measure

20.   _____Asset

21.   _____Liability

22.   _____Stockholders' equity

23.   _____Contributed capital

24.   _____Sarbanes-Oxley Act

25.   _____Exchange rate

e.   The statement that shows the financial position of a company on a certain date

f.   The repetitive recordkeeping process

g.   An economic resource of a business

h.   An information system that measures, processes, and communicates economic information

i.   A business owned and managed by two or more persons

j.   An expert accountant licensed by the state

k.   Representation on the balance sheet of stockholders' investments in a corporation

l.   The statement that shows a company's profit or loss over a certain period

m.   The statement that discloses the operating, investing, and financing activities during a period

n.   The branch of accounting concerned with providing external users with financial information needed to make decisions

o.   An electronic tool that processes information with great speed

p.   The balance sheet section that represents the owners' economic interest in a company

q.   The statement that shows the changes in the Retained Earnings account during a period

r.   An information network that links a company's functions

s.   Assets = Liabilities + Stockholders' Equity

t.   The accounting concept that treats a business as distinct from its owners, creditors, and customers

u.   The guidelines that define acceptable accounting practice at a given point in time

v.   A business owned and managed by one person

w.   The branch of accounting concerned with providing managers with financial information needed to make decisions

x.   Legislation that regulates financial reporting and the accounting profession

y.   A debt of a business

Note to student: The matching quiz might be completed more efficiently by starting with the definition and searching for the corresponding term.

Short Answer

Use the lines provided to answer each item.

1.   On the lines that follow, insert the correct heading for the annual income statement of Tolan Corporation on July 31, 20xx.

_____

_____

_____

2.   Briefly distinguish between *bookkeeping* and *accounting*.

_____

_____

_____

3.   Briefly define the terms below, all of which relate to the accountant's Code of Professional Conduct.

a.   Integrity _____

_____

b.   Objectivity _____

_____

c.   Independence _____

_____

d.   Due care _____

_____

4. What three broad groups use accounting information?

    _____

    _____

    _____

5. What two objectives must be met for a company to survive?

    _____

    _____

6. List the four principal financial statements and briefly state the purpose of each.

    ### *Statement*

    a. _____

        _____

    b. _____

        _____

    c. _____

        _____

    d. _____

        _____

    ### *Purpose*

    a. _____

        _____

    b. _____

        _____

    c. _____

        _____

    d. _____

        _____

True-False

Circle T if the statement is true, and F if it is false. Provide explanations for false answers, using the blank lines below.

1. T   F   Financial position can best be determined by referring to the balance sheet.

2. T   F   The IRS is responsible for interpreting and enforcing GAAP.

3. T   F   One form of the accounting equation is Assets – Liabilities = Stockholders' Equity.

4. T   F   Revenues have the effect of increasing stockholders' equity.

5. T   F   The existence of Accounts Receivable on the balance sheet indicates that the company has one or more creditors.

6.   T   F   When expenses exceed revenues, a company has suffered a net loss.

7.   T   F   The number of outstanding shares of stock cannot exceed the number of authorized shares.

8.   T   F   Dividends appear as a deduction on the income statement.

9.   T   F   The current authoritative body dictating accounting practice is the PCAOB.

10. T   F   A sole proprietor is personally liable for all debts of the business.

11. T   F   The statement of cash flows would disclose whether or not land was purchased for cash during the period.

12. T   F   The statement of retained earnings links a company's income statement to its balance sheet.

13. T   F   The IASB is responsible for setting guidelines for state and local governments.

14. T   F   A corporation is managed directly by its stockholders.

15. T   F   Generally accepted accounting principles are not like laws of math and science; they are guidelines that define correct accounting practice at a given point in time.

16. T   F   Net assets equal assets plus liabilities.

17. T   F   The major sections of a balance sheet are assets, liabilities, stockholders' equity, revenues, and expenses.

18. T   F   A business transaction must always involve an exchange of money.

19. T   F   A management information system deals not only with accounting, but with other activities of a business as well.

20. T   F   The income statement is generally considered to be the most important financial statement.

21. T   F   A business should be understood as an entity that is separate and distinct from its owners, customers, and creditors.

22. T   F   Economic planners are accounting information users with a direct financial interest.

23. T   F   The essence of an asset is that it is expected to benefit future operations.

24. T   F   Cash flow is a measure of profitability.

25. T   F   Violation of the Sarbanes-Oxley Act can result in criminal penalties.

26. T   F   Investments by stockholders appear in the statement of cash flows as an investing activity.

27. T   F   The return on assets is expressed in terms of a dollar amount.

28. T   F   Contributed capital is comprised of the par value of stock, as well as any additional paid-in capital.

_____

_____

_____

_____

_____

_____

_____

_____

_____

_____

_____

_____

_____

_____

_____

_____

_____

_____

_____

_____

_____

_____

_____

_____

_____

_____

_____

_____

Multiple Choice

Circle the letter of the best answer.

1. Which of the following accounts would *not* appear on the balance sheet?
    a.   Utilities Expense
    b.   Common Stock
    c.   Accounts Receivable
    d.   Wages Payable

2. Companies whose stock is publicly traded must file financial statements with the

    a.   FASB.
    b.   GASB.
    c.   SEC.
    d.   AICPA.

3. One characteristic of a corporation is

    a. unlimited liability of its owners.
    b. the ease with which ownership is transferred.
    c. ownership by the board of directors.
    d. dissolution upon the death of an owner.

4. Which of the following statements does *not* involve a distinct period of time?

    a. Income statement
    b. Balance sheet
    c. Statement of cash flows
    d. Statement of retained earnings

5. The principal purpose of an audit by a CPA is to

    a. express an opinion on the fairness of a company's financial statements.
    b. detect fraud by a company's employees.
    c. prepare the company's financial statements.
    d. assure investors that the company will be profitable in the future.

6. The intentional preparation of fraudulent financial statements can result from all of the following *except*

    a. fictitious sales or order.
    b. the manipulation of inventory records.
    c. recording an expense that has been incurred but not yet paid.
    d. the misapplication of accounting principles.

7. In a partnership,

    a. profits are always divided equally among partners.
    b. management consists of the board of directors.
    c. no partner is liable for more than a proportion of the company's debts.
    d. dissolution results when any partner leaves the partnership.

8. Which of the following is *not* a major heading on a balance sheet or income statement?

    a. Accounts receivable
    b. Stockholders' equity
    c. Liabilities
    d. Revenues

9. Which of the following is *not* an activity listed on the statement of cash flows?

    a. Investing activities
    b. Funding activities
    c. Operating activities
    d. Financing activities

10. Which of the following transactions does *not* involve an exchange of value?

    a. Purchase of land on credit
    b. The sale of goods and services
    c. The wear and tear on equipment
    d. Payment on a loan

APPLYING YOUR KNOWLEDGE

Exercises

1. Atlantic Siding Corporation always publishes annual financial statements. This year, however, it has suffered a very large loss, and it therefore would like to limit access to its financial statements. Why might each of the following insist on seeing Atlantic's financial statements?

   a. Potential investors in Atlantic

   b. The Securities and Exchange Commission

   c. The bank, which is considering a loan request by Atlantic

   d. Present stockholders of Atlantic

   e. Atlantic's management

2. Indian Ridge Corporation had assets of $120,000 and liabilities of $80,000 at the beginning of the year. During the year assets decreased by $15,000 and stockholders' equity increased by $10,000. What is the amount of liabilities at year end?

   $_____

3.   Following are the accounts of Philo's TV Repair Corporation as of December 31, 20xx:

Accounts Payable	$ 1,300
Accounts Receivable	1,500
Building	8,000
Cash	?
Common Stock	14,500
Equipment	850
Land	1,000
Retained Earnings	3,000
Truck	4,500

Using this information, prepare a balance sheet *in good form*. (You must derive the dollar amount for Cash.)

Philo's TV Repair Corporation
Balance Sheet
December 31, 20xx

Assets

Liabilities

Stockholders' Equity

Crossword Puzzle: Chapter 1

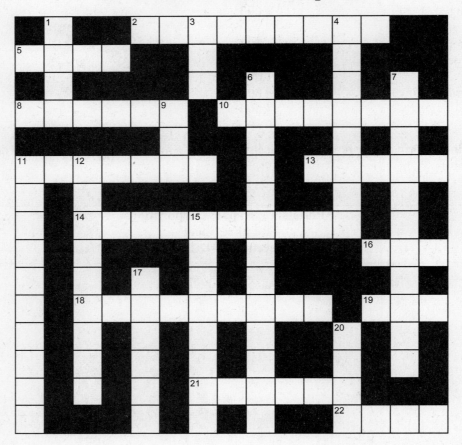

ACROSS

2 Accounting mainly for external use
5 _____ of professional conduct
8 Economic resources of a company
10 One to whom another is indebted
11 _____ sheet
13 Professional organization of accountants
14 The "A" in FASB
16 IRS's concern
18 Measure of debt-paying ability
19 Data-generating network
21 Separate _____ concept
22 _____ proprietorship

DOWN

1 See 3-Down
3 With 1-Down, income statement measure
4 Independent CPA activity
6 Measure of business performance
7 Form of business organization
9 Regulatory agency of publicly-held corporations
11 Recorder of business transactions
12 Debt of a company
15 Impartial
17 Stockholders' _____
20 Settles an account payable

SUPPLEMENT TO CHAPTER 1

How to Read an Annual Report

REVIEWING THE SUPPLEMENT

1. Most of the more than four million corporations in the United States are small, family-owned businesses. They are called *private* or *closely held* corporations because their stock is not available to the general public. *Public companies,* though fewer in number, have a far greater economic impact than their closely held counterparts. They are often owned by thousands of stockholders.

2. Public companies must register their common stock with the Securities and Exchange Commission (SEC), which regulates the issuance and trading of the stock of public companies. Public companies must also submit to their stockholders an *annual report,* which contains the financial statements and other vital information about the company's financial position and performance. Called the *10-K* when filed with the SEC, the annual report is available to the public through a number of sources (including the Internet and such electronic media as *Compact Disclosure*).

3. In addition to the financial statements, an annual report ordinarily contains a list of the corporation's directors and officers, a letter to the stockholders, a multiyear summary of financial highlights, a description of the business, management's discussion of operating results and financial conditions, notes to the financial statements, a report of management's responsibilities, the auditors' report, and supplementary information notes.

4. *Consolidated financial statements* are the combined financial statements of a company and its subsidiaries. The financial statements may present data from consecutive periods side by side for comparison. Such statements are called *comparative financial statements.*

5. The statement of earnings (income statement) should contain information regarding net income and earnings per share. A measure of a company's profitability, earnings per share equals net income divided by the weighted average number of shares of common stock outstanding.

6. The balance sheet usually contains such classifications as current assets, current liabilities, and long-term debt, which are useful in assessing a company's liquidity. In addition, the stockholders' equity section of the balance sheet normally contains information on stock issued and bought back by the corporation, on retained earnings, and on certain unusual items, such as adjustments for foreign currency translations.

7. Whereas the statement of earnings reflects a company's profitability, the consolidated statement of cash flows reflects its liquidity. It provides information about a company's cash receipts, cash payments, and operating, investing, and financing activities during an accounting period.

8. A corporation's annual report usually presents a *statement of stockholders' equity* in place of a statement of retained earnings. This statement explains the changes in each of the components of stockholders' equity.

9. A section called *notes to the financial statements* is an integral part of the financial statements. Its purpose is to help the reader interpret some of the more complex items presented in the statements.

10.   A *summary of significant accounting policies* discloses the generally accepted accounting principles used in preparing the statements. It usually appears as the first note to the statements or as a separate section just before the notes.

11.   In addition to management's discussion and analysis of operating performance, an annual report usually includes a report of management's responsibilities for the financial statements and the internal control structure.

12.   The *independent auditors' report* conveys to third parties that the financial statements were examined in accordance with generally accepted auditing standards (*scope section*) and expresses the auditors' opinion on how fairly the financial statements reflect the company's financial condition (*opinion section*). In addition, the auditors' report clarifies the nature and purpose of the audit and emphasizes management's ultimate responsibility for the financial statements.

13.   Corporations are often required to issue *interim financial statements*. These statements present financial information covering less than a year (e.g., quarterly data). Ordinarily, they are reviewed but not audited by the independent CPA.

CHAPTER 2

Analyzing Business Transactions

REVIEWING THE CHAPTER

Objective 1: Explain how the concepts of recognition, valuation, and classification apply to business transactions and why they are important factors in ethical financial reporting.

1. Before recording a business transaction, the accountant must determine three things:

    a. When the transaction should be recorded (the **recognition** issue)

    b. What value, or dollar amount, to place on the transaction (the **valuation** issue)

    c. How the components of the transaction should be categorized (the **classification** issue)

2. Normally, a sale is recognized (entered into the accounting records) when title to the merchandise passes from the supplier to the purchaser, regardless of when payment is made or received. This point of sale is referred to as the **recognition point.**

    a. Some business events, such as the hiring of a new employee, are *not* recordable transactions.

    b. Other business events, such as payment to an employee for work performed, *are* recordable transactions.

3. The **cost principle** states that business transactions should be recognized at their original cost (also called *historical cost*). In this case, **cost** refers to a transaction's **exchange price**—a verifiable measure based on the agreement between the buyer and the seller—at the point of recognition. Generally, any change in value that occurs after the original transaction is not reflected in the accounting records.

4. Ethical financial reporting requires that accountants apply generally accepted accounting principles when dealing with recognition, valuation, and classification issues. For example, when a company overstates its revenue, it has violated the guideline of recognition. When an asset is reported at an inflated dollar amount, for example, the guideline of valuation has been violated. And when expenses, for example, are treated as assets, the guideline of classification has been violated. Significant, intentional violations are viewed as fraudulent.

Objective 2: Explain the double-entry system and the usefulness of T accounts in analyzing business transactions.

5. Every business transaction is classified in a filing system consisting of accounts. An **account** is the basic storage unit for accounting data. Each asset, liability, and component of stockholders' equity, including revenues and expenses, has a separate account.

6. The **double-entry system** of accounting requires that one or more accounts be debited and one or more accounts be credited for each transaction and that total dollar amounts of debits equal total dollar amounts of credits.

7. A **T account** shows an account in its simplest form. It has three parts:

    a. A title that expresses the name of the asset, liability, or stockholders' equity account

    b. A left side, which is called the **debit** side

    c. A right side, which is called the **credit** side

8. To prepare the financial statements at the end of an accounting period, the accountant calculates the **balance** of each account (also called the *account balance*). Using T accounts to determine the account balances involves the following steps:

    a. Foot (add) the debit entries, and do the same with the credit entries.

    b. Write the **footings** (totals) for debits and credits in small numbers beneath the last entry in each column.

    c. Subtract the smaller total from the larger to determine the account balance. A debit balance exists when total debits exceed total credits; a credit balance exists when the opposite is true.

9. To determine which accounts are debited and which are credited in a given transaction, accountants use the following rules:

    a. Increases in assets are debited.

    b. Decreases in assets are credited.

    c. Increases in liabilities and stockholders' equity are credited.

    d. Decreases in liabilities and stockholders' equity are debited.

    e. Revenues, common stock, and retained earnings increase stockholders' equity, and are therefore credited.

    f. Dividends and expenses decrease stockholders' equity, and are therefore debited.

10. A normal balance for an account is determined by whether it is increased by entries to the debit side or by entries to the credit side. The side on which increases are recorded dictates the account's **normal balance.** For example, asset accounts have a normal debit balance, and liability accounts have a normal credit balance.

11. In its simplest form, stockholders' equity consists of Common Stock and Retained Earnings. The latter account is increased by revenues, but decreased by expenses and dividends. Dividends, however, are reported in the statement of retained earnings, and revenues and expenses appear in the income statement.

Objective 3: Demonstrate how the double-entry system is applied to common business transactions.

12. Analyzing and processing transactions involves five steps:

    a. Determine the effect (increase or decrease) of the transaction on assets, liabilities, and stockholders' equity accounts. Each transaction should be supported by a **source document,** such as an invoice or a check.

    b. Apply the rules of double entry.

    c. In **journal form,** enter the transaction into the journal (discussed in paragraph 21). A single transaction can have more than one debit or credit; this is called a **compound entry.**

d. Post the journal entry to the ledger (discussed in paragraph 23).

e. Prepare the trial balance (discussed in paragraphs 15 and 16).

13. To record a transaction, one must obtain a description of the transaction, determine the accounts involved in the transaction and the type of each account (e.g., asset or revenue), ascertain the accounts that are increased and decreased by the transaction, and apply the rules described in paragraph 9.

14. For example, if the transaction is described as "purchased office supplies on credit," the transaction analysis would proceed as follows: From the wording, one can determine that the accounts involved are Office Supplies and Accounts Payable. One can also determine that the transaction has increased both accounts. Applying the rules of double entry, an increase in an asset—Office Supplies, in this case—is debited, and an increase in a liability—Accounts Payable—is credited.

Objective 4: Prepare a trial balance, and describe its value and limitations.

15. Periodically, the accountant must check the equality of the total of debit and credit balances in the ledger. This is done formally by preparing a **trial balance.** The trial balance is not a published financial statement, but simply a work-paper listing of the accounts (typically in their order of appearance in the financial statements) with their end-of-period balances (debit or credit).

16. If the trial balance does not balance, one or more errors have been made in the journal, ledger, or trial balance. The accountant must locate the errors to put the trial balance in balance. It is important to realize that certain errors will not put the trial balance out of balance (such as the accidental omission of an entry); in other words, the trial balance cannot detect all errors.

a. Incorrectly recording a debit as a credit, or vice versa, will cause the trial balance to be out of balance by an amount that is evenly divisible by 2.

b. Transposing two digits (for example, writing $137 instead of $173) will cause the trial balance to be out of balance by an amount that is evenly divisible by 9.

Objective 5: Show how the timing of transactions affects cash flows and liquidity.

17. One of the most important objectives of management is to maintain an adequate level of liquidity. Stated simply, a business must be able to pay its bills on time. Thus, it is important to understand which transactions will generate immediate cash (or require immediate payment), and which will not. When a business generates revenue or incurs an expense, it hasn't necessarily experienced an accompanying cash flow. Management can help manage its cash flows by, for example, giving customers incentives for paying early and doing business with suppliers who will allow them to buy now and pay later.

Supplemental Objective 6: Define the *chart of accounts*, record transactions in the general journal, and post transactions to the ledger.

18. All of a company's accounts are contained in a book or file called the **general ledger** (or simply the *ledger*). In a manual accounting system, each account appears on a separate page. The accounts generally are in the following order: assets, liabilities, stockholders' equity, revenues, and expenses. A list of the accounts with their respective account numbers, called a **chart of accounts,** is presented at the beginning of the ledger for easy reference.

19. Although the accounts that companies use vary, some are common to most businesses. Typical asset accounts are Cash, Notes Receivable, Accounts Receivable, Prepaid Expenses, Land, Buildings, and Equipment. Typical liability accounts are Notes Payable, Accounts Payable, and Mortgage Payable.

20.   The stockholders' equity section of a corporation's balance sheet contains a Common Stock account and a Retained Earnings account. The Common Stock account represents the amount of capital invested by stockholders. The Retained Earnings account represents cumulative profits and losses, less cumulative dividends declared. Dividends are distributions of assets (generally cash) to stockholders and may be declared and paid only when sufficient retained earnings (and cash) exist.

21.   A separate account is kept for each type of revenue and expense. The exact revenue and expense accounts used vary according to the type of business and the nature of its operations. Revenues cause an increase in retained earnings, whereas expenses cause a decrease.

22.   As transactions occur, they are first recorded chronologically in a book called the **journal** (sometimes called the *book of original entry*). A separate **journal entry** is made to record each transaction; the process of recording the transactions is called **journalizing.** The **general journal** is the simplest and most flexible type of journal. Each entry in the general journal contains the date of the transaction, the account names, the dollar amounts debited and credited, an explanation of the transaction, and the account numbers if the transaction has been posted to the ledger. A line should be skipped after each journal entry.

23.   The general journal records the details of each transaction; the general ledger summarizes these details. Each day's journal entries must be transferred to the appropriate account in **ledger account form.** The process of transferring information from the journal to the general ledger, which updates each account balance, is called **posting.** The dates and amounts are posted to the ledger, and new account balances are calculated. The Post. Ref. columns are used for cross-referencing between the journal and the ledger.

24.   Ruled lines appear in financial reports before each subtotal, and a double line customarily is placed below the final amount. Although dollar signs are required in financial statements, they are omitted in journals and ledgers. On paper with ruled columns, commas and decimal points are omitted, and a dash frequently is used to designate zero cents. On unruled paper, however, commas and decimal points are used.

25.   **Cash return on assets** is a measure of liquidity that shows how much cash is generated by each dollar of assets. Expressed in terms of a percentage, it equals Net Cash Flows from Operating Activities divided by Average Total Assets.

Summary of Journal Entries Introduced in Chapter 2

A. (LO 3)   Cash   XX (amount received)
                Common Stock   XX (amount invested)
                    Owner invested cash into business

B. (LO 3)   Prepaid Rent   XX (amount paid)
                Cash   XX (amount paid)
                    Paid rent in advance

C. (LO 3)   Office Supplies   XX (purchase price)
                Accounts Payable   XX (amount paid)
                    Purchased office supplies on account

D. (LO 3)   Office Equipment   XX (purchase price)
                Cash   XX (amount paid)
                Accounts Payable   XX (amount owed)
                    Purchased office equipment, partial payment made

E. (LO 3)   Accounts Payable   XX (amount paid)
                Cash   XX (amount paid)
                    Made payment on a liability

F. (LO 3)   Cash   XX (amount received)
                Design Revenue   XX (amount earned)
                    Received payment for services rendered

G. (LO 3)   Accounts Receivable   XX (amount to be received)
                Design Revenue   XX (amount earned)
                    Rendered service, payment to be received at later time

H. (LO 3)   Cash   XX (amount received)
                Unearned Design Revenue   XX (amount received)
                    Received payment for services to be performed

I. (LO 3)   Cash   XX (amount received)
                Accounts Receivable   XX (amount received)
                    Received payment from credit customer

J. (LO 3)   Wages Expense   XX (amount incurred)
                Cash   XX (amount paid)
                    Recorded and paid wages for the period

K. (LO 3)   Utilities Expense   XX (amount incurred)
                Accounts Payable   XX (amount owed)
                    Recorded utility bill, payment to be made at later time

L. (LO 3)   Dividends   XX (amount declared)
                Cash   XX (amount paid)
                    Declared and paid a cash dividend

SELF-TEST

Test your knowledge of the chapter by choosing the best answer for each item below.

1. Deciding whether to record a sale when the order for services is received or when the services are performed is an example of a

    a. recognition issue.
    b. valuation issue.
    c. classification issue.
    d. communication issue.

2. Which of the following statements is *true*?

    a. The chart of accounts usually is presented in alphabetical order.
    b. The general ledger contains all the accounts found in the chart of accounts.
    c. The general journal contains a list of the chart of accounts.
    d. Companies generally use the same chart of accounts.

3. Which of the following is a liability account?

    a. Accounts Receivable
    b. Dividends
    c. Rent Expense
    d. Unearned Design Revenue

4. An entry on the left side of an account is called

    a. the balance.
    b. a debit.
    c. a credit.
    d. a footing.

5. Although debits increase assets, they also

    a. decrease assets.
    b. increase stockholders' equity.
    c. increase expenses.
    d. increase liabilities.

6. Payment for a two-year insurance policy is recorded as a debit to

    a. Prepaid Insurance.
    b. Insurance Expense.
    c. Cash.
    d. Accounts Payable.

7. An agreement to spend $250 a month on advertising beginning next month requires

    a. a debit to Advertising Expense.
    b. a debit to Prepaid Advertising.
    c. no entry.
    d. a credit to Cash.

8. Transactions initially are recorded in the

    a. trial balance.
    b. T account.
    c. journal.
    d. ledger.

9.   In posting from the general journal to the general ledger, the page number on which the transaction is recorded appears in the
   a.   Post. Ref. column of the general ledger.
   b.   Item column of the general ledger.
   c.   Post. Ref. column of the general journal.
   d.   Description column of the general journal.

10.   To test that the total of debits and the total of credits are equal, the accountant periodically prepares a
   a.   trial balance.
   b.   T account.
   c.   general journal.
   d.   ledger.

TESTING YOUR KNOWLEDGE

Matching*

Match each term with its definition by writing the appropriate letter in the blank.

1.   _____ Cost

2.   _____ Account

3.   _____ Debit

4.   _____ Credit

5.   _____ Account balance

6.   _____ Ledger

7.   _____ Posting

8.   _____ Prepaid expenses

9.   _____ Accounts Payable

10.   _____ Common Stock

11.   _____ Retained Earnings

12.   _____ Double-entry system

13.   _____ Trial balance

14.   _____ Journal

15.   _____ Post. Ref.

16.   _____ Footing

17.   _____ Compound entry

18.   _____ Unearned revenue

19.   _____ Dividends

20.   _____ Valuation

a.   Transferring data from the journal to the ledger

b.   The amount in an account at a given point in time

c.   An entry with more than one debit or credit

d.   A distribution of assets to stockholders resulting from profitable operations

e.   A procedure for checking the equality of debits and credits in the ledger accounts

f.   A record that occupies a page of the ledger

g.   The book or file that contains all of a company's accounts

h.   Adding a column of numbers

i.   A liability that arises when payment for services is received before the services are rendered

j.   Cumulative profits and losses, less dividends declared

k.   A transaction's exchange price at the point of recognition

l.   Amounts owed to others for purchases on credit

m.   Amounts paid in advance for goods or services

n.   The assignment of a dollar amount to a business transaction

o.   The right side of a ledger account

p.   The column in the journal and ledger that provides for cross-referencing between the two

q.   The left side of a ledger account

r.   The method that requires both a debit and a credit for each transaction

s.   The account that represents stockholders' claims arising from their investments in the corporation

t.   The book of original entry

Note to student: The matching quiz might be completed more efficiently by starting with the definition and searching for the corresponding term.

Short Answer

Use the lines provided to answer each item.

1. Indicate which part of the following journal entry applies to each measurement issue listed below:

    Apr. 22   Cash   200
               Accounts Receivable   200
                   Collected on account

    a.   Recognition issue _____

    b.   Valuation issue _____

    c.   Classification issue _____

2. Describe a transaction that would require a debit to one asset and a credit to another asset.

    _____

    _____

    _____

3. Describe a transaction that would require a debit to a liability and a credit to an asset.

    _____

    _____

    _____

4. List the three account types that affect the Retained Earnings account.

_____

_____

_____

5. List the three account types that are credited when increased.

_____

_____

_____

True-False

Circle T if the statement is true, and F if it is false. Provide explanations for the false answers, using the blank lines at the end of the section.

1.   T   F   A sale should be recorded on the date of payment.

2.   T   F   When a company hires a new employee, a recordable event has occurred.

3.   T   F   There must be a separate account for each asset, liability, and component of stockholders' equity, including revenues and expenses.

4.   T   F   The credit side of an account implies something favorable.

5.   T   F   In a given account, total debits must always equal total credits.

6.   T   F   Management can determine cash on hand quickly by referring to the journal.

7.   T   F   The number and titles of accounts vary among businesses.

8.   T   F   Promissory Note is an example of an account title.

9.   T   F   Prepaid expenses are classified as assets.

10.   T   F   Increases in liabilities are indicated with a credit.

11.   T   F   In all journal entries, at least one account must be increased and another decreased.

12.   T   F   Journal entries are made after transactions have been entered into the ledger accounts.

13.   T   F   In the journal, all liabilities and stockholders' equity accounts must be indented.

14.   T   F   A debit is never indented in the journal.

15.   T   F   Posting is the process of transferring data from the journal to the ledger.

16.   T   F   The Post. Ref. column of a journal or ledger should be empty until posting is done.

17.   T   F   In practice, the ledger account form is used, but the T account form is not.

18.   T   F   The chart of accounts is a table of contents to the general journal.

19.   T   F   Unearned Revenue has a normal debit balance.

20.   T   F   Retained Earnings is a cash account that appears in the assets section of the balance sheet.

21.   T   F   The Common Stock account represents stockholders' investments but not corporate profits and losses.

22. T F   Errors caused by transposing digits are evenly divisible by 9.

23. T F   Dollar signs are omitted from journals and ledgers.

24. T F   The ordering of a product from a supplier is considered a recordable transaction.

_____

_____

_____

_____

_____

_____

_____

_____

_____

_____

_____

_____

_____

_____

_____

_____

_____

_____

_____

_____

Multiple Choice

Circle the letter of the best answer.

1. Which of the following is *not* an issue when a business transaction is initially recorded?
    a. Classification
    b. Recognition
    c. Summarization
    d. Valuation

2. When a liability is paid, which of the following is *true*?

    a. Total assets and total liabilities remain the same.
    b. Total assets and total stockholders' equity decrease.
    c. Total assets decrease by the same amount that total liabilities increase.
    d. Total assets and total liabilities decrease.

3. Which of the following is *not* true about a proper journal entry?

    a. All credits are indented.
    b. All debits are listed before the first credit.
    c. An explanation is needed for each debit and each credit.
    d. A debit is never indented, even if a liability or stockholders' equity account is involved.

4. What is the last step taken when posting an entry?

    a. The explanation must be transferred.
    b. The account number is placed in the reference column of the ledger.
    c. The journal page number is placed in the reference column of the journal.
    d. The account number is placed in the reference column of the journal.

5. Which of the following errors would the preparation of a trial balance probably disclose (i.e., would cause it to be out of balance)?

    a. Failure to post an entire journal entry
    b. Failure to record an entire journal entry
    c. Failure to post part of a journal entry
    d. Posting the debit of a journal entry as a credit and the credit as a debit

6. When cash is received in payment of an account receivable, which of the following is *true*?

    a. Total assets increase.
    b. Total assets remain the same.
    c. Total assets decrease.
    d. Total assets and total stockholders' equity increase.

7. Which of the following is increased by debits?

    a. Dividends
    b. Unearned Revenue
    c. Wages Payable
    d. Retained Earnings

8. Which of the following accounts is an asset?

    a. Unearned Revenue
    b. Prepaid Rent
    c. Retained Earnings
    d. Service Revenue

9. Which of the following accounts is a liability?

    a. Interest Payable
    b. Interest Expense
    c. Interest Receivable
    d. Interest Income

10. A company that rents an office (i.e., is a lessee or tenant) would never have an entry for which of the following accounts?

    a. Prepaid Rent
    b. Unearned Rent
    c. Rent Payable
    d. Rent Expense

11. Which of the following accounts has a normal credit balance?

  a.   Prepaid Insurance
  b.   Dividends
  c.   Fees Earned
  d.   Advertising Expense

12. Payment of a $40 debt was accidentally debited and posted to Accounts Receivable instead of to Accounts Payable. As a result of the error, the trial balance will

  a.   be out of balance by $20.
  b.   be out of balance by $40.
  c.   be out of balance by $80.
  d.   not be out of balance.

APPLYING YOUR KNOWLEDGE

Exercises

1.   Following are all the transactions of Newton Printing, Inc., for the month of May. For each transaction, provide *in good form* the journal entries required. Use the journal provided.

  May   2   Newton Printing, Inc., was granted a charter by the state, and investors contributed $28,000 in exchange for 2,800 shares of $10 par value common stock.

  3   Rented part of a building for $300 per month. Paid three months' rent in advance.

  5   Purchased a small printing press for $10,000 and photographic equipment for $3,000 from Irvine Press, Inc. Paid $2,000 and agreed to pay the remainder as soon as possible.

  8   Hired a pressman, agreeing to pay him $200 per week.

  9   Received $1,200 from Raymond's Department Store as an advance for brochures to be printed.

  11   Purchased paper for $800 from Pacific Paper Company. Issued Pacific a promissory note for the entire amount.

  14   Completed a $500 printing job for Sunrise Shoes. Sunrise paid for half, agreeing to pay the remainder next week.

  14   Paid the pressman his weekly salary.

  15   Paid Irvine Press, Inc., $1,000 of the amount owed for the May 5 transaction.

  18   Received the remainder due from Sunrise Shoes for the May 14 transaction.

  20   A $700 cash dividend was declared and paid by the corporation.

  24   Received an electric bill of $45. Payment will be made in a few days.

  30   Paid the electric bill.

General Journal				
Date		**Description**	**Debit**	**Credit**
May	2	Cash	28,000	
		Common Stock		28,000
		Recorded the stockholders' original investment		

2. Following are three balance sheet accounts, selected at random, from Moger Company's ledger. For each, determine the account balance.

Accounts Receivable			Accounts Payable	
2,000	500		1,200	4,200
750			2,000	

Cash	
15,000	1,000
4,000	1,200
	2,200

a. Accounts Receivable has a (debit or credit) balance of $_____.

b. Accounts Payable has a (debit or credit) balance of $_____.

c. Cash has a (debit or credit) balance of $_____.

3. Two journal entries are presented below. Post both entries to the ledger accounts provided. Only those accounts needed have been provided, and previous postings have been omitted to simplify the exercise.

General Journal					Page 4
Date		**Description**	**Post. Ref.**	**Debit**	**Credit**
May	3	Cash		2,000	
		Revenue from Services			2,000
		Received payment from Rodgers Company for services			
	5	Accounts Payable		700	
		Cash			700
		Paid Grant Supply Company for supplies purchased on March 31 on credit			

Cash						Account No. 11	
			Post. Ref.			**Balance**	
Date		**Item**		**Debit**	**Credit**	**Debit**	**Credit**

Accounts Payable   Account No. 21

Date		Item	Post. Ref.	Debit	Credit	Balance Debit	Credit

Revenue from Services   Account No. 41

Date		Item	Post. Ref.	Debit	Credit	Balance Debit	Credit

CHAPTER 3

Measuring Business Income

REVIEWING THE CHAPTER

Objective 1: Define *net income*, and explain the assumptions underlying income measurement and their ethical application.

1. Profitability, or earning a **profit,** is a very important business goal. A major function of accounting is to measure and report a company's success or failure in achieving this goal. This is done by preparing an income statement that shows a company's net income or net loss.

2. **Net income** is the net increase in stockholders' equity that results from a company's operations. Net income occurs when revenues exceed expenses; if expenses exceed revenues, a **net loss** occurs.

3. **Revenues** are increases in stockholders' equity resulting from selling goods, rendering services, or performing other business activities. The revenue for a given period equals the total cash and receivables from goods and services provided to customers during the period.

4. Also described as the *cost of doing business* or as *expired costs,* **expenses** are the costs of goods and services used in the process of earning revenues. Examples of expenses are Telephone Expense, Wages Expense, and Advertising Expense. Expenses decrease stockholders' equity; typically, they also result in an outflow of cash or the incurrence of a liability.

5. Not all increases in stockholders' equity arise from revenues, nor are all decreases in stockholders' equity produced by expenses. Similarly, not all increases in cash arise from revenues, nor are all decreases in cash produced by expenses.

6. The issue of **continuity** addresses the difficulty of allocating certain expenses and revenues over several accounting periods when one cannot be certain how long the business will survive. Unless there is evidence to the contrary (such as an imminent bankruptcy), the accountant assumes the business is a **going concern**—that it will continue to operate indefinitely.

7. Another difficult accounting issue is the assignment of revenues and expenses to a short period of time. In dealing with this problem, accountants make an assumption about **periodicity**—that is, that while measurements of net income for short periods are approximate, they are nonetheless useful estimates of a firm's profitability for the period. To make the comparison of income statements easier, the accounting periods are usually of equal length. Accounting periods of less than a year are called *interim periods*. A **fiscal year** covers any 12-month accounting period. Many firms use a fiscal year that corresponds to a calendar year, the 12-month period ending on December 31. Others choose a fiscal year that corresponds to their yearly business cycles and ends during a slow season. The financial statements should always show the time period covered.

8. The matching issue has to do with the difficulty of assigning revenues and expenses to a period of time. When the **cash basis of accounting** is used, revenues are recorded when cash is received, and expenses are recorded when cash is paid. This method can lead to distortion of net income for the period. According to the **matching rule,** revenues must be recorded in the period(s) in which they are actually earned, and expenses must be recorded in the period(s) in which they are used to produce revenue; the timing of cash payments or receipts is irrelevant.

9. The manipulation of revenues and expenses to achieve a specific outcome (such as meeting a previously announced goal) is called **earnings management.** Though not illegal, earnings management is considered unethical when the judgments and estimates involved produce misleading financial statements.

Objective 2: Define *accrual accounting*, and explain how it is accomplished.

10. **Accrual accounting** consists of all the techniques accountants use to apply the matching rule. Three broad ways of accomplishing accrual accounting are by recognizing revenues when earned (**revenue recognition**), recording expenses when incurred, and adjusting accounts at the end of the period.

    a. Revenue should be recognized when (1) a purchase or sale arrangement exists, (2) goods have been delivered or services rendered, (3) the selling price is fixed or determinable, and (4) collectibility is reasonably assured.

    b. Expenses should be recognized when (1) a purchase or sale arrangement exists, (2) goods have been received or services rendered, (3) the price is fixed or determinable, and (4) the product or service has been used to generate revenue.

    c. Some transactions invariably span the cutoff point for an accounting period. Thus, to ensure that the financial statements for the period are accurate, some accounts will need to be adjusted.

11. Because adjusting entries do not affect cash flow, they never involve the Cash account. They are, however, necessary for the accurate measurement of performance. Good judgment must be exercised when preparing adjusting entries to avoid the abuse and misrepresentation that can occur.

Objective 3: Identify four situations that require adjusting entries, and illustrate typical adjusting entries.

12. When revenues or expenses apply to more than one accounting period, **adjusting entries** are made at the end of the accounting period. The adjusting entries allocate to the current period the revenues and expenses that apply to the period, deferring the remainder to future periods. A **deferral** is the postponement of the recognition of an expense already paid or of a revenue already received. An **accrual** is the recognition of an expense or revenue that has arisen but that has not yet been recorded.

13. Adjusting entries have several purposes:

    a. To allocate recorded costs (such as the cost of machinery or prepaid rent) between two or more accounting periods

    b. To recognize unrecorded expenses (such as wages earned by employees after the last pay period in an accounting period)

    c. To allocate recorded, but unearned revenues (such as commissions collected in advance) between two or more accounting periods

    d. To recognize unrecorded, but earned revenues (such as commissions that have been earned but that have not yet been billed to customers)

14. When an expenditure will benefit more than just the current period, the initial debit is usually made to an asset account rather than to an expense account. At the end of the accounting period, the amount that has been used is transferred from the asset account to an expense account.

    a. **Prepaid expenses** (expenses paid in advance, such as Prepaid Rent and Prepaid Insurance) are debited when paid.

b.   An account for supplies, such as Office Supplies, is debited when supplies are purchased. At the end of the accounting period, an inventory of supplies is taken. The difference between supplies available for use during the period and ending inventory is the amount used during the period.

c.   A long-lived asset, such as a building, a truck, or a piece of office equipment, is debited to an asset account when purchased. At the end of each accounting period, an adjusting entry must be made to transfer a part of the original cost of each long-lived asset to an expense account. The amount transferred or allocated is called **depreciation** or *depreciation expense*.

d.   **Accumulated depreciation accounts** are contra-asset accounts used to total the past depreciation expense on specific long-term assets. A **contra account** is so called because on the balance sheet it is subtracted from its associated asset account. Thus, proper balance sheet presentation will show the original cost, the accumulated depreciation as of the balance sheet date, and the undepreciated balance (called **carrying value** or *book value*). In making the adjusting entry to record depreciation, Depreciation Expense is debited and Accumulated Depreciation is credited.

15.   At the end of an accounting period, a company usually has incurred some expenses that have not been recorded in the accounts because it has not yet paid cash for them. An adjusting entry must be made to record these **accrued expenses.** For example, interest on a loan may have accrued during the current period but does not have to be paid until the next period. A debit to Interest Expense and a credit to Interest Payable will record the current period's interest for the income statement. A similar adjusting entry would be made for estimated income taxes and accrued wages. These entries will also record the liabilities for the balance sheet.

16.   A company sometimes receives payment for goods or services before delivering them. In such cases, a liability account, such as **Unearned Revenues** or Unearned Fees, appears on the balance sheet. This account is a liability because it represents revenues that must be earned by providing the product or service that is still owed.

17.   Often at the end of an accounting period, revenues have been earned but not recorded because no payment has been received. An adjusting entry must be made to record these **accrued (unrecorded) revenues.** For example, interest that has been earned might not be received until the next period. A debit must be made to Interest Receivable and a credit to Interest Income to record the current period's interest for the income statement. This entry will also record the asset for the balance sheet.

Objective 4: Prepare financial statements from an adjusted trial balance.

18.   After all the adjusting entries have been posted to the ledger accounts and new account balances have been computed, an **adjusted trial balance** should be prepared. Once in balance, the adjusted trial balance is used to prepare the financial statements (income statement first, then the statement of retained earnings and the balance sheet). The adjusted trial balance will probably contain some accounts, such as Depreciation Expense, that were not in the trial balance.

Objective 5: Describe the accounting cycle, and explain the purposes of closing entries.

19.   The steps in the **accounting cycle** are as follows:

a.   *Analyze* business transactions from the source documents.

b.   *Record* the transactions in the general journal.

c.   *Post* the entries to the ledger and prepare a trial balance.

d.   *Adjust* the accounts at the end of the period and prepare an adjusted trial balance.

e.   *Prepare* the financial statements.

f.   *Close* the accounts, and prepare a post-closing trial balance.

20. Balance sheet accounts are called **permanent** (or *real*) **accounts** because their balances can extend past the end of an accounting period. They are *not* set back to zero.

21. Revenue and expense accounts are called **temporary** (or *nominal*) **accounts** because of their transient nature. Their purpose is to record revenues and expenses during a particular accounting period. At the end of that period, their totals are transferred to Retained Earnings (via the Income Summary account), leaving zero balances to begin the next accounting period.

22. **Closing entries** serve two purposes. First, they set the stage for the new accounting period by clearing revenue and expense accounts of their balances. (So that the Retained Earnings account can be updated, the Dividends account is also closed.) Second, they summarize the period's revenues and expenses by transferring the balance of revenue and expense accounts to the **Income Summary** account. The Income Summary account exists only during the closing process and does not appear in the financial statements. Closing entries must be made at the end of each period for which financial statements are prepared (such as at the end of each quarter).

23. There are four closing entries:

a.   Temporary credit balances are closed. This is accomplished with a compound entry that debits each revenue account for the amount required to give it a zero balance and credits Income Summary for the revenue total.

b.   Temporary debit balances are closed. This is accomplished with a compound entry that credits each expense for the amount required to give it a zero balance and debits Income Summary for the expense total.

c.   The Income Summary account is closed. After the revenue and expense accounts have been closed, the Income Summary account will have either a debit balance or a credit balance (or a zero balance, in the unlikely event of neither a profit nor a loss). If a credit balance exists (i.e., when a profit has been realized), then Income Summary must be debited for the amount required to give it a zero balance, and Retained Earnings is credited for the same amount. The reverse is done when Income Summary has a debit balance.

d.   The Dividends account is closed. This is accomplished by crediting Dividends for the amount required to give it a zero balance, and debiting Retained Earnings for the same amount. Note that the Income Summary account is not involved in this closing entry.

24. The closing process prepares the books for the next accounting period. After closing, the revenue, expense, and Dividends accounts (temporary accounts) have zero balances. The updated Retained Earnings account reflects dividend declarations and net income or net loss for the period just ended. The balance sheet accounts (permanent accounts) show the correct balances, which are carried forward to the next period.

25. After the closing entries are posted to the ledger, a **post-closing trial balance** must be prepared to verify again the equality of the debits and credits in the ledger. Only balance sheet accounts appear in the post-closing trial balance because all income statement accounts, as well as the Dividends account, have zero balances at this point.

Objective 6: Use accrual-based information to analyze cash flows.

26. Liquidity, or the ability to pay debts when they fall due, relies on cash flow (not accrual-based) information. Fortunately, cash receipts and payments can be calculated from accrual-based net income and related information. The general rule for determining cash flow received from any revenue or paid for any expense (except depreciation) is to determine the potential cash payments or cash receipts and then deduct the amount not paid or received. For example, cash payments for rent would equal rent expense plus an increase (or minus a decrease) in prepaid rent occurring during the period.

27. Management can assess how well it is controlling its expenses in relation to its revenues by computing the **profit margin.** Expressed in terms of a percentage, the profit margin is obtained by dividing net income by net revenues.

Cash Flow Formulas (LO 6)

Type of Account	Potential Payment or Receipt Not Paid or Received	Result
Prepaid Expense	Ending Balance + Expense for the Period − Beginning Balance =	Cash Payments for Expenses
Unearned Revenue	Ending Balance + Revenue for the Period − Beginning Balance =	Cash Receipts from Revenues
Accrued Payable	Beginning Balance + Expense for the Period − Ending Balance =	Cash Payments for Expenses
Accrued Receivable	Beginning Balance + Revenue for the Period − Ending Balance =	Cash Receipts from Revenues

Summary of Journal Entries Introduced in Chapter 3 and Its Supplement

A.   (LO 3)   Rent Expense   XX (amount expired)
              Prepaid Rent   XX (amount expired)
                    Prepaid rent expired

B.   (LO 3)   Office Supplies Expense   XX (amount consumed)
              Office Supplies   XX (amount consumed)
                    Consumed office supplies

C.   (LO 3)   Depreciation Expense, Office Equipment   XX (amount allocated to period)
              Accumulated Depreciation, Office Equipment   XX (amount allocated to period)
                    Recorded depreciation expense

D.   (LO 3)   Wages Expense   XX (amount incurred)
              Wages Payable   XX (amount to be paid)
                    Accrued unrecorded expense

E.   (LO 3)   Income Taxes Expense   XX (amount estimated)
              Income Taxes Payable   XX (amount estimated to be paid)
                    Accrued estimated income taxes

F.   (LO 3)   Unearned Design Revenue   XX (amount earned)
              Design Revenue   XX (amount earned)
                    Performed services paid for in advance

G.   (LO 4)   Accounts Receivable   XX (amount due)
              Design Revenue   XX (amount earned)
                    Accrued unrecorded revenue

H.   (LO 5)   Design Revenue   XX (current credit balance)
              Income Summary   XX (sum of revenue amounts)
                    To close the revenue account

I.   (LO 5)   Income Summary   XX (sum of expense amounts)
              Wages Expense   XX (current debit balance)
              Utilities Expense   XX (current debit balance)
              Rent Expense   XX (current debit balance)
              Office Supplies Expense   XX (current debit balance)
              Depreciation Expense—Office Equipment   XX (current debit balance)
              Income Tax Expense   XX (current debit balance)
                    To close the expense accounts

J.   (LO 5)   Income Summary   XX (current credit balance)
              Retained Earnings   XX (net income amount)
                    To close the Income Summary account

K.   (LO 5)   Retained Earnings   XX (dividends for period)
              Dividends   XX (dividends for period)
                    To close the Dividends account

SELF-TEST

Test your knowledge of the chapter by choosing the best answer for each item below.

1. One important purpose of closing entries is to
   a. update the accounting records.
   b. set balance sheet accounts to zero to begin the next accounting period.
   c. set nominal accounts to zero to begin the next accounting period.
   d. close the Retained Earnings account.
2. Which of the following accounts is an example of a contra account?
   a. Unearned Art Fees
   b. Depreciation Expense, Buildings
   c. Prepaid Insurance
   d. Accumulated Depreciation, Office Equipment
3. A business can choose a fiscal year that corresponds to
   a. the calendar year.
   b. the yearly business cycle.
   c. any 12-month period.
   d. any of the above.
4. Which of the following sequences of actions describes the sequence of the accounting cycle?
   a. Post, record, analyze, prepare, close, adjust
   b. Analyze, record, post, adjust, prepare, close
   c. Prepare, record, post, adjust, analyze, close
   d. Enter, record, close, prepare, adjust, analyze
5. Accrual accounting involves all of the following *except*
   a. recording all revenues when cash is received.
   b. applying the matching rule.
   c. recognizing expenses when incurred.
   d. adjusting the accounts.
6. Which of the following items is an example of a deferral?
   a. Accruing year-end wages
   b. Recognizing revenues earned but not yet recorded
   c. Recording prepaid rent
   d. Recognizing expenses incurred but not yet recorded
7. Prepaid Insurance shows an ending balance of $2,300. During the period, insurance in the amount of $1,200 expired. The adjusting entry would include a debit to
   a. Prepaid Insurance for $1,200.
   b. Insurance Expense for $1,200.
   c. Prepaid Insurance for $1,100.
   d. Insurance Expense for $1,100.
8. The post-closing trial balance contains
   a. nominal accounts only.
   b. real accounts only.
   c. both nominal and real accounts.
   d. neither nominal nor real accounts.

9. On July 31, Wages Payable had a balance of $500; on August 31, the balance was $300. Wages Expense for August was $2,600. How much cash was expended for wages during August?

    a. $2,100
    b. $2,400
    c. $2,600
    d. $2,800

10. Which of the following accounts would probably be contained in an adjusted trial balance but *not* in a trial balance?

    a. Unearned Revenue
    b. Cash
    c. Depreciation Expense
    d. Utilities Expense

TESTING YOUR KNOWLEDGE

Matching*

Match each term with its definition by writing the appropriate letter in the blank.

1. _____Net income
2. _____Revenue
3. _____Expense
4. _____Expired cost
5. _____Unexpired cost
6. _____Deferral
7. _____Accrual
8. _____Fiscal year
9. _____Going concern assumption
10. _____Cash basis of accounting
11. _____Accrual accounting
12. _____Matching rule
13. _____Adjusting entry
14. _____Depreciation expense
15. _____Accumulated Depreciation
16. _____Contra account
17. _____Unearned revenue
18. _____Adjusted trial balance
19. _____Closing entries
20. _____Temporary (nominal) accounts

a. Accounts that begin each period with zero balances

b. A liability that represents an obligation to deliver goods or render services

c. The portion of an asset that has not yet been charged as an expense

d. The means of transferring net income or net loss (and dividends) to the Retained Earnings account

e. The assumption that a business will continue indefinitely

f. Recognition of an expense or revenue that has arisen but has not yet been recorded

g. A second check that the accounts are still in balance

h. The requirement that an expense be recognized in the same period as the revenue produced by that expense

i. The amount by which revenues exceed expenses

j. An account that is subtracted from an associated account

21. _____Permanent (real) accounts

22. _____Income Summary

23. _____Accounting cycle

k.   Accounts whose balances extend beyond the end of an accounting period

l.   An example of a contra account to assets

m.   An end-of-period allocation of revenues and expenses relevant to that period

n.   An account used only during the closing process

o.   Recording revenues and expenses when payment is received or made

p.   The expired cost of a plant asset for a particular accounting period

q.   Postponement of the recognition of an expense already paid or of a revenue already received

r.   A descriptive term for expense

s.   All the techniques used to apply the matching rule

t.   Any 12-month accounting period used by a business

u.   The sequence of steps following in the accounting system

v.   A general term for the price of goods sold or services rendered

w.   A cost of doing business

Note to student: The matching quiz might be completed more efficiently by starting with the definition and searching for the corresponding term.

Short Answer

Use the lines provided to answer each item.

1.   Briefly summarize the four situations that require adjusting entries.

_____

_____

_____

_____

2.   Briefly explain the matching rule.

_____

_____

_____

_____

3.   Define *depreciation*.

_____

_____

_____

4.   Distinguish between prepaid expenses and unearned revenues.

_____

_____

_____

_____

5.   List the four conditions that must exist before revenue should be recognized.

_____

_____

_____

_____

6.   What four accounts or types of accounts are closed each accounting period?

_____

_____

_____

_____

True-False

Circle T if the statement is true, and F if it is false. Provide explanations for the false answers, using the blank lines at the end of the section.

1.   T   F   Failure to record accrued wages will result in the understatement of total liabilities.

2.   T   F   Expired costs are listed on the income statement.

3.   T   F   A calendar year refers to any 12-month period.

4.   T   F   The cash basis of accounting often violates the matching rule.

5.   T   F   In accrual accounting, the timing of cash receipts and payments is vital for recording revenues and expenses.

6.   T   F   Adjusting entries must be made immediately after the financial statements have been prepared.

7.   T   F   Prepaid insurance represents an unexpired cost.

8.   T   F   Office Supplies Expense must be debited for the amount of office supplies in ending inventory.

9.   T   F   Because Accumulated Depreciation appears in the asset section of the balance sheet, it has a debit balance.

10.   T   F   As a machine is depreciated, its accumulated depreciation increases and its carrying value decreases.

11.   T   F   On the income statement, Unearned Revenues is a contra account to Earned Revenues.

12.   T   F   When an expense has accrued but payment has not yet been made, a debit is needed for the expense and a credit for Prepaid Expenses.

13.   T   F   The adjusted trial balance is the same as the trial balance, except that it has been modified by adjusting entries.

14.   T   F   If one has made a sale for which the money has not yet been received, one would debit Unearned Revenues and credit Earned Revenues.

15.   T   F   The original cost of a long-lived asset should appear on the balance sheet even after depreciation expense has been recorded.

16.   T   F   Adjusting entries help make financial statements comparable from one period to the next.

17.   T   F   The Income Summary account appears in the statement of retained earnings.

18.   T   F   Closing entries convert real and nominal accounts to zero balances.

19.   T   F   When revenue accounts are closed, the Income Summary account is credited.

20.   T   F   The Dividends account is closed to the Income Summary account.

21.   T   F   When the Income Summary account is closed, it always requires a debit.

22.   T   F   The post-closing trial balance would contain the Dividends account.

23.   T   F   Retained Earnings is an example of a permanent (real) account.

24.   T   F   Earnings management refers to the efforts put forth to produce as accurate a net income figure as possible.

_____

_____

_____

_____

_____

_____

_____

_____

_____

_____
_____
_____
_____
_____
_____
_____
_____
_____
_____
_____
_____
_____
_____

Multiple Choice

1. Which of the following is an unlikely description for an adjusting entry?
   a. Debit to an expense, credit to an asset
   b. Debit to a liability, credit to a revenue
   c. Debit to an expense, credit to a revenue
   d. Debit to an expense, credit to a liability

2. Depreciation does *not* apply to
   a. trucks.
   b. office supplies.
   c. machinery.
   d. office equipment.

3. An account called Unearned Fees is used when
   a. recorded costs have to be divided among periods.
   b. recorded unearned revenues have to be divided among periods.
   c. unrecorded (accrued) expenses have to be recorded.
   d. unrecorded (accrued) revenues have to be recorded.

4. Depreciation best applies to
   a. recorded costs that must be divided among periods.
   b. recorded revenues that must be divided among periods.
   c. unrecorded expenses that must be recorded.
   d. unrecorded revenues that must be recorded.

5. Which of the following would *not* appear in an adjusted trial balance?
   a. Prepaid Insurance
   b. Unearned Management Fees
   c. Net income
   d. Depreciation Expense

6.   Which of the following accounts would appear in a post-closing trial balance?

   a.   Interest Income
   b.   Income Summary
   c.   Retained Earnings
   d.   Dividends

7.   The periodicity assumption recognizes that

   a.   net income over a short period of time is a useful estimate.
   b.   a business is likely to continue indefinitely.
   c.   revenues should be recorded in the period earned.
   d.   a 12-month accounting period must be used.

8.   Prepaid Rent is a(n)

   a.   expense.
   b.   contra account.
   c.   liability.
   d.   asset.

9.   An adjusting entry would *never* include

   a.   Unearned Revenue.
   b.   Cash.
   c.   Prepaid Advertising.
   d.   Wages Expense.

10.   Which of the following accounts would probably contain a lower dollar amount on the adjusted trial balance than on the trial balance?

   a.   Accounts Receivable
   b.   Dividends
   c.   Office Supplies
   d.   Rent Expense

11.   Which of the following accounts would *not* be involved in closing entries?

   a.   Unearned Commissions
   b.   Retained Earnings
   c.   Telephone Expense
   d.   Dividends

12.   When a net loss has occurred,

   a.   all expense accounts are closed with debits.
   b.   the Income Summary account is closed with a credit.
   c.   the Dividends account is closed with a debit.
   d.   all revenue accounts are closed with credits.

13.   Which of the following is *not* an objective of closing entries?

   a.   To transfer net income or loss to Retained Earnings
   b.   To produce zero balances in all nominal accounts
   c.   To update the revenue and expense accounts
   d.   To be able to begin measuring income or loss for the following period

14.   Which of the following is an example of a temporary account?

   a.   Prepaid Rent
   b.   Unearned Revenues
   c.   Wages Expense
   d.   Accumulated Depreciation, Building

15. A corporation began the accounting period with $50,000 in retained earnings and ended it with $75,000 in retained earnings. During the period it declared $30,000 in dividends. What was the corporation's net income or loss for the period?

    a. $55,000 net income
    b. $30,000 net loss
    c. $5,000 net loss
    d. $5,000 net income

APPLYING YOUR KNOWLEDGE

Exercises

1. On January 1, 20x3, Newton Transit Company began its business by buying a new bus for $24,000. One-eighth of the cost of the bus is depreciated each year. Complete *in good form* the company's partial balance sheet as of December 31, 20x5.

Newton Transit Company
Partial Balance Sheet
December 31, 20x5

Assets

Cash	$5,000
Accounts receivable	3,000
Company vehicles	
Total assets	$_____

---

2. For each set of facts that follows, provide the dollar amount that would be recorded.

    a. The cost of supplies at the beginning of the period was $510. During the period, supplies that cost $800 were purchased. At the end of the period, supplies that cost $340 remained. Supplies Expense should be recorded for $_____.

    b. The company signed a lease and paid $14,000 on July 1, 20x4, to cover the four-year period beginning July 1, 20x4. How much Rent Expense should it record on December 31, 20x4? $_____

    c. The company was paid $600 in advance for services to be performed. By the end of the period, only one-fourth of the sum had been earned. How much of the $600 will appear as Unearned Revenues on the balance sheet? $_____

3. In the next column is the trial balance of Milman Company, which operates on a calendar year. The facts that follow are based on this trial balance. For each item, make the adjusting entry in the journal provided.

Milman Company
Trial Balance
December 31, 20xx

	Debit	Credit
Cash	$ 77,300	
Notes Receivable	5,000	
Accounts Receivable	9,000	
Prepaid Advertising	8,000	
Prepaid Insurance	1,000	
Supplies	500	
Buildings	90,000	
Accumulated Depreciation, Buildings		$ 6,000
Notes Payable		1,500
Unearned Revenues		2,800
Common Stock		100,000
Dividends	13,000	
Revenues from Services		212,000
Wages Expense	118,500	
	$322,300	$322,300

a. Cost of supplies on hand, based on a physical count, is $375.

b. Wages of $2,500 for the five-day workweek ($500 per day) are recorded and paid every Friday. December 31 falls on a Thursday.

c. During 20x6, services amounting to $600 were rendered for customers who had paid for the services in advance.

d. Five percent of the cost of buildings is taken as depreciation for 20x6.

e. One-quarter of the prepaid advertising expired during 20x6.

f. All the insurance shown on the trial balance was paid for on July 1, 20x6, and covers the two-year period beginning July 1, 20x6.

g. Work performed for customers that has not been billed or recorded amounts to $2,200.

h. Accrued income tax expense for the year amounts to $21,700. This amount will be paid early next year.

General Journal

Date	Description	Debit	Credit

4. At the beginning and end of the year, Elton Industries had the following account balances on its balance sheet:

	Jan. 1	Dec. 31
Wages payable	$1,200	$3,700
Unearned revenue	500	900
Prepaid rent	2,400	1,800

    The company's income statement for the year showed these figures:

Wages expense	$ 8,700
Revenue from services	35,000
Rent expense	3,600

    a. Cash paid for wages during the year = $_____.

    b. Cash received for revenue during the year = $_____.

    c. Cash paid for rent during the year = $_____.

5. Following are the accounts of an adjusted trial balance for the month of July. In the journal provided below, make the necessary closing entries. All accounts have normal balances.

Accounts Payable	$ 1,000
Accounts Receivable	2,000
Cash	13,500
Common Stock	10,000
Dividends	2,500
Rent Expense	500
Retained Earnings	3,000
Revenue from Services	4,700
Telephone Expense	50
Utilities Expense	150

General Journal			
Date	Description	Debit	Credit

6.   Using the information from Exercise 5, complete the following statement of retained earnings.

Frank's Fix-It Services, Inc.
Statement of Retained Earnings
For the Month Ended July 31, 20xx

Crossword Puzzle: Chapters 2 and 3

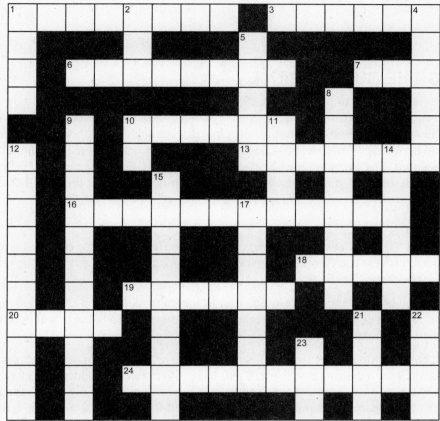

ACROSS

1 Cash _____ assets (2 words)
3 _____ Summary
6 Postponement of a revenue or expense
7 Cost of doing business (abbr.)
10 Where accounts are kept
13 Source of revenue
16 Test of debit and credit equality (2 words)
18 Left side of an account
19 Monthly or yearly compensation
20 See 23-Down
24 _____ bookkeeping (hyph.)

DOWN

1 Prepaid _____
2 Post. _____ column
4 Become an expense
5 Hourly or piecework-rate compensation
8 Income statement item
9 _____ trial balance (hyph.)
10 Journal column title (same as 2-Down)
11 Opposite of nominal
12 Record a transaction
14 Right side of an account
15 Assignment of a dollar amount to
17 Recognition of unrecorded revenues or expenses
21 Written promise to pay
22 Remits
23 With 20-Across, possible bottom-line result

SUPPLEMENT TO CHAPTER 3

Closing Entries and the Work Sheet

REVIEWING THE SUPPLEMENT

1. Closing entries serve two purposes. First, they set the stage for the new accounting period by clearing revenue and expense accounts of their balances. (So that the Retained Earnings account can be updated, the Dividends account also is closed.) Second, they summarize the period's revenues and expenses by transferring the balance of revenue and expense accounts to the Income Summary account. The Income Summary account exists only during the closing process and does not appear in the financial statements. Closing entries must be made at the end of each period for which financial statements are prepared (such as at the end of each quarter).

2. There are four closing entries:

    a. Temporary credit balances are closed. This is accomplished with a compound entry that debits each revenue account for the amount required to give it a zero balance and credits Income Summary for the revenue total.

    b. Temporary debit balances are closed. This is accomplished with a compound entry that credits each expense for the amount required to give it a zero balance and debits Income Summary for the expense total.

    c. The Income Summary account is closed. After the revenue and expense accounts have been closed, the Income Summary account will have either a debit balance or a credit balance. If a credit balance exists, then Income Summary must be debited for the amount required to give it a zero balance, and Retained Earnings is credited for the same amount. The reverse is done when Income Summary has a debit balance.

    d. The Dividends account is closed. This is accomplished by crediting Dividends for the amount required to give it a zero balance, and debiting Retained Earnings for the same amount. Note that the Income Summary account is not involved in this closing entry.

3. The closing process prepares the books for the next accounting period. After closing, the revenue, expense, and Dividends accounts (temporary accounts) have zero balances. The updated Retained Earnings account reflects dividend declarations and net income or net loss for the period just ended. The balance sheet accounts (permanent accounts) show the correct balances, which are carried forward to the next period.

4. After the closing entries are posted to the ledger, a post-closing trial balance must be prepared to verify again the equality of the debits and credits in the ledger. Only balance sheet accounts appear in the post-closing trial balance because all income statement accounts, as well as the Dividends account, have zero balances at this point.

5. Accountants use working papers to help organize their work and to provide evidence in support of the financial statements. The *work sheet* is one such working paper. The work sheet decreases the chance of overlooking an adjustment, acts as a check on the arithmetical accuracy of the accounts, and helps in preparing the financial statements. The work sheet is never published and is rarely seen by management. It is a useful tool for the accountant.

6. The five steps in the preparation of the work sheet are as follows:

    a. Enter and total the account balances in the Trial Balance columns.

    b. Enter and total the adjustments in the Adjustments columns. (A letter identifies the debit and credit for each adjustment and can act as a key to a brief explanation at the bottom of the work sheet.)

    c. Enter and total (by means of crossfooting, or adding and subtracting horizontally) the adjusted account balances in the Adjusted Trial Balance columns.

    d. Extend (transfer) the account balances from the Adjusted Trial Balance columns to the Income Statement columns or the Balance Sheet columns (depending on which type of account is involved).

    e. Total the Income Statement columns and the Balance Sheet columns. Enter the net income or net loss in both pairs of columns (one will be a debit and the other a credit) as a balancing figure, and recompute the column totals.

7. Once the work sheet is completed, the accountant can use it to (a) record the adjusting entries, (b) record the closing entries, thus preparing the records for the new period, and (c) prepare the financial statements.

    a. Formal adjusting entries must be recorded in the journal and posted to the ledger so that the account balances on the books will agree with those on the financial statements. This is easily accomplished by referring to the Adjustments columns (and footnoted explanations) of the work sheet.

    b. Formal closing entries are entered into the journal and posted to the ledger, as explained above. This is accomplished by referring to the work sheet's Income Statement columns (for the revenue and expense accounts) and its Balance Sheet columns (for the Dividends account).

    c. The income statement may be prepared from the information found in the work sheet's Income Statement columns. Calculations of the change in retained earnings for the period are shown on the statement of retained earnings. Information for this calculation may be found in the Balance Sheet columns of the work sheet (beginning retained earnings, net income, and dividends). The balance sheet may be prepared from information found in the work sheet's Balance Sheet columns and in the statement of retained earnings.

APPLYING YOUR KNOWLEDGE

Exercise

1. The items below provide the information needed to make adjustments for Mike's Maintenance, Inc., as of December 31, 20xx. Complete the entire work sheet on the next page using this information. Remember to use key letters for each adjustment.

    a. On December 31, there is $200 of unexpired rent on the storage garage.

    b. Depreciation taken on the lawn equipment during the period amounts to $1,500.

    c. An inventory of lawn supplies shows $100 remaining on December 31.

    d. Accrued wages on December 31 amount to $280.

    e. Grass-cutting fees earned but as yet uncollected amount to $50.

f.   Of the $300 landscaping fees paid for in advance, $120 had been earned by December 31.

g.   Accrued income tax expense for the year amounts to $1,570. This amount will be paid early next year.

Mike's Maintenance, Inc.
Work Sheet
For the Year Ended December 31, 20xx

Account Name	Trial Balance Debit	Trial Balance Credit	Adjustments Debit	Adjustments Credit	Adjusted Trial Balance Debit	Adjusted Trial Balance Credit	Income Statement Debit	Income Statement Credit	Balance Sheet Debit	Balance Sheet Credit
Cash	2,560									
Accounts Receivable	880									
Prepaid Rent	750									
Lawn Supplies	250									
Lawn Equipment	10,000									
Accum. Deprec., Lawn Equipment		2,000								
Accounts Payable		630								
Unearned Landscaping Fees		300								
Common Stock		5,000								
Retained Earnings		1,000								
Dividends	6,050									
Grass-Cutting Fees Earned		15,000								
Wages Expense	3,300									
Gasoline Expense	140									
	23,930	23,930								
Rent Expense										
Depreciation Expense, Lawn Equipment										
Lawn Supplies Expense										
Wages Payable										
Landscaping Fees Earned										
Income Taxes Expense										
Income Taxes Payable										
Net Income										

CHAPTER 4

Financial Reporting and Analysis

REVIEWING THE CHAPTER

Objective 1: Describe the objectives and qualitative characteristics of financial reporting and the ethical responsibilities that financial reporting involves.

1. Financial reporting should fulfill three objectives. It should (a) furnish information that is useful in making investment and credit decisions; (b) provide information that is useful in assessing cash flow prospects; and (c) provide information about business resources, claims to those resources, and changes in them. General-purpose external financial statements are the main way of presenting financial information to interested parties. They consist of the balance sheet, income statement, statement of retained earnings, and statement of cash flows.

2. Accounting attempts to provide decision makers with information that displays certain **qualitative characteristics,** or standards:

    a. **Understandability** is the qualitative characteristic of information that enables users to perceive its meaning. To understand accounting information, users must be familiar with the **accounting conventions**, or rules of thumb (discussed in paragraph 4 below), used in preparing financial statements.

    b. Another very important standard is **usefulness.** To be useful, information must be relevant and reliable. **Relevance** means that the information is capable of influencing a decision. Relevant information provides feedback, helps in making predictions, and is timely. **Reliability** means that the information accurately reflects what it is meant to reflect, that it is credible, verifiable, and neutral.

3. Users of financial statements depend on a company's management and accountants to act ethically and with good judgment in preparing the statements. One product of the Sarbanes-Oxley Act is that the chief executive officers and chief financial officers of all publicly traded companies are required to certify that, to their knowledge, the quarterly and annual statements filed with the SEC are accurate and complete. Persons found guilty of fraudulent financial reporting are subject to criminal penalties and fines.

Objective 2: Define and describe the conventions of *comparability* **and** *consistency, materiality, conservatism, full disclosure,* **and** *cost-benefit.*

4. To help users interpret financial information, accountants depend on five conventions: comparability and consistency, materiality, conservatism, full disclosure, and cost-benefit.

    a. **Comparability** means that the information allows the decision maker to compare the same company over two or more accounting periods or different companies over the same accounting period. **Consistency** means that a particular accounting procedure, once adopted, should not be changed unless management decides it is no longer appropriate or unless reporting requirements change. The nature of the change, its justification, and its dollar effect on income should be disclosed in the notes to the financial statements.

    b. The **materiality** convention states that strict accounting practice need not be applied to items of insignificant dollar value. Whether a dollar amount is material is a matter of professional judgment, which should be exercised in a fair and accurate manner.

c.   The **conservatism** convention states that an accountant who has a choice of acceptable accounting procedures should choose the one that is least likely to overstate assets and income. Applying the lower-of-cost-or-market rule to inventory valuation is an example of conservatism.

d.   The **full disclosure** convention states that financial statements and their notes should contain all information relevant to the user's understanding of the statements. Disclosures of such matters as accounting changes, commitments and contingencies, and the accounting methods used are essential for a full understanding of the financial statements.

e.   The **cost-benefit** convention states that the benefits to be gained from providing accounting information should be greater than the cost of providing it.

Objective 3: Identify and describe the basic components of a classified balance sheet.

5.   **Classified financial statements** are general-purpose external financial statements that divide assets, liabilities, stockholders' equity, revenues, and expenses into subcategories, thus making the statements more useful to readers.

6.   On a classified balance sheet, assets are usually divided into four categories: (a) current assets; (b) investments; (c) property, plant, and equipment; and (d) intangible assets. These categories are listed in order of liquidity (the ease with which an asset can be turned into cash). For simplicity, some companies group investments, intangible assets, and miscellaneous assets (i.e., all assets other than current assets and property, plant, and equipment) into a category called **other assets.**

a.   **Current assets** are cash and other assets (including short-term investments, accounts and notes receivable, prepaid expenses, supplies, and inventory) that are expected to be turned into cash or used up within a company's normal operating cycle or within one year, whichever is longer. (From here on, we will call this time period the *current period.*) A company's **normal operating cycle** is the average time between the purchase of inventory and the collection of cash from the sale of that inventory.

b.   Examples of **investments** include stocks and bonds held for long-term investment, land held for future use, plant or equipment that is not used in the business, special funds, and large permanent investments made to control another company.

c.   **Property, plant, and equipment** (also called *operating assets, fixed assets, tangible assets, long-lived assets,* or *plant assets*) include things like land, buildings, delivery equipment, machinery, office equipment, and natural resources. Most of the assets in this category are subject to depreciation.

d.   **Intangible assets** have no physical substance. Their value stems from the rights or privileges they extend to their owners. Examples are patents, copyrights, goodwill, franchises, and trademarks.

7.   Liabilities on a classified balance sheet are divided into current and long-term liabilities.

a.   **Current liabilities** are obligations for which payment (or performance) is due in the current period. They are paid from current assets or by incurring new short-term liabilities. Examples of current liabilities include notes payable, accounts payable, taxes payable, and unearned revenues.

b.   **Long-term liabilities** are debts that are due after the current period or that will be paid from noncurrent assets. Examples are mortgages payable, long-term notes payable, bonds payable, employee pension obligations, and long-term leases.

8. The owners' equity section of a classified balance sheet is usually called owner's equity, partners' equity, or stockholders' equity. The exact name depends on whether the business is a sole proprietorship, a partnership, or a corporation. Other descriptive terms for owners' equity are *proprietorship, capital,* and the somewhat misleading term *net worth.*

    a. The stockholders' equity section consists of contributed capital and retained earnings. Contributed capital is generally shown on the balance sheet at the par value of the issued stock and at the amount contributed in excess of par value (called *additional paid-in capital*).

    b. In a sole proprietorship or partnership, the owner's or partners' equity section shows the name of the owner or owners. Each is followed by the word *capital* and the dollar amount of investment as of the balance sheet date.

Objective 4: Describe the features of multistep and single-step classified income statements.

9. An income statement may be presented in either multistep or single-step form. The **multistep income statement** is the more detailed of the two, containing several subtractions and subtotals. A merchandiser's or manufacturer's multistep income statement has separate sections for cost of goods sold, operating expenses, and other (nonoperating) revenues and expenses.

10. On the multistep income statements of **merchandising companies** (which buy and sell finished products) and **manufacturing companies** (which make and sell products), net income is computed as follows:

    Net sales
    − Cost of goods sold
    = Gross margin
    − Operating expenses
    = Income from operations
    ± Other revenues and expenses
    = Income before income taxes
    − Income taxes
    = Net income

    The multistep income statement of a service company is prepared in the same manner, except that it does not contain cost of goods sold or gross margin.

    a. **Net sales** (also called *sales*) consist of gross proceeds from the sale of merchandise (**gross sales**) less **sales returns and allowances** and sales discounts.

    b. **Cost of goods sold** (also called *cost of sales*) is the amount a merchandising company paid for the goods that it sold during an accounting period. If, for example, a merchandiser sells for $100 a radio that cost the firm $70, then revenue from the sale is $100, cost of goods sold is $70, and **gross margin** (also called *gross profit*) is $30. The gross margin helps pay for **operating expenses** (all expenses other than cost of goods sold and income taxes). What is left after subtracting operating expenses represents **income from operations** (also called *operating income*).

   c.   Operating expenses consist of selling expenses and general and administrative expenses. Selling expenses are directly related to the sales effort. They include advertising expenses, salespeople's salaries, sales office expenses, and freight out expense. General and administrative expenses are not directly related to the manufacturing or sales effort. Examples are general office expenses and executive salaries.

   d.   **Other revenues and expenses** are nonoperating items, such as interest income and interest expense. They are added to or deducted from income from operations to arrive at **income before income taxes.** A corporate income statement should disclose **income taxes** (also called *provision for income taxes*) separately from the other expenses. (The income statement of a sole proprietorship or a partnership does not contain a provision for income taxes because these forms of business are not taxable units.)

   e.   **Net income,** often described as the *bottom line,* is what remains of the gross margin after operating expenses have been deducted, other revenues and expenses have been added or deducted, and income taxes have been deducted.

   f.   **Earnings per share,** also called *net income per share,* equals net income divided by the average number of shares of common stock outstanding. It usually appears below net income in the income statement and is a measure of the company's profitability.

11.   In the **single-step income statement**, the revenues section lists all revenues, including other revenues, and the costs and expenses section lists all expenses (except for income taxes), including cost of goods sold and other expenses. A condensed version of the single-step form (omitting earnings per share data) is as follows:

	Revenues	X
−	Costs and expenses	X
=	Income before income taxes	X
−	Income taxes	X
=	Net income	X

Objective 5: Use classified financial statements to evaluate liquidity and profitability.

12.   Classified financial statements help the reader evaluate liquidity and profitability.

13.   Liquidity refers to a company's ability to pay its bills when they are due and to meet unexpected needs for cash. Two measures of liquidity are working capital and the current ratio.

   a.   **Working capital** equals current assets minus current liabilities. It is the amount of current assets that would remain if all current debts were paid.

   b.   The **current ratio** equals current assets divided by current liabilities. A current ratio of 1:1, for example, shows that current assets are just enough to pay current liabilities. A 2:1 current ratio is considered more satisfactory.

14.   Profitability refers to a company's ability to earn a satisfactory income. To draw conclusions about profitability, one must compare profitability measures with past performance and industry averages. Five common measures of profitability are profit margin, asset turnover, return on assets, debt to equity ratio, and return on equity.

   a.   The **profit margin** equals net income divided by net sales. A 12.5 percent profit margin, for example, means that 12½ cents have been earned on each dollar of sales.

   b.   **Asset turnover** equals net sales divided by average total assets. This measure shows how efficiently a company is using its assets to produce sales.

c.   **Return on assets** equals net income divided by average total assets. This measure shows how efficiently a company is using its assets to produce income.

d.   The **debt to equity ratio** measures the proportion of a business financed by creditors relative to the proportion financed by owners. It equals total liabilities divided by stockholders' equity. A debt to equity ratio of 1.0, for instance, indicates equal financing by creditors and owners.

e.   **Return on equity** shows what percentage was earned on the owners' investment. It equals net income divided by average stockholders' equity.

SELF-TEST

Test your knowledge of the chapter by choosing the best answer for each item below.

1.   Trademarks are categorized as
   a.   a current asset.
   b.   revenue.
   c.   an intangible asset.
   d.   property, plant, and equipment.

2.   Accounting information is said to be useful if it is
   a.   timely and unbiased.
   b.   relevant and reliable.
   c.   relevant and certain.
   d.   accurate and faithful.

3.   To expense an item that would normally be recorded as an asset because the item is insignificant in amount is an application of
   a.   materiality.
   b.   conservatism.
   c.   full disclosure.
   d.   comparability.

4.   Which of the following would *not* appear in an income statement?
   a.   Cost of goods sold
   b.   Gross margin
   c.   Additional paid-in capital
   d.   Sales returns and allowances

5.   Land held for future use is classified as
   a.   a current asset.
   b.   an investment.
   c.   property, plant, and equipment.
   d.   an intangible asset.

6.   The current portion of long-term debt is normally classified as
   a.   current assets.
   b.   current liabilities.
   c.   long-term liabilities.
   d.   stockholders' equity.

7.   A disadvantage of the single-step income statement is that
   a.   gross margin is not disclosed separately.
   b.   other revenues and expenses are separated from operating items.
   c.   interest expense is not disclosed.
   d.   the cost of goods sold cannot be determined.

8. Net income is a component in determining each of the following ratios *except*
   a. profit margin.
   b. return on assets.
   c. debt to equity ratio.
   d. return on equity.

9. Asset turnover is expressed
   a. in dollars.
   b. as a percentage.
   c. in times.
   d. in days.

10. Which of the following terms does *not* mean the same as the others listed?
    a. Net worth
    b. Owners' equity
    c. Proprietorship
    d. Working capital

TESTING YOUR KNOWLEDGE

Matching*

Match each term with its definition by writing the appropriate letter in the blank.

1. _____ Qualitative characteristics
2. _____ Relevance
3. _____ Reliability
4. _____ Manufacturing company
5. _____ Classified financial statements
6. _____ Liquidity
7. _____ Current assets
8. _____ Property, plant, and equipment
9. _____ Intangible assets
10. _____ Current liabilities
11. _____ Long-term liabilities
12. _____ Other revenues and expenses
13. _____ Earnings per share
14. _____ Merchandising company
15. _____ Cost of goods sold
16. _____ Gross margin
17. _____ Operating expenses

a. A buyer and seller of goods in finished form
b. Long-lived tangible assets
c. A business that both produces and sells products
d. All expenses except for cost of goods sold and income taxes
e. Guidelines for evaluating the quality of accounting reports
f. Short-term obligations
g. Financial reports broken down into subcategories
h. What a merchandising company paid for the goods it sold during an accounting period
i. Net income divided by the average number of shares of common stock outstanding
j. The income statement section that contains nonoperating items
k. The subcategory of assets that are expected to be turned into cash or used up within one year or the normal operating cycle, whichever is longer

l.   The standard that accounting information should be related to the user's needs

m.   Long-term assets that lack physical substance and that grant rights or privileges to their owner

n.   Net sales minus cost of goods sold

o.   Obligations due after the current period

p.   The standard that accounting information should accurately reflect what it is meant to represent

q.   The ability to pay bills when due and to meet unexpected needs for cash

Note to student: The matching quiz might be completed more efficiently by starting with the definition and searching for the corresponding term.

Short Answer

Use the lines provided to answer each item.

1.   List the three forms of business organization and each one's name for the owners' equity section of the balance sheet.

Business Organization

_____

_____

_____

Name for Equity Section

_____

_____

_____

2.   What does each of the following ratios show about a company's profitability?

Profit margin

_____

_____

Asset turnover

_____

_____

Return on assets

_____

_____

_____

Return on equity

_____

_____

_____

Debt to equity ratio

_____

_____

_____

3.   Define each of the following liquidity ratios:

Working capital

_____

_____

Current ratio

_____

_____

4.   Explain the basic point of each of the following conventions:

Consistency and comparability

_____

_____

_____

Materiality

_____

_____

_____

Cost-benefit

_____

_____

_____

Conservatism

_____

_____

_____

Full disclosure

_____

_____

_____

True-False

Circle T if the statement is true, and F if it is false. Provide explanations for the false answers, using the blank lines below.

1. T F   Receivables are not current assets if collection requires more than one year.

2. T F   The lower-of-cost-or-market method of accounting for inventory is an application of conservatism.

3. T F   Gross margin minus operating expenses equals income from operations.

4. T F   Operating expenses consist of selling expenses and cost of goods sold.

5. T F   Accounting information is relevant if it could make a difference to the outcome of a decision.

6. T F   The net income figure is needed to compute the profit margin, the return on assets, and the return on equity.

7. T F   The investments section of a balance sheet includes both short- and long-term investments in stock.

8. T F   One meaning of the term _profitability_ is the ease with which an asset can be converted to cash.

9. T F   A company's normal operating cycle cannot be less than one year.

10. T F   Net worth refers to the current value of a company's assets.

11. T F   Other revenues and expenses is a separate category in a multistep income statement.

12. T F   Multistep and single-step income statements for the same company in the same accounting period will produce the same net income figures.

13. T F   Working capital equals current assets plus current liabilities.

14. T F   The debt to equity ratio shows the proportion of a company financed by the owners.

15. T F   The qualitative characteristic of relevance means that independent parties can confirm or duplicate accounting information.

16. T F   Earnings per share is an important measure of liquidity.

17. T F   The customary dividing line between a material amount and an immaterial one is $1,000.

_____
_____
_____
_____
_____
_____
_____
_____
_____
_____
_____
_____
_____
_____

Multiple Choice

Circle the letter of the best answer.

1.   The basis for classifying assets as current or noncurrent is the period of time that a business normally needs to turn cash invested in
   a.   noncurrent assets back into current assets.
   b.   receivables back into cash, or one year, whichever is shorter.
   c.   inventories back into cash, or one year, whichever is longer.
   d.   inventories back into cash, or one year, whichever is shorter.

2.   Which of the following will *not* be found anywhere in a single-step income statement?
   a.   Cost of goods sold
   b.   Net sales
   c.   Gross margin
   d.   Operating expenses

3.   The current ratio would probably be of *most* interest to
   a.   stockholders.
   b.   creditors.
   c.   management.
   d.   customers.

4.   Which of the following would *not* appear in the stockholders' equity section of a corporation's balance sheet?
   a.   Retained earnings
   b.   Common stock
   c.   Additional paid-in capital
   d.   Dawn Roberts, Capital

5. Net income divided by net sales equals

    a. profit margin.
    b. return on assets.
    c. working capital.
    d. income from operations.

6. Operating expenses consist of

    a. other expenses and cost of goods sold.
    b. selling expenses and cost of goods sold.
    c. selling expenses and general and administrative expenses.
    d. selling expenses, general and administrative expenses, and other expenses.

7. All of the following are objectives of financial reporting, as prescribed by the FASB, *except*

    a. to provide information about the timing of cash flows
    b. to provide information to investors and creditors
    c. to provide information about business resources
    d. to provide information to management

8. If a company has a profit margin of 4.0 percent and an asset turnover of 3.0 times, its return on assets is approximately

    a. 1.3 percent.
    b. 3.0 percent.
    c. 4.0 percent.
    d. 12.0 percent.

9. The multistep income statement of a service company would *not* contain which of the following components?

    a. Income taxes
    b. Gross margin
    c. Other revenues and expenses
    d. Operating expenses

APPLYING YOUR KNOWLEDGE

Exercises

1. Oakdale Company uses the following headings on its classified balance sheet:

    a. Current Assets

    b. Investments

    c. Property, Plant, and Equipment

    d. Intangible Assets

    e. Current Liabilities

    f. Long-Term Liabilities

    g. Stockholders' Equity

    Indicate by the letters preceding these headings where each of the following items should be placed. Write an *X* next to items that do not belong on the balance sheet.

    _____ 1. Goodwill

    _____ 2. Short-term advances from customers

    _____ 3. Accumulated depreciation

_____ 4. Common stock

_____ 5. Prepaid rent

_____ 6. Delivery truck

_____ 7. Office supplies

_____ 8. Fund for the purchase of land

_____ 9. Notes payable due in ten years

_____ 10. Bonds payable currently due (payable out of current assets)

_____ 11. Patents

_____ 12. Short-term investments

_____ 13. Provision for income taxes

_____ 14. Inventory

_____ 15. Accounts payable

2.   The following information relates to Spiffy Appliance, Inc., for 20xx:

Current Assets	$ 60,000
Average Total Assets	200,000
Current Liabilities	20,000
Long-Term Liabilities	30,000
Average Stockholders' Equity	150,000
Net Sales	250,000
Net Income	25,000

Using this information, compute the following measures of liquidity and profitability:

a.   Working capital = $ _____

b.   Current ratio = _____

c.   Profit margin = _____%

d.   Return on assets = _____%

e.   Return on equity = _____%

f.   Asset turnover = _____ times

3.   The following data relate to Newcastle Corporation for 20xx:

Cost of Goods Sold	$150,000	
Interest Income	2,000	
Income Taxes	5,000	
Net Sales	200,000	
Common Stock Outstanding	3,500	shares
Operating Expenses	30,000	

a.   In the space provided on the next page, complete a condensed multistep income statement in good form. Include earnings per share information in the proper place.

Newcastle Corporation Income Statement (Multistep) For the Year Ended December 31, 20xx		

b. In the space provided below, complete a condensed single-step income statement in good form. Include earnings per share information in the proper place.

Newcastle Corporation Income Statement (Single-Step) For the Year Ended December 31, 20xx		

CHAPTER 5

The Operating Cycle and Merchandising Operations

REVIEWING THE CHAPTER

Objective 1: Identify the management issues related to merchandising businesses.

1. A **merchandising business** earns income by buying and selling goods, also known as **merchandise inventory.** This type of firm, whether wholesale or retail, uses the same basic accounting methods as a service company. However, accounting for a merchandising concern is more complicated because, unlike a service firm, a merchandiser must account for the inventory of goods it holds for resale.

2. A merchandiser engages in a series of transactions known as the **operating cycle.** The transactions involved in the operating cycle are (a) the purchase of merchandise inventory for cash or on credit, (b) payment for purchases made on credit, (c) sale of the merchandise inventory for cash or on credit, and (d) collection of cash from credit sales.

3. Cash flow can be improved by reducing the **financing period** (also called the *cash gap*), which is the length of time a business will be without cash from merchandise inventory transactions. Technically, it is the amount of time from the purchase of inventory to the collection of cash from its sale minus the time the business takes to pay for the inventory.

4. A merchandising company must choose a system or a combination of systems to account for its inventory. The two basic systems are the perpetual inventory system and the periodic inventory system.

    a. Under the **perpetual inventory system,** continuous records are kept of the quantity and, usually, the cost of individual items as they are bought and sold. The detailed data available from the perpetual inventory system (which is often computerized) enable managers to quickly determine product availability, avoid running out of stock, and control the costs of carrying inventory. A physical count of the inventory should still be taken periodically to make sure that the actual number of goods on hand matches the accounting records.

    b. Merchandisers use the **periodic inventory system** when it is unnecessary or impractical to keep track of the quantity of inventory or the cost of each item (e.g., when a retailer sells a high volume of low-value items). With this system, no detailed records of inventory are kept during the accounting period; the merchandiser waits until the end of the period to take a physical count of the inventory. The periodic inventory system is simpler and less costly to maintain than the perpetual inventory system. However, its lack of detailed records may lead to inefficiencies, lost sales, and higher operating costs.

5. Most merchandising and manufacturing firms conduct some of their business overseas. Transactions with foreign businesses are often denominated in the foreign currency, which must be translated to the domestic currency (the U.S. dollar for an American company) by means of an *exchange rate*, or the value of one currency in terms of another.

6.   No accounting problem arises when the domestic company bills and receives payment from the foreign company in the domestic currency. However, when a transaction involves foreign currency, the domestic company will probably realize and record an **exchange gain or loss.** This exchange gain or loss, which is reported in the income statement, reflects the change in the exchange rate between the transaction date and the date of payment.

7.   A merchandising business typically handles a great deal of cash and inventory—assets that are very susceptible to theft and embezzlement. Thus, a good system of **internal control** must be established to protect the company's assets.

    a.   A **physical inventory**—an actual count of the merchandise on hand—is a means of maintaining control over merchandise inventory. Such a count is conducted under both the perpetual and periodic inventory systems. It usually takes place on the last day of the fiscal year. To simplify the process, many retailers end their fiscal year during a slow season, when inventories are relatively low.

    b.   Merchandise inventory appears as an asset on the balance sheet and includes all salable goods owned by the company, no matter where the goods are located. Goods in transit to which a company has acquired title are included in ending inventory; goods that the company has formally sold are not included even if they are still in transit.

    c.   Inventory losses from theft and spoilage are included in the cost of goods sold. It is easier to track such losses under the perpetual inventory system than under the periodic inventory system.

8.   The Sarbanes-Oxley Act holds a public company's chief executive officer, its chief financial officer, and its auditors fully responsible for the company's system of internal control. Such a system must (a) safeguard the company's assets, (b) ensure the reliability of its accounting records, (c) see that its employees comply with all legal requirements, and (d) promote efficiency and effectiveness of operations.

Objective 2: Describe the terms of sale related to merchandising transactions.

9.   As a matter of convenience, manufacturers and wholesalers frequently quote prices of merchandise based on a discount from the list or catalogue price (called a **trade discount**). Neither the list price nor the trade discount is entered into the accounting records.

10.   When goods are sold on credit, terms vary as to when payment must be made. For instance, n/30 means that full payment is due within 30 days of the invoice date, and n/10 eom means that full payment is due 10 days after the end of the month. Terms of 2/10, n/30, for example, mean that a 2 percent discount will be given if payment is made within 10 days of the invoice date. Otherwise, the full amount is due within 30 days.

11.   Sales discounts for early payment are customary in some industries. When a merchandising firm gives a customer a discount for early payment, it records a **sales discount.** Cash and Sales Discounts are debited, and Accounts Receivable is credited. Sales Discounts is a contra account to sales in the income statement.

12.   **Purchases discounts** are discounts taken for early payment of merchandise purchased for resale. They are to the buyer what sales discounts are to the seller. A purchase is initially recorded at the gross purchase price. If the company makes payment within the discount period, it debits Accounts Payable, credits Purchases Discounts, and credits Cash. Purchases Discounts will reduce cost of goods sold or purchases, depending on the inventory method used.

13. The terms of sale designate whether the buyer or seller of the goods bears the freight charges. A buyer in Chicago, for instance, must pay the freight-in from Boston if the terms specify FOB (free on board) Boston or **FOB shipping point.** However, the seller in Boston pays if the terms are FOB Chicago or **FOB destination.** FOB terms also pertain to when the title of the merchandise passes from the seller to the buyer.

14. Transportation costs for goods *received* are recorded as **freight-in** (also called *transportation-in*), and—depending on the relative dollar amount—either added to the cost of merchandise purchased or included in the cost of goods sold. Delivery costs for goods *sold* are recorded as **delivery expense** (also called *freight-out*), and treated as a selling expense in the income statement.

15. Companies that allow customers to make purchases with credit cards (such as MasterCard or Visa) or debit cards (whereby a person's bank account is reduced directly) must follow special accounting procedures. In reimbursing a merchant for a sale, credit card companies take a 2 to 6 discount as payment for having established the customer's credit and for collecting money from the customer. When the merchant communicates its credit card sales to its bank (resulting in a cash deposit to its account), it debits Cash and Credit Card Discount Expense (a selling expense) and credits Sales.

Objective 3: Prepare an income statement and record merchandising transactions under the perpetual inventory system.

16. The net income of a merchandising firm is computed as follows:

	Net sales
−	Cost of goods sold
=	Gross margin
−	Operating expenses
=	Income before income taxes
−	Income taxes
=	Net income

17. Under the perpetual inventory system, the Cost of Goods Sold and Merchandise Inventory accounts are updated whenever a purchase, sale, or other inventory transaction takes place. Transactions are recorded under the perpetual inventory system as follows:

a. For the purchase of merchandise on credit, Merchandise Inventory is debited, and Accounts Payable is credited.

b. A return of goods to the supplier for credit is recorded with a debit to Accounts Payable and a credit to Merchandise Inventory.

c. Payment on account is recorded with a debit to Accounts Payable and a credit to Cash.

d. When goods are sold on credit, Accounts Receivable is debited, and Sales is credited. However, an *additional* entry must be made, debiting Cost of Goods Sold and crediting Merchandise Inventory. A cash sale is recorded with a debit to Cash and a credit to Sales (along with the additional entry shown above).

e. When a credit customer returns goods for a refund, **Sales Returns and Allowances** is debited and Accounts Receivable is credited. (The purpose in accumulating returns and allowances in a Sales Returns and Allowances account rather than in the Sales account is to make data on customer dissatisfaction readily available to managers.) A second entry is needed to reinstate Merchandise Inventory (a debit) and to reduce Cost of Goods Sold (a credit).

f.   The receipt of payment on account is recorded with a debit to Cash and a credit to Accounts Receivable.

Objective 4: Prepare an income statement and record merchandising transactions under the periodic inventory system.

18. Under the periodic inventory system, the Merchandise Inventory and Cost of Goods Sold accounts are *not* updated as purchases, sales, and other inventory transactions occur. Cost of goods sold is therefore computed on the income statement as follows:

    Beginning inventory
+   Net cost of purchases (see paragraph 19)
=   **Goods available for sale**
−   Ending inventory
=   Cost of goods sold

19. **Net cost of purchases** is calculated as follows:

    Purchases
−   Purchases returns and allowances
−   Purchases discounts
=   **Net purchases**
+   Freight-in
=   Net cost of purchases

20. Transactions are recorded under the periodic inventory system as follows:

a.   All purchases of merchandise are debited to the **Purchases account** and credited to Accounts Payable or Cash. The purpose of the Purchases account is to accumulate the cost of merchandise purchased for resale during the period.

b.   The return of goods to the supplier for credit is recorded with a debit to Accounts Payable and a credit to **Purchases Returns and Allowances.** The latter appears as a contra account to purchases on the income statement.

c.   Payment on account is recorded with a debit to Accounts Payable and credit to Cash.

d.   When a cash sale is made, Cash is debited and Sales is credited for the amount of the sale. When a credit sale is made, Accounts Receivable is debited and Sales is credited.

e.   Delivery costs for goods sold are recorded with a debit to Delivery Expense and a credit to Accounts Payable or Cash.

f.   When a credit customer returns goods for a refund, Sales Returns and Allowances is debited and Accounts Receivable is credited. The former functions as a contra account to sales on the income statement.

g.   The receipt of payment on account is recorded with a simple debit to Cash and credit to Accounts Receivable.

Objective 5: Describe the components of internal control, control activities, and limitation on internal control.

21. **Internal control** encompasses all the policies and procedures management uses to ensure the reliability of financial reporting, compliance with laws and regulations, and the effectiveness and efficiency of operations. To achieve these objectives, management must establish five components of internal control: the control environment, risk assessment, information and communication, control activities, and monitoring.

   a.   The **control environment** reflects management's integrity and ethics, philosophy and operating style, method of assigning authority and responsibility, as well as the company's organizational structure and personnel policies and practices.

   b.   **Risk assessment** entails identifying areas in which risk of asset loss or inaccuracy of accounting records is especially high.

   c.   **Information and communication** relates to the accounting system that management sets up and to the communication of individual responsibilities within that system.

   d.   **Control activities** are the procedures and policies that management establishes to ensure that the objectives of internal control are met.

   e.   **Monitoring** consists of management's regular assessment of the quality of internal control.

22. Examples of control activities are (a) requiring authorization for all transactions, (b) recording all transactions, (c) using well-designed documents, (d) instituting physical controls, as over the accounting records, (e) making periodic independent checks of records and assets, (f) separating duties, and (g) employing sound personnel procedures. **Bonding** an employee (a good example of a sound personnel procedure) means insuring the company against theft by that person.

23. A system of internal control relies on the people who carry out the control procedures. In addition to human error, collusion and changing conditions can limit the effectiveness of a system of internal control.

Objective 6: Apply internal control activities to common merchandising transactions.

24. Proper controls over merchandising transactions not only help prevent losses from theft or fraud; they also help ensure accuracy in the accounting records. In addition, they can foster balanced inventory levels, help a company keep enough cash on hand to make timely payments for purchases discounts, and enable a company to avoid credit losses.

25. Some common procedures for maintaining control over cash are (a) separating the authorization, recordkeeping, and custodianship of cash; (b) limiting access to cash; (c) specifying the persons responsible for handling cash; (d) maximizing the use of banking facilities and minimizing cash on hand; (e) bonding employees who have access to cash; (f) physically protecting cash on hand by using cash registers, safes, and similar equipment; (g) performing unannounced audits of the cash on hand; (h) recording cash receipts promptly; (i) depositing cash receipts promptly; (j) paying by check; and (k) having someone who does not deal with cash reconcile the Cash account.

26. Cash received by mail should be handled by two or more employees. Cash received from sales over the counter should be controlled through the use of cash registers and prenumbered sales tickets. At the end of each day, total cash receipts should be reconciled and recorded in the cash receipts journal. All these tasks should be performed in accordance with the separation of duties.

27. All cash payments for purchases should be made by check and only with authorization. The system of authorization and the documents used differ among companies. The most common documents are described below.

   a. When a department needs to acquire materials, it fills out a **purchase requisition** form requesting that the company purchase them.

   b. The department responsible for the company's purchasing activities completes a **purchase order** and sends it to the vendor.

   c. After shipping the goods, the vendor sends an **invoice,** or bill, to the company.

   d. When the goods arrive, the receiving department completes a **receiving report** and forwards it to the accounting department; it contains information about the quantity and condition of the goods received.

   e. A **check authorization**, issued by the accounting department, is a document attached to the purchase order, invoice, and receiving report; it indicates that the information on those three documents is in agreement and that payment is approved.

   f. When payment is approved, the company's treasurer issues a check to the vendor for the amount of the invoice less any appropriate discount. A remittance advice, which shows what the check is paying, should be attached to the check.

Summary of Journal Entries Introduced in Chapter 5

(Note: In most instances, the text instead described the entry or presented it in T-account form.)

A.	(LO 2)	Cash	XX	(amount net of fee)
		Credit Card Discount Expense	XX	(fee charged)
		Sales	XX	(gross amount sold)
		Made sales on credit cards		

Perpetual Inventory System

B.	(LO 3)	Merchandise Inventory	XX	(purchase price)
		Accounts Payable	XX	(amount due)
		Purchased merchandise on credit		
C.	(LO 3)	Freight-In	XX	(price charged)
		Accounts Payable	XX	(amount due)
		Received bill for transportation charges		
D.	(LO 3)	Accounts Payable	XX	(amount returned)
		Merchandise Inventory	XX	(amount returned)
		Returned merchandise to supplier for credit		
E.	(LO 3)	Accounts Payable	XX	(amount paid)
		Cash	XX	(amount paid)
		Made payment on account to supplier		

F.   (LO 3)   Accounts Receivable (or Cash)   XX (amount due or received)
                  Sales   XX (sales price)
                       Sold merchandise on credit (or for cash)

               Cost of Goods Sold   XX (inventory cost)
                  Merchandise Inventory   XX (inventory cost)
                       Transferred cost of merchandise inventory
                       to Cost of Goods Sold account

G.   (LO 3)   Delivery Expense   XX (amount incurred)
                  Cash   XX (amount paid)
                       Paid delivery costs for goods shipped
                       to customer

H.   (LO 3)   Sales Returns and Allowances   XX (price of goods returned)
                  Accounts Receivable   XX (amount credited to
                                                                    account)

                       Accepted return of merchandise for credit

               Merchandise Inventory   XX (inventory cost)
                  Cost of Goods Sold   XX (inventory cost)
                       Transferred cost of merchandise returned to
                       Merchandise Inventory account

I.   (LO 3)   Cash   XX (amount received)
                  Accounts Receivable   XX (amount settled)
                       Received payment on account from customer

---

Periodic Inventory System

J.   (LO 4)   Purchases   XX (purchase price)
                  Accounts Payable   XX (amount due)
                       Purchased merchandise on credit

K.   (LO 4)   Accounts Payable   XX (amount returned)
                  Purchases Returns and Allowances   XX (amount returned)
                       Returned merchandise to supplier for credit

L.   (LO 4)   Accounts Payable   XX (amount paid)
                  Cash   XX (amount paid)
                       Made payment on account to supplier

M.   (LO 4)   Accounts Receivable (or Cash)   XX (amount due or received)
                  Sales   XX (sales price)
                       Sold merchandise on credit (or for cash)

| N. | (LO 4) | Delivery Expense | | XX (amount incurred) |
| | | Cash | | XX (amount paid) |

Paid delivery costs for goods shipped
to customer

| O. | (LO 4) | Sales Returns and Allowances | | XX (price of goods returned) |
| | | Accounts Receivable | | XX (amount credited to account) |

Accepted return of merchandise,
account credited

P.	(LO 4)	Cash		XX (amount received)
		Accounts Receivable		XX (amount settled)
		Received payment on account from customer		

SELF-TEST

Test your knowledge of the chapter by choosing the best answer for each item below.

1. When a company purchases goods, it would prepare all of the following business documents, *except* a(n)

   a. invoice.
   b. purchase order.
   c. check authorization.
   d. purchase requisition.

2. A pretax income always results when

   a. cost of goods sold exceeds operating expenses.
   b. revenues exceed the cost of goods sold.
   c. revenues exceed operating expenses.
   d. the gross margin exceeds operating expenses.

3. Which of the following appears as an operating expense on the income statement of a merchandising concern?

   a. Freight-In
   b. Delivery Expense
   c. Sales Returns and Allowances
   d. Purchases Returns and Allowances

4. If a firm's beginning merchandise inventory is $400, its ending merchandise inventory is $700, and its cost of goods sold is $3,400, the net cost of purchases

   a. is $3,700.
   b. is $3,400.
   c. is $3,100.
   d. cannot be determined.

5. A sale is made on June 1 for $200, terms 2/10, n/30, on which a sales return of $50 is granted on June 7. The dollar amount received for payment in full on June 9 is

   a. $200.
   b. $150.
   c. $147.
   d. $196.

6. Under a periodic inventory system, a purchase of merchandise for $750 that includes freight of $50 under terms of n/30, FOB shipping point, would result in a

   a. debit to Freight-In of $50.
   b. debit to Purchases of $750.
   c. credit to Accounts Payable of $700.
   d. credit to Freight Payable of $50.

7. A firm that maintains perpetual inventory records sells on account for $2,000 goods that cost the firm $1,400. The entries to record this transaction should include a

   a. debit to Merchandise Inventory for $1,400.
   b. debit to Sales for $2,000.
   c. credit to Accounts Receivable for $2,000.
   d. debit to Cost of Goods Sold for $1,400.

8. Which of the following is *not* a component of internal control?

   a. Monitoring
   b. Risk assessment
   c. Reporting
   d. Control activities

9. The separation of duties in terms of cash transactions means that different persons should be responsible for authorization, custody, and

   a. approval.
   b. recordkeeping.
   c. control.
   d. protection.

10. Which of the following documents must be presented and in agreement before a check authorization is prepared?

    a. Purchase requisition and purchase order
    b. Purchase order and receiving report
    c. Purchase requisition, purchase order, and invoice
    d. Purchase order, invoice, and receiving report

TESTING YOUR KNOWLEDGE

Matching*

Match each term with its definition by writing the appropriate letter in the blank.

1. _____ Trade discount

2. _____ Invoice

3. _____ Receiving report

4. _____ Check authorization

5. _____ Sales Returns and Allowances

6. _____ Sales Discounts

7. _____ Delivery expense

8. _____ Purchases

9. _____ Goods available for sale

a. Transportation cost for goods purchased

b. A document that authorizes payment

c. Freight charge for goods sold

d. A system that maintains continuous records of the quantity and, usually, the cost of goods as they are bought and sold

e. A vendor's bill

f. The point after which the buyer must bear the transportation cost

10. _____Perpetual inventory system

11. _____Periodic inventory system

12. _____Freight-in

13. _____FOB (free on board)

14. _____Purchases Returns and Allowances

15. _____Purchases Discounts

16. _____Internal control

17. _____Purchase requisition

18. _____Purchase order

g. Under the periodic inventory system, the account used to accumulate the cost of goods bought during the period

h. A deduction off a list or catalogue price

i. Beginning inventory plus net cost of purchases

j. A document that asks the purchasing department to order certain items

k. The account used by sellers when a buyer pays for goods within the discount period

l. The account used by sellers when a buyer returns goods

m. A system that does *not* maintain continuous records of merchandise inventory

n. The account used by buyers when they pay for goods within the discount period

o. An order for goods that is sent to a vendor

p. Under the periodic inventory system, the account used by buyers when they return goods

q. A description of goods received by a company

r. A system designed to ensure the reliability of financial reporting, compliance with laws and regulations, and the effectiveness and efficiency of operations

Note to student: The matching quiz might be completed more efficiently by starting with the definition and searching for the corresponding term.

Short Answer

Use the lines provided to answer each item.

1. List seven control activities that help make a system of internal control effective.

    _____

    _____

    _____

    _____

    _____

    _____

    _____

2. List any six procedures that may be employed to control and safeguard cash.

    _____

    _____

    _____

    _____

    _____

    _____

3. What three documents should be in agreement before an invoice is paid?

    _____

    _____

    _____

4. Assuming a company uses the periodic inventory system, list the items that would appear in a condensed cost of goods sold section of its income statement. Use mathematical signs to indicate their relationship.

    _____

    _____

    _____

    _____

5. Using mathematical signs, list the sequence of items involved in computing net cost of purchases in a periodic inventory system.

    _____

    _____

    _____

    _____

True-False

Circle T if the statement is true, and F if it is false. Provide explanations for the false answers, using the blank lines at the end of the section.

1.   T   F   Ending merchandise inventory is needed to calculate goods available for sale.

2.   T   F   Terms of n/10 eom mean that payment must be made ten days before the end of the month.

3.   T   F   If the exchange rate changes between the transaction date and the date the foreign currency changes hands, an exchange gain or loss is recorded.

4.   T   F   Inventory losses are normally included in the cost of goods sold.

5.   T   F   FOB destination means that the seller bears the transportation cost.

6.   T   F   Sales Discounts is a contra account to Net Sales.

7.   T   F   Under the periodic inventory system, ending inventory is a necessary component of both the balance sheet and the income statement.

8.   T   F   Cost of goods available for sale minus cost of goods sold equals ending inventory.

9.   T   F   The perpetual inventory system requires more detailed recordkeeping than the periodic system.

10. T   F   The beginning inventory of an accounting period is the same as the ending inventory of the previous period.

11. T   F   Sales Returns and Allowances normally has a credit balance.

12. T   F   Under the periodic inventory system, a cash purchase of office supplies for use in daily operations requires a debit to Purchases and a credit to Cash.

13. T   F   A Purchases Returns and Allowances account is not used in the perpetual inventory system.

14. T   F   Merchants treat Credit Card Discount Expense as a contra account to Sales.

15. T   F   Under the periodic inventory system, the cost of goods sold must be recorded and the inventory account must be decreased as soon as a sale is made.

16. T   F   An example of a trade discount is 2/10, n/30.

17. T   F   When goods are shipped FOB shipping point, title passes when the buyer receives the goods.

18. T   F   A good system of internal control will guarantee that the accounting records are accurate.

19. T   F   *Collusion* refers to a secret agreement between two or more persons to defraud a company.

20. T   F   Mail should be opened in the accounting department so that transactions can be recorded immediately.

21. T   F   A company orders goods by sending the supplier a purchase requisition.

22. T   F   Rotating employees in job assignments is poor internal control because employees are continually forced to learn new job skills.

23. T   F   One of the five components of internal control is "information and communication."

_____
_____
_____
_____
_____
_____
_____
_____
_____
_____
_____
_____
_____
_____
_____
_____
_____
_____
_____
_____
_____
_____

Multiple Choice

Circle the letter of the best answer.

1. Bob (who uses a periodic inventory system) buys $600 of merchandise from Allen, with terms of 2/10, n/30. Bob immediately returns $100 of goods and pays for the remainder eight days after the purchase. Bob's entry on the date of payment would include a

    a. debit to Accounts Payable for $600.
    b. debit to Sales Discounts for $12.
    c. credit to Purchases Returns and Allowances for $100.
    d. credit to Purchases Discounts for $10.

2. Which of the following accounts normally has a credit balance?

    a. Sales Discounts
    b. Merchandise Inventory
    c. Purchases Returns and Allowances
    d. Freight-In

3.   Under a periodic inventory system, which of the following accounts is irrelevant in computing cost of goods sold?

   a.   Freight-In
   b.   Delivery Expense
   c.   Merchandise Inventory, beginning
   d.   Merchandise Inventory, ending

4.   When a company is buying goods, which of the following documents is prepared first?

   a.   Purchase order
   b.   Receiving report
   c.   Check authorization
   d.   Purchase requisition

5.   Which of the following is an example of poor internal control?

   a.   Having the receiving department compare goods received with the related purchase order
   b.   Forcing employees to take earned vacations
   c.   Requiring someone other than the petty cash custodian to enter petty cash transactions in the accounting records
   d.   Bonding employees

6.   Which of the following accounts is *not* used in conjunction with a perpetual inventory system?

   a.   Cost of Goods Sold
   b.   Freight-In
   c.   Purchases
   d.   Merchandise Inventory

7.   Which of the following transactions is *not* part of the operating cycle?

   a.   Sale of inventory
   b.   Cash payment for operating expenses
   c.   Purchase of inventory
   d.   Cash collection from inventory sales

8.   A company has credit card sales for the day of $1,000. If the credit card company charges 5 percent, the company's journal entry to record sales and the receipt of cash when it deposits the credit card invoices at its bank would include a

   a.   credit to Sales for $950.
   b.   credit to Credit Card Discount Expense for $50.
   c.   debit to Sales for $1,000.
   d.   debit to Cash for $950.

9.   On average, it takes Meadows Corporation 45 days to sell its inventory and 60 days to collect payment from customers. Meadows normally pays for inventory purchases within 30 days. Its financing period is

   a.   75 days.
   b.   135 days.
   c.   15 days.
   d.   105 days.

APPLYING YOUR KNOWLEDGE

Exercises

1. Davis Merchandising Company uses the periodic inventory system. Listed below are its transactions during the month of May. Record each transaction in the journal provided below.

May	1	Purchased merchandise for $500 on credit, terms n/30.
	3	Sold merchandise for $500 on credit, terms n/30.
	4	Paid $42 for freight charges relating to a merchandise purchase in April.
	5	Purchased office supplies for $100, on credit.
	6	Returned $20 of the May 5 office supplies, for credit.
	7	Returned $50 of merchandise purchased on May 1, for credit.
	9	Sold merchandise for $225, on credit, terms n/30.
	10	Paid for the merchandise purchased on May 1, less the return.
	14	The customer of May 9 returned $25 of merchandise, for credit.
	22	The customer of May 9 paid for the merchandise, less the return.
	26	The customer of May 3 paid for the merchandise purchased on that date.

General Journal

Date		Description	Debit	Credit

2.   The following data are from the records of the Mammoth Merchandising Company:

Advertising Expense	$ 5,000
Dividends	12,000
Freight-In	2,000
Delivery Expense	4,000
Income Taxes Expense	4,780
Income Taxes Payable	4,780
Interest Income	150
Merchandise Inventory (Jan. 1)	10,000
Merchandise Inventory (Dec. 31)	8,000
Purchases	50,000
Purchases Discounts	500
Purchases Returns and Allowances	500
Rent Expense	3,000
Retained Earnings	15,000
Sales	100,000
Sales Discounts	300
Sales Returns and Allowances	200
Wages Expense	7,000

Using this information, complete the form below, showing only the computation of gross margin.

Mammoth Merchandising Company Partial Income Statement For the Year Ended December 31, 20xx			

Crossword Puzzle: Chapters 4 and 5

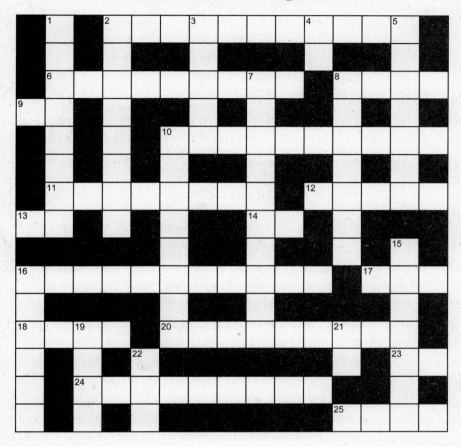

ACROSS

2   FOB _____
6   Pertinence to a decision
8   Exchange _____
9   Return _____ equity
10 _____ of duties
11 _____ per share
12 The opposite of "net"
13 Lower-of-cost-_____-market
14 Additional paid-_____ capital
16 Relative importance
17 End-of-month, for short
18 Internal-control assessment
20 Cost of _____ (2 words)
23 Freight-_____
24 Property, plant, and _____
25 Hourly pay

DOWN

1   Asset _____ (ratio)
2   Transportation of goods
3   Catalog discount
4   Debt _____ equity ratio
5   Possible bottom-line result (2 words)
7   Financial statement form
8   Sales _____ and allowances
10 FOB _____ point
15 Insuring against employee theft
16 Gross _____
19 Single-_____ income statement
21 Cost _____ sales
22 Payable

CHAPTER 6

Inventories

REVIEWING THE CHAPTER

Objective 1: Explain the management decisions related to inventory accounting, evaluation of inventory level, and the effects of inventory misstatements on income measurement.

1.   Inventory is considered a current asset because it normally is sold within one year or the operating cycle (whichever is longer). The inventory of a merchandising company consists of only completed goods that it owns and holds for sale in the regular course of business. The inventory of a manufacturer, on the other hand, consists of raw materials, work in process, and finished goods. The costs of work in process and finished goods inventories include the costs of raw material, labor, and overhead (indirect manufacturing costs) incurred in producing the finished product.

2.   The objective of accounting for inventory is the proper determination of income through the matching of costs and revenues, not the determination of the most realistic inventory value. Thus, in accounting for inventory, the following two questions must be answered:

   a.   How much of the asset has been used up (expired) during the current period and should be transferred to expense?

   b.   How much of the asset is unused (unexpired) and should remain on the balance sheet as an asset?

3.   A company has a number of choices with regard to inventory systems and methods. Because these systems and methods usually produce different amounts of reported net income, the choices that a company makes affect external evaluations of the company, as well as such internal evaluations as performance reviews. In addition, because income is affected, the valuation of inventory can have a considerable effect on the amount of income taxes paid, which will in turn affect cash flows.

4.   Once a company has chosen the systems and methods it will use for its inventory, the consistency convention allows a change to be made only when it can be justified by management. When a justifiable change is made, the full disclosure convention requires the notes to the financial statements to contain a description of the change, as well as its effects.

5.   It is important for a merchandiser to maintain a sufficient level of inventory to satisfy customer demand. However, the higher the level maintained, the more costly it is for the business to handle and store its goods. Management can evaluate the level of inventory by calculating and analyzing its inventory turnover and days' inventory on hand.

   a.   **Inventory turnover** indicates the number of times a company's average inventory is sold during an accounting period. It equals cost of goods sold divided by average inventory.

   b.   **Days' inventory on hand** indicates the average number of days required to sell the inventory on hand. It equals 365 divided by the inventory turnover.

6. To reduce their levels of inventory, many companies use supply-chain management in conjunction with a just-in-time operating environment. With **supply-chain management**, a company manages its inventory and purchasing through business-to-business transactions conducted over the Internet. In a **just-in-time operating environment,** companies work closely with suppliers to coordinate and schedule shipments so that the goods arrive just in time to be used or sold. As a result, the costs of carrying inventory are greatly reduced.

7. It is important to match the cost of goods sold with sales so that income before income taxes is reasonably accurate. Because both beginning and ending inventory are figured into the calculation of cost of goods sold, errors in inventory valuation will produce errors in income determination. Recall that beginning inventory plus net cost of purchases equals the cost of goods available for sale. The cost of goods sold is determined indirectly by deducting ending inventory from the cost of goods available for sale. Thus, if the value of ending inventory is understated or overstated, a corresponding error—dollar for dollar—will be made in both gross margin and income before income taxes. Below are some good rules of thumb to remember for inventory errors.

    a. If ending inventory for 20xx is *overstated*, then income before income taxes for 20xx will also be overstated.

    b. If ending inventory for 20xx is *understated*, then income before income taxes for 20xx will also be understated.

    c. If beginning inventory for 20xx is *overstated*, then income before income taxes for 20xx will be understated.

    d. If beginning inventory for 20xx is *understated*, then income before income taxes for 20xx will be overstated.

8. Because the ending inventory of one period becomes the beginning inventory of the next period, a misstatement in inventory will affect both periods. Although over a two-year period, the errors in income before income taxes will counterbalance each other, the misstatements are a violation of the matching rule. Moreover, management, investors, and creditors make many annual decisions on an annual basis, and in doing so, they rely on the accuracy of the net income figure.

Objective 2: Define *inventory cost,* contrast goods flow and cost flow, and explain the lower-of-cost-or-market (LCM) rule.

9. **Inventory cost** includes the invoice price of the inventory less purchases discounts, plus freight-in (including insurance in transit), plus applicable taxes and tariffs.

10. When identical items of merchandise are purchased at different prices during the year, it is usually impractical to monitor the actual **goods flow** and record the corresponding costs. Instead, the accountant makes an assumption about the **cost flow** using one of the following costing methods: specific identification; average-cost; first-in, first-out (FIFO); or last-in, first-out (LIFO). These four costing methods are discussed below.

11. Goods in transit should be included in inventory only if the company has title to the goods. When goods are sent FOB (free on board) shipping point, title passes to the buyer when the goods reach the common carrier. When goods are sent FOB destination, title passes when the goods reach the buyer.

12. Goods that have been sold but are awaiting delivery to the buyer should not be included in the seller's inventory count. When goods are held on **consignment,** the consignee (who earns a commission on making the sale) has possession of the goods, but the consignor retains title until the consignee sells the goods. The consignor therefore includes them in its physical inventory.

13. The **market** (current replacement cost) of inventory can fall below its historical cost as a result of physical deterioration, obsolescence, or a decline in price level. When that happens, the inventory valuation should be based on the **lower-of-cost-or-market (LCM) rule.** In addition, a loss should be reported in the income statement. The lower-of-cost-or-market rule is an application of the conservatism convention because the loss is recognized when it is anticipated, rather than when it actually occurs (i.e., when the goods are ultimately sold). In addition, full disclosure requires that the use of LCM be disclosed in the notes to the financial statements.

Objective 3: Calculate inventory cost under the periodic inventory system using various costing methods.

14. If the units of ending inventory can be identified as having come from specific purchases, the **specific identification method** can be used. In this case, the flow of costs reflects the actual flow of goods. However, the specific identification method is not practical in most cases.

15. Under the **average-cost method,** inventory is priced at the average cost of the goods available for sale during the period. Average cost is computed by dividing the total cost of goods available for sale by the total units available for sale. The average cost per unit is then multiplied by the number of units in ending inventory to arrive at the cost of ending inventory.

16. Under the **first-in, first-out (FIFO) method,** the costs of the first items purchased are assigned to the first items sold. Thus, ending inventory cost is determined from the prices of the most recent purchases. During periods of rising prices, FIFO yields a higher income before income taxes than any of the other three costing methods.

17. Under the **last-in, first-out (LIFO) method,** the costs of the last items purchased are assigned to the first items sold. Thus, the ending inventory cost is determined from the prices of the earliest purchases. During periods of rising prices, LIFO yields a lower income before income taxes than any of the other three methods. However, it matches current merchandise costs with current sales prices.

Objective 4: Explain the effects of inventory costing methods on income determination and income taxes.

18. During periods of rising prices, FIFO produces a higher net income figure than LIFO. During periods of falling prices, the reverse is true. The average-cost method produces a net income figure somewhere between the figures produced by FIFO and LIFO. Because the specific identification method depends on the particular items sold, no generalization can be made about the effect of changing prices. LIFO is best suited for the income statement because it matches revenues and cost of goods sold. FIFO, however, provides a more up-to-date ending inventory figure for the balance sheet.

19. Several rules govern the valuation of inventory for federal income tax purposes. For example, even though a business has a wide choice of methods, once it has chosen a method, it must apply that method consistently (though it can make a change with approval from the IRS). In addition, several regulations apply to LIFO, such as the requirement that if LIFO is used for tax purposes, it must also be used in the accounting records. Moreover, lower-of-cost-or-market is allowed (for tax purposes) for every method *except* LIFO.

20. A **LIFO liquidation** occurs when sales have reduced inventories below the levels established in earlier years. When prices have been rising steadily, a LIFO liquidation produces unusually high profits. LIFO liquidation can normally be prevented by making enough inventory purchases before year-end to restore the desired inventory level.

21. The inventory method that a company uses will affect not only its reported profitability, but also its reported liquidity and cash flows (primarily through the amount of income taxes paid). LIFO, for example, will usually produce a lower figure for income before income taxes than will FIFO. However, the reduced tax liability under LIFO will have a positive effect on cash flows.

Supplemental Objective 5: Calculate inventory cost under the perpetual inventory system using various costing methods.

22. The pricing of inventories differs under the periodic and perpetual inventory systems. When the periodic system is used, only the ending inventory is counted and priced, and the cost of goods sold is calculated by subtracting ending inventory from the cost of goods available for sale. When the perpetual system is used, a company has more control over its inventory because a continuous record is kept of the balance of each inventory item; as goods are sold, costs are transferred from the Inventory account to the Cost of Goods Sold account.

23. The specific identification and FIFO methods produce the same figures for inventory and cost of goods sold under the periodic and perpetual inventory systems. The results differ for the average-cost method because under the perpetual system, an average is calculated after each purchase rather than at the end of the accounting period. The results for the LIFO method also differ because under the perpetual system, the cost components of inventory change constantly as goods are bought and sold.

Supplemental Objective 6: Use the retail method and gross profit method to estimate the cost of ending inventory.

24. The **retail method** of inventory estimation can be used when the difference between the cost and sale prices of goods is a constant percentage over a period of time. It can be used regardless of whether a business makes a physical count of goods. To apply the retail method, goods available for sale are figured both at cost and at retail. Next, a cost-to-retail ratio is computed. Sales for the period are then subtracted from goods available for sale at retail to produce ending inventory at retail. Finally, ending inventory at retail is multiplied by the cost-to-retail ratio to produce an estimate of the cost of ending inventory.

25. The **gross profit method** of inventory estimation (also called the *gross margin method*) assumes that a business's gross margin ratio remains relatively stable from year to year. This method is used when a business does not keep records of the retail prices of beginning inventory and purchases and when inventory records are lost or destroyed. To apply the gross profit method, the cost of goods available for sale is determined by adding purchases to beginning inventory. The cost of goods sold is then estimated by deducting the estimated gross margin from sales. Finally, the estimated cost of goods sold is subtracted from the cost of goods available for sale to arrive at the estimated cost of ending inventory.

SELF-TEST

Test your knowledge of the chapter by choosing the best answer for each item below.

1. An overstatement of ending inventory in one period results in
   a. an overstatement of the ending inventory in the next period.
   b. an understatement of income before income taxes in the next period.
   c. an overstatement of income before income taxes in the next period.
   d. no effect on income before income taxes in the next period.

2. Which of the following costs would *not* be included in the cost of inventory?

    a. Goods held on consignment
    b. Taxes and tariffs applicable to the goods
    c. Freight-in
    d. Invoice price

3.

    Sept. 1 Inventory 10 @ $4.00
           8 Purchased 40 @ $4.40
          17 Purchased 20 @ $4.20
          25 Purchased 30 @ $4.80   Sold 70

    Based on this information and assuming that the periodic inventory system is used, cost of goods sold under the average-cost method would be

    a. $133.20.
    b. $444.00.
    c. $310.80.
    d. $304.50.

4. Assuming the same facts as in **3,** cost of goods sold under the first-in, first-out (FIFO) method would be

    a. $144.00.
    b. $300.00.
    c. $388.50.
    d. $444.00.

5. Assuming the same facts as in **3,** ending inventory under the last-in, first-out (LIFO) method would be

    a. $316.
    b. $444.
    c. $300.
    d. $128.

6. Inventory turnover equals cost of goods sold divided by

    a. number of days in a year.
    b. cost of goods available for sale.
    c. number of months in a year.
    d. average inventory.

7. In a period of rising prices, which of the following inventory costing methods generally results in the lowest figure for income before income taxes?

    a. Average-cost method
    b. FIFO method
    c. LIFO method
    d. Cannot tell without more information

8. When applying the lower-of-cost-or-market rule to inventory, *market* generally means

    a. original cost less physical deterioration.
    b. resale value.
    c. original cost.
    d. current replacement cost.

9. Which of the following companies would be most likely to use the retail inventory method?
   a. A farm supply company
   b. A TV repair company
   c. A dealer in heavy machinery
   d. A men's clothing shop
10. A retail company has goods available for sale of $1,000,000 at retail and $600,000 at cost, and ending inventory of $100,000 at retail. What is the estimated cost of goods sold?
   a. $60,000
   b. $100,000
   c. $900,000
   d. $540,000

TESTING YOUR KNOWLEDGE

Matching*

Match each term with its definition by writing the appropriate letter in the blank.

1. _____ LIFO liquidation
2. _____ Merchandise inventory
3. _____ Specific identification method
4. _____ FIFO method
5. _____ LIFO method
6. _____ Average-cost method
7. _____ Lower of cost or market
8. _____ Retail method
9. _____ Gross profit method
10. _____ Periodic inventory system
11. _____ Perpetual inventory system
12. _____ Market
13. _____ Consignment
14. _____ Cost flow
15. _____ Goods flow
16. _____ Supply-chain management

a. The association of costs with their assumed flow

b. The current replacement cost of inventory

c. The inventory estimation method used when inventory records are lost or destroyed

d. The inventory method in which the assumed flow of costs matches the actual flow of goods

e. The inventory system that maintains continuous records

f. The actual physical movement of inventory

g. The inventory method that yields the highest net income figure during periods of rising prices

h. Goods that a merchandiser holds for sale in the regular course of business

i. A method of managing inventory and purchasing by conducting business-to-business transactions over the Internet

j. The inventory method that best follows the matching rule

k. An arrangement whereby one company sells goods for another company, for a commission

l.   The inventory system that does not maintain continuous records

m.   An occurrence that produces unusually high profits under steadily rising prices

n.   The inventory method that utilizes an average-cost-per-unit figure

o.   A rule that governs how inventory should be valued when its replacement cost falls below its historical cost

p.   The inventory estimation method that uses a cost-to-retail ratio

Note to student: The matching quiz might be completed more efficiently by starting with the definition and searching for the corresponding term.

Short Answer

Use the lines provided to answer each item.

1.   List the four basic methods used to determine the cost of merchandise inventory.

_____

_____

_____

_____

2.   List two methods of estimating ending inventory.

_____

_____

3.   Briefly distinguish between the periodic and perpetual inventory systems in terms of recordkeeping and inventory taking.

_____

_____

_____

_____

4.   List the three types of inventory involved in the manufacture of goods.

_____

_____

_____

True-False

Circle T if the statement is true, and F if it is false. Provide explanations for the false answers, using the blank lines at the end of the section.

1. T   F   The inventory turnover figure is needed to calculate days' inventory on hand.

2. T   F   When beginning inventory is understated, the cost of goods sold for the period is also understated.

3. T   F   When ending inventory is overstated, income before income taxes for the period is also overstated.

4. T   F   An error in 20x1's ending inventory will cause income before income taxes to be misstated in both 20x1 and 20x2.

5. T   F   Goods in transit belong in a buyer's inventory only if the buyer has paid for them.

6. T   F   If prices never changed, all methods of inventory valuation would result in identical figures for income before income taxes.

7. T   F   Under FIFO, goods are sold in exactly the same order as they are purchased.

8. T   F   Of the four inventory costing methods, LIFO yields the lowest net income figure during periods of falling prices.

9. T   F   Under the retail method, inventory must be figured both at cost and at retail.

10. T   F   Under the gross profit method, the cost of goods sold is estimated by multiplying the gross margin percentage by sales.

11. T   F   In periods of rising prices, the average-cost method results in a lower income before income taxes than LIFO does.

12. T   F   If FIFO is used for tax purposes, it must be used for financial reporting purposes as well.

13. T   F   When goods are held on consignment, the consignee retains possession of the goods as well as title to them until they are sold.

14. T   F   The inventory costing method that produces the highest profitability will not necessarily generate the highest cash flow.

15. T   F   In a just-in-time operating environment, a significant amount of money is tied up in inventories.

_____

_____

_____

_____

_____

_____

_____

_____

_____

_____

_____

_____

_____

_____

Multiple Choice

Circle the letter of the best answer.

1. Which of the following is least likely to be included in the cost of inventory?

    a. Freight-in
    b. The cost of storing goods
    c. The purchase cost of goods
    d. The excise tax on goods purchased

2. In periods of rising prices, which inventory method yields the highest income before income taxes?

    a. FIFO
    b. LIFO
    c. Specific identification
    d. Average-cost

3. If an item of merchandise in a warehouse is overlooked and not included in inventory, it results in

    a. overstated income before income taxes.
    b. overstated total assets.
    c. understated stockholders' equity.
    d. understated cost of goods sold.

4. Which inventory method is best suited for costing low-volume, high-priced goods?

    a. FIFO
    b. LIFO
    c. Specific identification
    d. Average-cost

5. Which of the following does the retail method of estimating inventory _not_ use or compute?

    a. Ending inventory at retail
    b. Freight-in at retail
    c. Beginning inventory at cost
    d. Sales during the period

6. The cost of merchandise inventory becomes an expense in the period in which the merchandiser

    a. sells the inventory.
    b. obtains title to the inventory.
    c. pays for the inventory.
    d. receives payment for the inventory that it has sold.

7. Goods in transit should be included in the inventory of

    a. neither the buyer nor the seller.
    b. the buyer when the goods have been shipped FOB destination.
    c. the seller when the goods have been shipped FOB shipping point.
    d. the company that has title to the goods.

8. Insurance companies often verify the extent of inventory lost or destroyed by applying the
    a. specific identification method.
    b. retail method.
    c. lower-of-cost-or-market method.
    d. gross profit method.
9. For a manufacturer, the cost of work in process and finished goods inventories includes all of the following *except*
    a. indirect materials costs.
    b. office wages.
    c. indirect labor costs.
    d. factory rent.

APPLYING YOUR KNOWLEDGE

Exercises

1. Gatlin Company uses the periodic inventory system. The company had a beginning inventory of 100 units that cost $20 each. It then made the following purchases:

    Feb.   20 Purchased 200 units at $22 each
    May   8 Purchased 150 units at $20 each
    Oct.   17 Purchased 250 units at $24 each

    Calculate the cost that would be assigned to an ending inventory of 310 units and the cost of goods sold under the LIFO, FIFO, and average-costing methods.

		Cost of Ending Inventory	Cost of Goods Sold
a.	LIFO	$_____	$_____
b.	FIFO	$_____	$_____
c.	Average-cost	$_____	$_____

2. The records of Pincus Company show the following data for the month of May:

Sales	$156,000
Beginning inventory, at cost	70,000
Beginning inventory, at retail	125,000
Net purchases, at cost	48,000
Net purchases, at retail	75,000
Freight-in	2,000

    Use the retail method to compute the estimated cost of ending inventory.

3. At the beginning of Madera Company's accounting period, the cost of merchandise inventory was $150,000. During the period, net sales were $300,000, and net purchases totaled $120,000; the historical gross margin has been 20 percent. Compute the estimated cost of ending inventory using the gross profit method.

4. Morris Enterprises uses the perpetual inventory system and the LIFO costing method. On May 1, its inventory consisted of 100 units that cost $10 each. Successive purchases and sales for May were as follows:

    May   4   Purchased 60 units at $12 each
          8   Sold 50 units
          17 Purchased 70 units at $11 each
          31 Sold 100 units

    Calculate ending inventory and cost of goods sold.

5. Assume the same facts as in Exercise **4,** except that Morris uses the average-cost method. Calculate ending inventory and cost of goods sold (round dollar amounts to the nearest cent).

CHAPTER 7

Cash and Receivables

REVIEWING THE CHAPTER

Objective 1: Identify and explain the management and ethical issues related to cash and receivables.

1. To maintain adequate liquidity, management must carefully monitor its cash and receivables. To accomplish this, it must address five key issues: managing cash needs, setting credit policies, evaluating the level of accounts receivable, financing receivables, and making ethical estimates of credit losses.

2. **Cash** consists of currency and coins on hand, checks and money orders from customers, and deposits in checking and savings accounts. Cash may also include a **compensating balance,** the minimum amount a bank requires a company to keep in its bank account as part of a credit-granting arrangement.

3. During the course of a year, most businesses experience periods of both strong and weak sales and variations in cash flow. To remain liquid throughout these seasonal cycles, a business must carefully plan for cash inflows, cash outflows, borrowing, and investing. Excess cash, for example, must be invested wisely, while providing for access when needed. On the other hand, periods of cash shortages must be anticipated so that short-term borrowing (or other means of obtaining funds) can be arranged in advance.

4. A company must use its assets to maximize income while maintaining liquidity. **Short-term financial assets** are assets that arise from cash transactions, the investment of cash, and the extension of credit. Examples are cash, accounts receivable, and notes receivable.

5. **Accounts receivable** are short-term financial assets of a wholesaler or retailer that represent payment due from credit customers. This type of credit is often called **trade credit. Installment accounts receivable** are receivables that will be collected in a series of payments; they usually are classified on the balance sheet as current assets. When loans or credit sales are made to a company's employees, officers, or owners, they are shown separately on the balance sheet with a title like "receivables from employees" rather than "assets receivable." Accounts Receivable should appear on the balance sheet as the sum of all accounts with debit balances. Customers' accounts sometimes show credit balances because of overpayment; the sum of the credit balances should appear on the balance sheet as a current liability.

6. Companies that sell on credit do so to be competitive and to increase sales. To minimize the risk of incurring bad debts, they establish policies and procedures for checking the financial backgrounds of potential credit customers. The effectiveness of a company's credit policies is commonly measured by the **receivable turnover** (net sales divided by average accounts receivable) and the **days' sales uncollected** (365 divided by the receivable turnover).

7. Companies sometimes cannot afford to wait until their receivables are collected. They can use the receivables to obtain cash by borrowing funds and pledging the accounts receivable as collateral. They can also raise funds by selling or transferring their receivables to a **factor** (e.g., a bank or finance company) through a process called **factoring.** Receivables can be factored with recourse or without recourse. With recourse means that the seller of the receivable has a **contingent liability** (potential obligation) to "make good" on the debt if the debtor fails to pay the receivable. When receivables are factored without recourse (as with major credit cards), the factor bears any losses from uncollectible accounts; because the risk involved is greater, the factoring fee is also greater. **Securitization** is the process of grouping receivables into batches and selling them (with or without recourse) at a discount to companies and investors. **Discounting** is a method of selling notes receivable in which the holder of a note receives cash upon endorsing the note and turning it over to a bank. However, the bank has recourse against the note's endorser, who is contingently liable for payment if the note's maker fails to pay the bank at the maturity date.

8. A company will always have some customers who cannot or will not pay. **Uncollectible accounts** (also called *bad debts*) are an expense of selling on credit. A company can usually afford such an expense because extending credit typically allows it to sell more and thereby increase its earnings.

9. The matching rule requires that uncollectible accounts expense be recognized in the same accounting period as the corresponding sale. Of course, at the time of a credit sale, a company does not know which customers are not going to pay or how much money will be lost. An estimate must therefore be made at the end of the accounting period. Companies with high ethical standards try to be accurate in their estimates of uncollectible accounts; those with little regard for ethics often use such estimates to manipulate earnings to their advantage.

Objective 2: Define *cash equivalents,* and explain methods of controlling cash, including bank reconciliations.

10. When a business has idle cash, management often invests it in cash equivalents to realize some investment income in the short run. **Cash equivalents** consist of investments, such as certificates of deposit and U.S. Treasury notes, that have a term of 90 days or less. Cash and cash equivalents often are combined on the balance sheet.

11. Many companies use an imprest system to maintain control over the petty cash they keep on hand for cash registers, for paying for small purchases, and for making cash advances. The checking accounts that banks offer improve control by minimizing the amount of currency a company needs to keep on hand and by providing permanent records of payments. Today, instead of writing checks to pay for purchases or to repay loans, companies often use **electronic funds transfer (EFT)**—that is, the transfer of funds between banks through electronic communication. Automated teller machines (ATMs), banking by telephone, and *debit cards* have also become commonplace. When a purchase is made with a debit card, the purchase amount is deducted directly from the customer's bank account.

12. The end-of-period balance in a bank statement rarely agrees with the balance on the company's books for that date. Thus, the accountant must prepare a **bank reconciliation** to account for the difference and to locate any errors made by the bank or the company. The bank reconciliation begins with the balance per bank and balance per books figures as of the bank statement date. Each figure is adjusted by additions and deductions, resulting in two adjusted cash balance figures, which must agree. The balance per bank figure is adjusted by information that the company knew on the bank statement date but the bank did not. On the other hand, the balance per books figure is adjusted by information that the bank knew on the bank statement date but the company did not. For example:

   a. Deposits in transit are an addition to the balance per bank.

b.   Outstanding checks are a deduction from the balance per bank.

c.   Service charges by the bank appear on the bank statement and are a deduction from the balance per books.

d.   A customer's nonsufficient funds (NSF) check is deducted from the balance per books.

e.   Interested earned on a checking account is added to the balance per books.

f.   Miscellaneous charges (as evidenced by debit memoranda) are deducted from the balance per books. Miscellaneous credits (as evidenced by credit memoranda) are added to the balance per books.

g.   Errors must be identified and corrected.

13.   After the bank reconciliation has been prepared, journal entries must be made so that the accounting records will reflect the new information supplied by the bank statement. Each entry will update both the Cash account and one or more other accounts.

Objective 3: Apply the allowance method of accounting for uncollectible accounts.

14.   Small companies are allowed to recognize the loss from an uncollectible account at the time it is determined to be uncollectible. Because of government regulations, all companies use this method, called the **direct charge-off method,** for tax purposes. However, companies that follow GAAP do not use it for financial reporting purposes because it does not conform to the matching rule. Instead, they use the allowance method, which is described below.

15.   As previously explained, the matching rule requires that, for financial reporting purposes, uncollectible accounts expense be recognized in the same accounting period as the corresponding sale. An estimate must therefore be made at the end of the accounting period. At that time, an adjusting entry is made, debiting Uncollectible Accounts Expense and crediting Allowance for Uncollectible Accounts for the estimated amount. This method of accounting for uncollectible accounts is called the **allowance method.** Uncollectible Accounts Expense appears on the income statement as an operating expense and is closed out, as are other expenses. **Allowance for Uncollectible Accounts** (also called *Allowance for Doubtful Accounts and Allowance for Bad Debts*) is a contra account to Accounts Receivable; it reduces Accounts Receivable to the amount estimated to be collectible.

16.   Two common methods of estimating uncollectible accounts are the percentage of net sales method and the accounts receivable aging method.

a.   With the **percentage of net sales method,** the estimated percentage of uncollectible accounts is multiplied by net sales for the period to determine the amount of the adjusting entry for uncollectible accounts.

b.   With the **accounts receivable aging method,** accounts receivable are placed in a "not yet due" category or in one of several "past due" categories; this procedure is called the **aging of accounts receivable.** The amounts in each category are totaled, and each total is then multiplied by an estimated percentage for bad debts. The sum of these figures represents estimated bad debts in ending Accounts Receivable. As with the percentage of net sales method, the debit is to Uncollectible Accounts Expense, and the credit is to Allowance for Uncollectible Accounts. However, the entry is for the amount that will bring Allowance for Uncollectible Accounts to the figure arrived at in the aging calculation.

c. The percentage of net sales method can be described as an income statement approach to estimating uncollectible accounts because net sales (an income statement component) is the basis for the calculation. The accounts receivable aging method is more of a balance sheet approach because it uses accounts receivable (a balance sheet component) as its computational basis.

17. When it becomes clear that a specific account receivable will not be collected, it is written off by a debit to Allowance for Uncollectible Accounts (not to Uncollectible Accounts Expense, which was already charged when the allowance was set up) and a credit to Accounts Receivable. When this happens, Accounts Receivable and Allowance for Uncollectible Accounts decrease by a similar amount, and the estimated net figure for receivables stays the same.

18. When a customer whose account has been written off pays in part or in full, two entries must be made: one to reverse the earlier write-off (which is now incorrect) and another to show the collection of the account.

Objective 4: Define *promissory note,* and make common calculations for promissory notes receivable.

19. A **promissory note** is an unconditional written promise to pay a definite sum, or principal, on demand or at a future date. The person who signs the note and thereby promises to pay is called the *maker* of the note. The person to whom money is owed is called the *payee.* The payee records all promissory notes due in less than one year as short-term **notes receivable;** the maker records them as short-term **notes payable.**

20. The **maturity date** (the date on which the note must be paid) and the **duration of the note** (the length of time between its issuance and the maturity date) must be stated on the promissory note or be determinable from the facts stated on the note.

21. **Interest** is the cost of borrowing money or the reward for lending money, depending on whether one is the borrower or the lender. The amount of interest is based on the principal (the amount of money borrowed or lent), the interest rate (the annual charge for borrowing money, which is expressed as a percentage), and the loan's length of time. It is computed as follows:

Interest = Principal × Rate of Interest × Time (length of loan)

22. The **maturity value** of an interest-bearing note is the face value of the note (the principal) plus interest at the maturity date. A note can also be non-interest-bearing. In that case, maturity value is equal to the principal, but the principal includes implied interest.

23. End-of-period adjustments must be made for notes that apply to both the current and future periods. In this way, interest can be divided correctly among the periods. The note's payee would recognize both interest receivable and interest income.

24. A **dishonored note** is one that is not paid at the maturity date. When a note is dishonored, the payee transfers the total amount due (including interest income) from Notes Receivable to an account receivable from the maker of the note.

Summary of Journal Entries Introduced in Chapter 7

A. (LO 3)   Uncollectible Accounts Expense   XX (amount estimated)
                   Allowance for Uncollectible Accounts   XX (amount estimated)
                       To record the estimated uncollectible accounts
                       expense for the year

B. (LO 3)   Allowance for Uncollectible Accounts   XX (defaulted amount)
                   Accounts Receivable   XX (defaulted amount)
                       To write off receivable of a specific customer as
                       uncollectible

SELF-TEST

Test your knowledge of the chapter by choosing the best answer for each item below.

1. Because Tamara Company's sales are concentrated in the summer, its managers must carefully plan for borrowing needs and short-term investments. This is an example of management's responsibility to

    a.   finance receivables.
    b.   manage cash needs during seasonal cycles.
    c.   set reasonable credit policies.
    d.   finance purchases of long-term assets.

2. At year end, RJN Company has $3,400 on hand in currency and coins, deposits in checking accounts of $32,000, U.S. Treasury bills due in 60 days worth $58,000, and U.S. Treasury bonds due in 180 days worth $88,000. On its balance sheet, cash and cash equivalents will be shown as

    a. $3,400.
    b. $35,400.
    c. $93,400.
    d. $181,400.

3. On a bank reconciliation, which of the following items would be added to the balance per bank?

    a.   Deposits in transit
    b.   Bank service charge
    c.   Outstanding checks
    d.   Interest earned

4. The matching rule

    a.   necessitates the recording of an estimated amount for bad debts.
    b.   is violated when the allowance method is used.
    c.   results in the recording of an exact amount for losses from bad debts.
    d.   requires that losses from bad debts be recorded whenever a customer defaults.

5. Which of the following methods of recording uncollectible accounts expense would best be described as an income statement method?

    a.   Accounts receivable aging method
    b.   Direct charge-off method
    c.   Percentage of net sales method
    d.   Both **a** and **b**

6.   Using the percentage of net sales method, uncollectible accounts expense for the year is estimated to be $54,000. If the balance of Allowance for Uncollectible Accounts is a $16,000 credit before adjustment, what is the balance after adjustment?

    a. $16,000
    b. $38,000
    c. $54,000
    d. $70,000

7.   Using the accounts receivable aging method, estimated uncollectible accounts are $74,000. If the balance of Allowance for Uncollectible Accounts is an $18,000 credit before adjustment, what is the balance after adjustment?

    a. $18,000
    b. $56,000
    c. $74,000
    d. $92,000

8.   Each of the following is a characteristic of a promissory note *except* a(n)

    a.   payee who has an unconditional right to receive a definite amount on a definite date.
    b.   amount to be paid that can be determined on the date the note is signed.
    c.   due date that can be determined on the date the note is signed.
    d.   maker who agrees to pay a definite sum subject to conditions to be determined at a later date.

9.   The maturity value of a $6,000, three-month note at 10 percent is

    a. $600.
    b. $5,850.
    c. $6,600.
    d. $6,150.

10.   On a bank reconciliation, which of the following items would be added to the balance per books?

    a.   Note receivable collected by bank
    b.   NSF check from customer
    c.   Deposit made, but not shown on bank statement
    d.   Issued check for $52, but recorded it for $25

TESTING YOUR KNOWLEDGE

Matching*

Match each term with its definition by writing the appropriate letter in the blank.

1.   _____Trade credit

2.   _____Factoring

3.   _____Uncollectible accounts expense

4.   _____Allowance for uncollectible accounts

5.   _____Installment accounts receivable

6.   _____Promissory note

7.   _____Maker

8.   _____Payee

a.   Short-term investments of 90 days or less

b.   Coins, currency, checks, money orders, and bank deposits

c.   The charge for borrowing money, expressed as a percentage

d.   A note that is not paid at the maturity date

e.   A written promise to pay

f.   Estimated bad debts as shown on the income statement

9. _____Maturity date

10. _____Maturity value

11. _____Interest rate

12. _____Interest

13. _____Principal

14. _____Contingent liability

15. _____Dishonored note

16. _____Discounting

17. _____Compensating balance

18. _____Cash equivalents

19. _____Cash

20. _____Securitization

g.   Selling or transferring accounts receivable

h.   A potential obligation

i.   The date on which payment on a note is due

j.   Allowing customers to pay for merchandise over a period of time

k.   The grouping of receivables into batches for selling at a discount

l.   The creditor named in a promissory note

m.   Estimated bad debts as represented on the balance sheet

n.   Selling a note before its maturity date

o.   The charge for borrowing money, expressed in dollars

p.   Receivables that will be collected in a series of payments

q.   A minimum amount that a bank requires a company to keep in its account

r.   The debtor named in a promissory note

s.   The amount of money borrowed or lent

t.   A note's principal plus interest

Note to student: The matching quiz might be completed more efficiently by starting with the definition and searching for the corresponding term.

Short Answer

Use the lines provided to answer each item.

1.   List three methods used to compute uncollectible accounts expense.

_____

_____

_____

2. Explain the concept of contingent liability as it relates to factoring.

_____

_____

_____

_____

3. Under what circumstance would there be a debit balance in Allowance for Uncollectible Accounts?

_____

_____

_____

4. List three examples of short-term financial assets.

_____

_____

_____

True-False

Circle T if the statement is true, and F if it is false. Provide explanations for the false answers, using the blank lines at the end of the section.

1. T F Under the direct charge-off method, Allowance for Uncollectible Accounts does not exist.

2. T F The percentage of net sales method violates the matching rule.

3. T F Under the accounts receivable aging method, the balance in Allowance for Uncollectible Accounts is ignored in making the adjusting entry.

4. T F Allowance for Uncollectible Accounts is a contra account to Accounts Receivable.

5. T F Loans to a company's officers should not be included in Accounts Receivable on the balance sheet.

6. T F When a customer overpays, his or her account on the company's books has a credit balance.

7. T F Interest of 5 percent on $700 for 90 days would be computed as follows: 700 × .05 × 90.

8. T F *Trade credit* refers to sales that wholesalers and retailers make on credit.

9. T F When a note is discounted at a bank, the maker must make good on the note if the payee defaults.

10. T F A note dated December 14 and due February 14 has a duration of 60 days.

11. T F The figure for receivable turnover is a component in the calculation of days' sales uncollected.

12. T F Under the allowance method, the entry to write off a specific account as uncollectible decreases total assets.

13. T F   The maturity value of an interest-bearing note equals principal plus interest.

14. T F   Under the allowance method, a specific account is written off with a debit to Uncollectible Accounts Expense and a credit to Accounts Receivable.

15. T F   The payee of a dishonored note should record interest earned on the note.

16. T F   Uncollectible accounts are an expense of selling on credit.

17. T F   Accounts receivable are an example of a cash equivalent.

18. T F   The use of a major credit card (e.g., MasterCard) is an example of factoring with recourse.

19. T F   An *imprest system* refers to the mechanics of a petty cash fund.

20. T F   Securitization involves selling batched receivables at a discount.

21. T F   A check that is outstanding for two consecutive months should be included in both months' bank reconciliations.

22. T F   A debit memorandum on a bank statement indicates an addition to the bank balance.

23. T F   After a bank reconciliation has been completed, the company must make journal entries to adjust for all outstanding checks.

24. T F   A bank reconciliation for the month of September should begin with the balance per books and the balance per bank on September 1.

_____

_____

_____

_____

_____

_____

_____

_____

_____

_____

_____

_____

_____

_____

_____

_____

_____

_____

_____
_____
_____
_____
_____

Multiple Choice

Circle the letter of the best answer.

1. Which of the following does *not* equal the others?

    a. $600 for 60 days at 6 percent
    b. $1,200 for 120 days at 3 percent
    c. $300 for 120 days at 6 percent
    d. $600 for 30 days at 12 percent

2. At the balance sheet date, a company estimates that $1,500 of net sales for the year will not be collected. A debit balance of $600 exists in Allowance for Uncollectible Accounts. Under the percentage of net sales method, Uncollectible Accounts Expense would be debited and Allowance for Uncollectible Accounts would be credited for

    a. $600.
    b. $1,100.
    c. $1,500.
    d. $2,100.

3. A contingent liability exists when

    a. a note is discounted.
    b. a note is dishonored.
    c. interest accrues on a note.
    d. a note reaches maturity.

4. Based on the accounts receivable aging method, a company estimates that $850 of end-of-period accounts receivable will not be collected. A credit balance of $300 exists in Allowance for Uncollectible Accounts. Uncollectible Accounts Expense should be recorded for

    a. $300.
    b. $550.
    c. $850.
    d. $1,150.

5. Under the accounts receivable aging method, a specific customer's account is written off by debiting

    a. Uncollectible Accounts Expense and crediting Allowance for Uncollectible Accounts.
    b. Accounts Receivable and crediting Allowance for Uncollectible Accounts.
    c. Allowance for Uncollectible Accounts and crediting Accounts Receivable.
    d. Uncollectible Accounts Expense and crediting Accounts Receivable.

6. Which of the following *cannot* be determined from the information on a note?

    a. Discount rate
    b. Interest rate
    c. Interest
    d. Maturity date

7. Which of the following methods of handling bad debts often violates the matching rule?

   a. Percentage of net sales method
   b. Direct charge-off method
   c. Accounts receivable aging method
   d. Both **a** and **c**

8. Which of the following is *not* considered a short-term financial asset?

   a. Notes receivable
   b. Cash
   c. Inventory
   d. Accounts receivable

9. A company's bank statement erroneously shows a $1,000 deposit as $100, and the bank is notified. The $900 error appears on the bank reconciliation as a(n)

   a. addition to the balance per bank.
   b. deduction from the balance per bank.
   c. addition to the balance per books.
   d. deduction from the balance per books.

10. After the bank reconciliation has been completed, a company must make journal entries to adjust for all of the following *except*

   a. bank service charges.
   b. deposits in transit.
   c. a note collected by the bank.
   d. interest earned.

APPLYING YOUR KNOWLEDGE

Exercises

1. For the following set of facts, make the necessary entries for Doheny's Department Store in the journal provided.

Dec. 31 Interest of $75 has accrued on notes receivable.

Dec. 31 Net sales for the year were $600,000. It is estimated that 4 percent will not be collected. Make the entry for uncollectible accounts.

Jan. 3 Anna Kohn purchased $10,000 worth of goods on credit in November. She now issues Doherty's a $10,000, 30-day, 6 percent note, thus extending her credit period.

Jan. 8 Tom O'Brien goes bankrupt and notifies Doherty's that he cannot pay for the $1,000 worth of goods that he purchased last year on account.

General Journal			
Date	Description	Debit	Credit

2. Calculate interest on the following amounts:

    a. $7,200 at 4% for 20 days = _____

    b. $52,000 at 7% for 3 months = _____

    c. $4,317 at 6% for 60 days = _____

    d. $18,000 at 8% for 1 day = _____

3. Mackey's Hardware had net sales of $250,000 for 20x1. In addition, it had beginning accounts receivable of $46,000 and ending accounts receivable of $50,000. Based on this information, compute the following ratios, rounding amounts to one decimal place.

    a. The receivable turnover = _____ times.

    b. The days' sales uncollected = _____ days.

4.   The facts that follow are needed to prepare a bank reconciliation for Bernstein Company as of May 31, 20x2. For each, write the correct letter (a, b, c, or d) to indicate where it should appear.

a = Addition to the balance per bank

b = Deduction from the balance per bank

c = Addition to the balance per books

d = Deduction from the balance per books

_____ 1.   The service charge by the bank was $8.

_____ 2.   A $1,700 note receivable was collected for the company by the bank. No collection fee was charged.

_____ 3.   There were to outstanding checks, totaling $3,200.

_____ 4.   A $355 NSF check drawn by a customer was deducted from the company's bank account and returned to the company.

_____ 5.   A deposit of $725 was made after banking hours on May 31.

_____ 6.   Check no. 185 was drawn for $342 but was recorded erroneously in the company's books as $324.

CHAPTER 8

Current Liabilities and the Time Value of Money

REVIEWING THE CHAPTER

Objective 1: Identify the management issues related to current liabilities.

1. Liabilities, one of the three major parts of the balance sheet, are legal obligations for the future payment of assets or the future performance of services. The primary reason for incurring current liabilities is to meet needs for cash during the operating cycle.

2. If a company's cash flows are inadequate to meet its current liabilities, the company could be forced into bankruptcy; thus, careful management of cash flows related to current liabilities is critical. Another issue in managing cash flows and current liabilities is the length of time creditors allow for payment. Common measures of this time are payables turnover and days' payable. **Payables turnover** (measured in number of "times") shows the relative size of a company's accounts payable. The formula for calculating it is as follows:

$$\frac{\text{Cost of Goods Sold} \pm \text{Change in Merchandise Inventory}}{\text{Average Accounts Payable}}$$

Days' payable shows the average length of time a company takes to pay its accounts payable. It is computed as follows:

$$\frac{365 \text{ days}}{\text{Payables Turnover}}$$

3. Ethical reporting of liabilities requires that they be properly recognized, valued, classified, and disclosed. A liability should be recognized (recorded) at the time it is incurred. However, for accrued and estimated liabilities, it is necessary to make adjusting entries at the end of an accounting period. Contracts representing future obligations are not recorded as liabilities until they become current obligations.

4. Liabilities are valued at the actual or estimated amount of money necessary to satisfy the obligation or at the fair market value of the goods or services that must be delivered.

5. **Current liabilities** are obligations expected to be satisfied within one year or the normal operating cycle, whichever is longer. They are normally paid out of current assets or with cash generated from operations. **Long-term liabilities** are obligations due beyond one year or the normal operating cycle.

6. Supplemental disclosure of some liabilities may be required in the notes to the financial statements—for example, when a company has special credit arrangements that can influence potential investors' decisions.

Objective 2: Identify, compute, and record definitely determinable and estimated current liabilities.

7. Current liabilities consist of definitely determinable liabilities and estimated liabilities.

8. **Definitely determinable liabilities** are obligations that can be measured exactly. They include accounts payable, bank loans and commercial paper, notes payable, accrued liabilities, dividends payable, sales and excise taxes payable, current portions of long-term debt, payroll liabilities, and unearned revenues.

    a. Accounts payable, sometimes called *trade accounts payable,* are obligations currently due to suppliers of goods and services.

    b. To finance current operations by borrowing funds, companies often obtain a **line of credit** with a bank. Companies with excellent credit ratings can also borrow short-term funds by issuing **commercial paper** (unsecured loans sold to the public).

    c. Short-term notes payable are current obligations evidenced by promissory notes. Interest is usually stated separately on the face of the note.

    d. Accrued liabilities (also called *accrued expenses*) are actual or estimated liabilities that exist at the balance sheet date but are unrecorded at that date. An end-of-period adjustment is needed to record both the expenses and the accrued liabilities.

    e. Dividends payable represent a corporation's obligation to distribute earnings to stockholders. This obligation arises only when the board of directors declares a dividend.

    f. Most states and many cities levy a sales tax on retail transactions. The federal government also charges an excise tax on some products. The merchant must collect payment for these taxes at the time of the sale; the related journal entry records both the receipt of cash and the tax liabilities.

    g. If a portion of long-term debt is due within the next year and is to be paid from current assets, that amount should be classified as a current liability; the remaining debt should be classified as a long-term liability.

    h. Payroll liabilities are a business's employee-related obligations. Payroll accounting applies only to an organization's employees, who are under its direct supervision and control; it does not apply to independent contractors, such as lawyers and CPAs. A business is not only responsible for paying its employees **wages** or **salaries;** it is also obligated for such items as social security (FICA) taxes, Medicare, and unemployment taxes. In addition, it must withhold income taxes from its employees' gross earnings and remit them to the appropriate government agencies. Some companies also contribute to medical insurance for employees and to pension funds.

    i. **Unearned revenues** represent obligations to deliver goods or services in return for advance payment. When delivery takes place, Unearned Revenue is debited, and a revenue account is credited.

9. **Estimated liabilities** are definite obligations, but the amount of the obligations must be estimated at the balance sheet date because the exact figure will not be known until a future date. Examples of estimated liabilities are corporate income taxes, property taxes, promotional costs, product warranties, and vacation pay.

    a. A corporation's income tax depends on its net income, a figure that often is not determined until well after the balance sheet date.

    b. Property taxes are levied on real and personal property. Very often, a company's accounting period ends before property taxes have been assessed, and the company must therefore estimate the taxes.

    c. Promotional costs associated with such things as coupons, rebates, and frequent flyer programs are usually treated as a reduction in sales rather than as an expense.

d.   When a company sells a product with a warranty, a liability exists for the length of the warranty. Many warranties will remain in effect in subsequent accounting periods. However, the warranty expense and liability must be recorded in the period of the sale no matter when the company makes good on the warranty. Therefore, at the end of each accounting period, the company should make an estimate of future warranty expense that will apply to the present period's sales.

e.   In a company in which employees earn vacation pay for working a certain length of time, the company must estimate the vacation pay that applies to each payroll period. The debit is to Vacation Pay Expense, and the credit is to Estimated Liability for Vacation Pay. The liability decreases (is debited) when an employee receives vacation pay.

Objective 3: Distinguish *contingent liabilities* from *commitments*.

10.   Businesses are required to disclose contingent liabilities and commitments in the notes to their financial statements.

a.   A **contingent liability** is a potential liability that may or may not become an actual liability. The uncertainty about its outcome is settled when a future event does or does not occur. Contingent liabilities arise from things like pending lawsuits, tax disputes, and failure to follow government regulations. Two conditions must be met before a contingency is entered in the accounting records: the liability must be probable, and it can be reasonably estimated.

b.   A **commitment** is a legal obligation that does not qualify for recognition as a liability. Leases and purchase agreements are the most common examples of commitments.

Objective 4: Define the *time value of money*, and apply it to future and present values.

11.   The timing of the receipt and payment of cash (measured in interest) is an important consideration in making business decisions. The effect of the passage of time on holding or not holding money is called the **time value of money. Interest** is the cost of using money for a specific period of time; it may be calculated on a simple or compound basis.

a.   When **simple interest** is computed for one or more periods, the amount on which interest is computed does *not* increase each period (that is, interest is not computed on principal plus accrued interest).

b.   However, when **compound interest** is computed for two or more periods, the amount on which interest is computed *does* increase each period (that is, interest is computed on principal plus accrued interest).

12.   **Future value** is the amount an investment will be worth at a future date if invested at compound interest.

a.   Future value may be computed on a single sum invested at compound interest. Table 1 in your text facilitates this computation.

b.   Future value may also be computed on an **ordinary annuity** (i.e., a series of equal payments made at the end of equal intervals of time) at compound interest. Table 2 in your text facilitates this computation.

13.   **Present value** is the amount that must be invested now at a given rate of interest to produce a given future value or values.

a.   Present value may be computed on a single sum due in the future. Table 3 in your text facilitates this computation.

b.   Present value may also be computed on an ordinary annuity. Table 4 in your text facilitates this computation.

Objective 5: Apply the time value of money to simple accounting situations.

14. Present value may be used in accounting to (a) determine the value of an asset being considered for purchase, (b) calculate deferred payments for the purchase of an asset, (c) account for the investment of idle cash, (d) accumulate funds needed to pay off a loan, and (e) determine numerous other accounting quantities, such as the value of a bond, pension and lease obligations, and depreciation.

Summary of Journal Entries Introduced in Chapter 8

A.	(LO 2)	Cash		XX (amount received)
		Notes Payable		XX (face amount)
		Issued promissory note with interest stated separately		

B.	(LO 2)	Notes Payable		XX (face amount)
		Interest Expense		XX (amount incurred)
		Cash		XX (maturity amount)
		Payment of note with interest stated separately		

C.	(LO 2)	Interest Expense		XX (amount accrued)
		Interest Payable		XX (amount accrued)
		To record interest expense on note with interest stated separately		

D.	(LO 2)	Cash		XX (amount collected)
		Sales		XX (price charged)
		Sales Tax Payable		XX (amount to remit)
		Excise Tax Payable		XX (amount to remit)
		Sale of merchandise and collection of sales and excise taxes		

E.	(LO 2)	Wages Expense		XX (gross amount)
		Employees' Federal Income Taxes Payable		XX (amount withheld)
		Employees' State Income Taxes Payable		XX (amount withheld)
		Social Security Tax Payable		XX (employees' share)
		Medicare Tax Payable		XX (employees' share)
		Medical Insurance Premiums Payable		XX (employees' share)
		Pension Contributions Payable		XX (employees' share)
		Wages Payable		XX (take-home pay)
		To record payroll		

F.	(LO 2)	Payroll Taxes and Benefits Expense		XX (total employer payroll taxes)
		Social Security Tax Payable		XX (employer's share)
		Medicare Tax Payable		XX (employer's share)
		Medical Insurance Premiums Payable		XX (employer's share)
		Pension Contributions Payable		XX (employer's share)
		Federal Unemployment Tax Payable		XX (amount incurred)
		State Unemployment Tax Payable		XX (amount incurred)
		To record payroll taxes and other costs		

G.   (LO 2)   Cash   XX (amount prepaid)
                   Unearned Subscriptions   XX (amount to earn)
                       Receipt of annual subscriptions in advance

H.   (LO 2)   Unearned Subscriptions   XX (amount earned)
                   Subscription Revenues   XX (amount earned)
                       Delivery of monthly magazine issues

I.   (LO 2)   Income Taxes Expense   XX (amount estimated)
                   Income Taxes Payable   XX (amount estimated)
                       To record estimated federal income taxes

J.   (LO 2)   Product Warranty Expense   XX (amount estimated)
                   Estimated Product Warranty Liability   XX (amount estimated)
                       To record estimated product warranty expense

K.   (LO 2)   Cash   XX (fee charged)
                   Estimated Product Warranty Liability   XX (cost of part)
                   Service Revenue   XX (fee charged)
                   Merchandise Inventory   XX (cost of part)
                       Replacement of part under warranty

L.   (LO 2)   Vacation Pay Expense   XX (amount incurred)
                   Estimated Liability for Vacation Pay   XX (amount owed or
                                                                accrued)
                       Estimated vacation pay expense

M.   (LO 2)   Estimated Liability for Vacation Pay   XX (amount taken)
                   Cash (or Wages Payable)   XX (amount paid or payable)
                       Wages of employees on vacation

SELF-TEST

Test your knowledge of the chapter by choosing the best answer for each item below.

1.   Failure to record a liability will probably
      a.   have no effect on net income.
      b.   result in overstated net income.
      c.   result in overstated total assets.
      d.   result in overstated total liabilities and stockholders' equity.
2.   Which of the following is most likely to be a definitely determinable liability?
      a.   Property taxes payable
      b.   Product warranty liability
      c.   Income taxes payable
      d.   Interest payable
3.   Which of the following is a payroll tax borne by both employee and employer?
      a.   Excise tax
      b.   Income tax
      c.   FUTA tax
      d.   Medicare tax

4.   The present value of a single sum table would *not* contain the factor

   a.   1.000.
   b.   0.926.
   c.   0.744.
   d.   0.837.

5.   Which of the following is most likely to be an estimated liability?

   a.   Unearned revenues
   b.   Vacation pay liability
   c.   Current portion of long-term debt
   d.   Payroll liabilities

6.   If product J cost $100 and had a 2 percent failure rate, the estimated warranty expense in a month in which 1,000 units were sold would be

   a. $2,000.
   b. $100.
   c. $20.
   d. $20,000.

7.   Seventy percent of a company's employees typically qualify to receive two weeks' paid vacation per year. The amount of estimated vacation pay liability for a week in which the total payroll is $3,000 is

   a. $2,100.
   b. $42.
   c. $84.
   d. $120.

8.   A business accepts a $10,000, 12 percent note due in three years. Assuming simple interest, how much will the business receive when the note falls due?

   a. $10,360
   b. $14,049
   c. $10,000
   d. $13,600

9.   Marcia wishes to deposit an amount into her savings account that will enable her to withdraw $1,000 per year for the next four years. She should deposit $1,000 multiplied by the

   a.   future value of a single sum factor.
   b.   present value of a single sum factor.
   c.   future value of an ordinary annuity factor.
   d.   present value of an ordinary annuity factor.

10.   Payroll Taxes and Benefits Expense contains all of the following *except*

   a.   federal unemployment tax payable.
   b.   social security tax payable.
   c.   federal income tax payable.
   d.   state unemployment tax payable.

TESTING YOUR KNOWLEDGE

Matching*

Match each term with its definition by writing the appropriate letter in the blank.

1. _____Current liabilities
2. _____Long-term liabilities
3. _____Definitely determinable liabilities
4. _____Estimated liabilities
5. _____Unearned revenues
6. _____Vacation pay
7. _____Interest
8. _____Commercial paper
9. _____Simple interest
10. _____Compound interest
11. _____Future value
12. _____Present value
13. _____Commitment
14. _____Ordinary annuity
15. _____Contingent liabilities
16. _____Wages
17. _____Salaries
18. _____Line of credit

a. A legal obligation that does not qualify for recognition as a liability

b. Obligations that are expected to be satisfied within one year or the normal operating cycle, whichever is longer

c. An arrangement with a bank that allows a company to borrow funds when needed

d. Employee compensation at an hourly rate

e. Obligations that exist but cannot be measured exactly on the balance sheet date

f. The computation whereby interest is computed without considering accrued interest

g. Obligations that can be measured exactly

h. A series of equal payments made at the end of each period

i. The amount an investment will be worth at a future date

j. Payment for time off that an employee has earned

k. The computation whereby interest is computed on the original amount plus accrued interest

l. Unsecured loans sold to the public

m. The cost of using money for a specific period of time

n. The amount that must be invested now to produce a given future value

o. Obligations to deliver goods or services in return for advance payment

p.   Employment compensation at a
     monthly or yearly rate

q.   Potential liabilities that may or may
     not become actual liabilities

r.   Obligations that are not expected to
     be satisfied in the current period

Note to student: The matching quiz might be completed more efficiently by starting with the definition and searching for the corresponding term.

Short Answer

Use the lines provided to answer each item.

1. Current liabilities fall into two main categories. What are these categories?

    _____

    _____

2. Provide three examples of contingent liabilities.

    _____

    _____

    _____

3. Provide three examples of estimated liabilities.

    _____

    _____

    _____

4. Provide three examples of definitely determinable liabilities.

    _____

    _____

    _____

5. List the two most common examples of commitments.

    _____

    _____

6. List the four time value of money concepts illustrated in this chapter.

    _____

    _____

    _____

    _____

7.   List four withholdings from an employee's salary that are always or almost always required.

_____

_____

_____

_____

True-False

Circle T if the statement is true, and F if it is false. Provide explanations for the false answers, using the blank lines at the end of the section.

1.   T   F   Unearned revenues appear on the income statement.

2.   T   F   A contract to purchase goods in the future does not require that a current liability be recorded.

3.   T   F   The failure to record an accrued liability results in an overstatement of net income.

4.   T   F   The current portion of a long-term debt is a current liability if it is to be satisfied with cash.

5.   T   F   Sales tax payable is an example of an estimated liability.

6.   T   F   Warranties fall into the category of definitely determinable liabilities.

7.   T   F   The factors incorporated into the "present value of a single sum to be received in the future" table are all less than 1.000.

8.   T   F   An ordinary annuity is a series of equal payments made at the beginning of equal periods of time.

9.   T   F   FUTA is a tax borne by both the employer and the employee.

10. T   F   Every contingent liability must eventually become an actual liability or no liability at all.

11. T   F   The higher the interest rate applied, the higher the present value of an amount or annuity to be received in the future.

12. T   F   Liabilities basically are obligations that result from past transactions.

13. T   F   The payables turnover is expressed in terms of days.

14. T   F   If a refrigerator is sold with a warranty in year 1 and repairs are made in year 2, Product Warranty Expense should be recorded in year 2.

15. T   F   Interest on a $5,000, 10%, 90-day note is obtained by taking $5,000 × .1 × 90.

16. T   F   Unearned Subscriptions is recorded as a credit and eliminated with a debit.

17. T   F   Typically, unemployment taxes are a component of Payroll Taxes and Benefits Expense.

18. T   F   A decrease in the payables turnover will produce an increase in the days' payable.

_____

_____

_____

_____
_____
_____
_____
_____
_____
_____
_____
_____
_____
_____
_____
_____
_____

Multiple Choice

Circle the letter of the best answer.

1. Which of the following is *not* a definitely determinable liability?
   a. Dividends payable
   b. Deferred revenues
   c. Property taxes payable
   d. Excise taxes payable

2. All of the following involve estimated liabilities *except*
   a. warranties.
   b. vacation pay.
   c. promotional costs.
   d. dividends.

3. Which of the following is *not* deducted from an employee's earnings?
   a. State unemployment tax
   b. Union dues
   c. Social security tax
   d. Charitable contributions

4. The amount of federal income tax withheld on behalf of an employee is recorded as a
   a. payroll expense.
   b. contra account.
   c. current asset.
   d. current liability.

5. When an employee receives vacation pay, the company should debit

    a. Vacation Pay Expense and credit Cash.
    b. Vacation Pay Receivable and credit Cash.
    c. Estimated Liability for Vacation Pay and credit Cash.
    d. Vacation Pay Expense and credit Estimated Liability for Vacation Pay.

6. Compound interest is computed semiannually on $100 in the bank for five years at 10 percent annual interest. The future value table is used by multiplying the $100 by which factor?

    a. 5 periods at 10 percent
    b. 10 periods at 5 percent
    c. 10 periods at 10 percent
    d. 5 periods at 5 percent

7. The journal entry to accrue interest at year-end on a note payable would be

    a. debit Interest Expense, credit Cash
    b. debit Notes Payable, credit Interest Expense
    c. debit Interest Expense, credit Notes Payable
    d. debit Interest Expense, credit Interest Payable

Use the following present and future value information to answer Questions 8 and 9.

Period	Present Value of $1 Discounted at 12% per Period	Future Value of $1 at 12% per Period
1	0.893	1.120
2	0.797	1.254

8. What amount should be deposited in a bank today at 12 percent interest (compounded annually) to grow to $100 two years from today?

    a. $100/0.797
    b. $100 × 0.893 × 2
    c. ($100 × 0.893) + ($100 × 0.797)
    d. $100 × 0.797

9. If $200 were placed in the bank today at 12 percent interest (compounded annually), what amount would be available two years from today?

    a. $200 × 1.120 × 2
    b. $200/1.254
    c. $200 × 1.254
    d. $200/1.120

APPLYING YOUR KNOWLEDGE

Exercises

1. During 20x5, Paul's Appliance Store sold 300 washing machines, each with a one-year guarantee. It estimated that 5 percent of the washing machines eventually would require some type of repair, at an average cost of $35. Prepare the adjusting entry that Paul's would make concerning the warranty, as well as the entry that it would make on April 9, 20x6, for a repair that cost $48.

General Journal

Date		Description	Debit	Credit

2. Pat Bauer, an office worker who is paid $6.50 per hour, worked 40 hours during the week that ended May 11. Social security taxes are 6.20 percent, Medicare taxes are 1.45 percent, union dues are $5, state taxes withheld are $8, and federal income taxes withheld are $52. Bauer's employer must pay (on the basis of gross earnings) social security taxes of 6.20 percent, Medicare taxes of 1.45 percent, federal unemployment taxes of 0.8 percent, and state unemployment taxes of 5.4 percent. In the journal provided below, record an entry that summarizes Pat Bauer's earnings for the week and an entry that records the employer's payroll taxes. Round amounts to the nearest cent.

General Journal

Date		Description	Debit	Credit

3. Tillit Corporation has current assets of $100,000 and current liabilities of $40,000, of which accounts payable are $30,000. Last year, its accounts payable were $20,000. Its cost of goods sold is $290,000, and its merchandise decreased by $15,000. Using the relevant data, compute the following short-term liquidity measures (round amounts to one decimal place):

a. Payables turnover: _____

b. Days' payable: _____

4. The manager of Westfield Lanes is considering replacing the existing automatic pinsetters with improved ones that cost $10,000 each. It is estimated that each new pinsetter will save $2,000 annually and will last for ten years. Using an interest rate of 18 percent and the time value of money tables in your text, what is the present value of the savings of each new pinsetter to Westfield Lanes?

    $_____

    Should the purchase be made? _____

5. Use the time value of money tables in your text to answer the following questions.

    a. What amount received today is equivalent to $1,000 receivable at the end of five years, assuming a 6 percent annual interest rate compounded annually?

        $_____

    b. If payments of $1,000 are invested at 8 percent annual interest at the end of each quarter for one year, compute the amount that will accumulate by the time the last payment is made.

        $_____

    c. If $1,000 is invested on June 30, 20x1, at 6 percent annual interest compounded semiannually, how much will be in the account on June 30, 20x3?

        $_____

    d. Compute the equal annual deposits required to accumulate a fund of $100,000 at the end of 20 years, assuming a 10 percent interest rate compounded annually.

        $_____

Crossword Puzzle: Chapters 6, 7, and 8

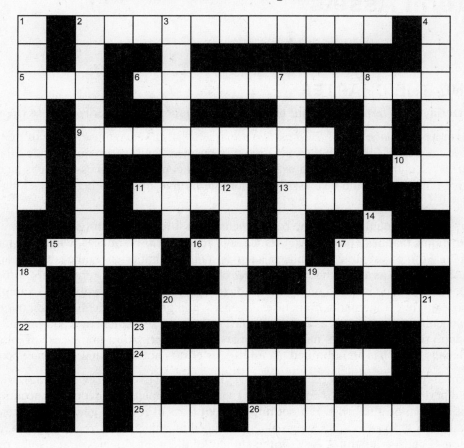

ACROSS

2 Goods-sold-by-one-for-another arrangement
5 Inventory valuation method (abbr.)
6 Goods
9 Liability imprecise in amount
10 The "I" in "LIFO"
11 Method that produces most up-to-date ending inventory (abbr.)
13 List receivables according to due date
15 _____ reconciliation
16 Like unproductive cash
17 Social security tax (abbr.)
20 Potential, as a liability
22 Bank advances
24 _____ cycle
25 Payable
26 Trade _____

DOWN

1 Compensating _____
2 Unsecured loans sold to the public (2 words)
3 _____ identification method
4 _____ value
7 _____ -cost method
8 Cost of using money (abbr.)
12 Type of annuity
14 _____ of credit
18 Percentage of net _____ method
19 Just-_____ operating environment
21 _____ value of money
23 Cost of goods _____

CHAPTER 9

Long-Term Assets

REVIEWING THE CHAPTER

Objective 1: Define *long-term assets*, and explain the management issues related to them.

1. **Long-term assets** (once called *fixed assets*) are assets that (a) have a useful life of more than one year, (b) are acquired for use in the operation of a business, and (c) are not intended for resale to customers. Assets that are not being used in the normal course of business, such as land held for speculative purposes, should be classified as long-term investments rather than as long-term assets.

2. Property, plant, and equipment is the balance sheet classification for **tangible assets,** which are long-term assets that have physical substance, and for **natural resources,** which are long-term assets in the form of valuable substances, such as standing timber, oil and gas fields, and mineral deposits. **Intangible assets** is the balance sheet classification for long-term assets without physical substance whose value is based on rights or advantages accruing to the owners; examples are patents, copyrights, trademarks, franchises, licenses, and goodwill. The allocation of costs to different accounting periods is called **depreciation** in the case of plant and equipment (plant assets), **depletion** in the case of natural resources, and **amortization** in the case of intangible assets. Because land has an unlimited useful life, its cost is not converted into an expense.

3. Long-term assets are generally reported at **carrying value** (also called *book value*), which is the unexpired part of a plant asset's cost. Carrying value is calculated by deducting accumulated depreciation from original cost. If **asset impairment** (loss of revenue-generating potential) occurs, the long-term asset's carrying value is reduced to reflect its current fair value (an application of conservatism). A loss for the amount of the write-down would also be recorded. Taking a large write-down in a bad year is often called "taking a bath," because it presumably will reduce future depreciation or amortization and, thus, raise the likelihood of profit realization.

4. Capital budgeting is the process of evaluating a decision to acquire a long-term asset. One common capital budgeting technique compares the amount and timing of cash inflows and outflows over the life of the asset under consideration. If the net present value of those cash flows is positive, the asset should probably be purchased. Information about long-term asset acquisitions may be found in the investing activities section of the statement of cash flows.

5. Long-term assets not purchased for cash must be financed. Common financing techniques include issuing stock, bonds, and long-term notes. **Free cash flow** is a good measure of a business's ability to finance long-term assets. Specifically, it is the amount of cash that remains after deducting the funds a company must commit to continue operating at its planned level, and is computed as follows:

Free Cash Flow = Net Cash Flows from Operating Activities – Dividends – Purchases of Plant Assets + Sales of Plant Assets

6. The major problem in accounting for long-term assets is to figure out how much of the asset has benefited the current period and how much should be carried forward as an asset that will benefit future periods. To resolve these issues, one must determine (a) the cost of the asset; (b) the method of matching the cost with revenues; (c) the treatment of subsequent expenditures, such as repairs and additions; and (d) the treatment of the asset at the time of disposal.

Objective 2: Distinguish between *capital expenditures* and *revenue expenditures*, and account for the cost of property, plant, and equipment.

7. Before recording an **expenditure** (a payment or the incurrence of liability) for a long-term asset, one must determine whether it was a capital expenditure or a revenue expenditure. A **capital expenditure** is an expenditure for the purchase or expansion of long-term assets. Capital expenditures are recorded in the asset accounts because they will benefit several future accounting periods. A **revenue expenditure** is an expenditure for ordinary repairs, maintenance, and anything else necessary to enable the asset to fulfill its originally estimated useful life. A revenue expenditure is charged as an expense in the period in which it is incurred because it benefits only the current accounting period.

8. Businesses make capital expenditures not only for plant assets, natural resources, and intangible assets, but also for **additions** (such as a building wing) and **betterments** (such as the installation of an air-conditioning system). **Extraordinary repairs** (such as the complete overhaul of a heating system) are expenditures that either increase an asset's residual value or lengthen its useful life. They are recorded by reducing Accumulated Depreciation, thereby increasing the asset's carrying value.

9. Treating a capital expenditure as a revenue expenditure, or vice versa, can result in a mismatching of revenues and expenses. Great care must therefore be taken to draw the appropriate distinction.

10. The acquisition cost of a long-term asset includes the purchase price, freight charges, insurance while in transit, installation, and other costs involved in acquiring the asset and getting it ready for use. These costs are allocated to the useful life of the asset rather than charged as expenses in the current period. Also included in the acquisition cost is interest incurred during the construction of a plant asset. However, interest incurred in the purchase of an asset is expensed when incurred. Small expenditures for such items as office supplies are also often expensed immediately because the amounts involved are immaterial.

    a. When land is purchased, the Land account should be debited not only for the price paid for the land, but also for such expenses as real estate commissions, lawyers' fees, back taxes paid by the buyer; the cost (less salvage value) of razing buildings on the land; draining, clearing, and grading costs; assessments for local improvements; and (usually) the cost of landscaping. Land is not subject to depreciation because of its unlimited useful life.

    b. Unlike land, land improvements, such as fences, driveways, and parking lots, have a limited life and are therefore subject to depreciation. They are recorded in a Land Improvements account rather than in the Land account.

    c. When a business constructs a building for its own use, it debits the Buildings account for such costs as materials, labor, overhead, architects' fees, insurance during construction, interest on construction loans, legal fees, and building permits. Because they have a limited useful life, buildings are considered depreciable assets.

    d. **Leasehold improvements** are improvements to leased property that become the property of the lessor when the lease expires. Examples are light fixtures and carpeting.

e.   The cost of equipment includes the invoice price less cash discounts, freight charges (including insurance), excise taxes and tariffs, buying expenses, installation costs, and test runs. Like land improvements and buildings, equipment is subject to depreciation.

f.   When long-term assets are purchased for a lump sum, the cost should be divided among the assets acquired in proportion to their appraised values.

Objective 3: Compute depreciation under the straight-line, production, and declining-balance methods.

11.   *Depreciation,* as the term is used in accounting, refers to the allocation of the cost (less the residual value) of a tangible asset to the periods benefited by the asset. It does not refer to the asset's physical deterioration or to a decrease in its market value. Thus, depreciation is not a process of valuation but of allocating the cost of the asset over the asset's estimated useful life. All tangible assets except land have limited useful lives, generally because of **physical deterioration** (resulting from use and exposure to the elements) and **obsolescence** (the process of becoming out of date).

12.   Depreciation is computed after the asset's cost, residual value, depreciable cost, and estimated useful life have been determined. **Residual value** (often called *salvage value* or *disposal value*) is the estimated value of the asset at the estimated disposal date. **Depreciable cost** is the asset's cost less its residual value. **Estimated useful life** can be measured in time or in units and requires the accountant's careful consideration.

13.   The most common depreciation methods are the straight-line, production, and declining-balance methods. The last is described as an accelerated method.

a.   Under the **straight-line method,** the depreciable cost is spread evenly over the life of the asset. Depreciation for each year is computed as follows:

$$\frac{\text{Cost} - \text{Residual Value}}{\text{Estimated Useful Life (Years)}}$$

b.   Under the **production method,** depreciation is based not on time, but on use of the asset in units. Under this method, depreciation for each year is computed as follows:

$$\frac{\text{Cost} - \text{Residual Value}}{\substack{\text{Estimated Units of} \\ \text{Useful Life}}} \times \substack{\text{Actual Units} \\ \text{of Output}}$$

c.   The declining-balance method is called an **accelerated method** because depreciation is greatest in the first year and decreases each year thereafter. This method is consistent with the matching rule because the highest depreciation is charged in the most productive years, when the asset is new, and because of the smoothing effect that results when annual depreciation and repair expense are combined (i.e., over the years, depreciation charges decrease, while repair costs increase). With the **declining-balance method,** depreciation is computed by multiplying the remaining carrying value (the unexpired part of the cost) of the asset by a fixed percentage. The **double-declining-balance method** is a form of the declining-balance method; it uses a fixed percentage that is twice the straight-line percentage. Under the double-declining-balance method, depreciation for each year is computed as follows:

$$2 \times \frac{100\%}{\text{Useful Life in Years}} \times \substack{\text{Remaining} \\ \text{Carrying Value}}$$

Under the declining-balance or double-declining-balance method, as under the other methods, an asset should not be depreciated below its residual value.

14. When a company has a number of plant assets that are similar in nature, such as trucks or pieces of office equipment, it may use a method known as **group depreciation** rather than individual depreciation. Under group depreciation, the original costs of all similar assets are lumped together in one summary account. Depreciation is then figured for the group of assets as a whole.

15. When an asset is purchased after the beginning of the year or discarded before the end of the year, depreciation should be recorded for only part of the year. The accountant figures the year's depreciation and multiplies this figure by the fraction of the year that the asset was in use. As a matter of convenience, some companies compute depreciation to the nearest month or use the half-year convention.

16. Often, the estimated useful life or residual value of an asset is found to be significantly over- or understated after some depreciation has been taken. In that case, the accountant must produce a revised figure for the asset's remaining useful life or remaining depreciable cost. Future depreciation is then calculated by spreading the remaining depreciable cost over the remaining useful life, leaving previous depreciation unchanged.

17. Depreciation for federal income tax purposes differs considerably from depreciation for financial reporting purposes. Tax law, for example, disregards estimated useful life and residual value, and allows rapid write-offs of expenditures recorded as assets. Small businesses can expense the first $100,000 of equipment on their taxes, and most property (other than real estate) is depreciated using a 200 percent declining balance with a half-year convention. Income tax depreciation is not normally acceptable for financial reporting because the recovery period is typically shorter than the asset's useful life.

Objective 4: Account for the disposal of depreciable assets.

18. When an asset is still in use after it has been fully depreciated, no more depreciation should be recorded, but the asset should not be written off until its disposal. Disposal occurs when the asset is discarded, sold, or traded in for another asset.

19. When a business disposes of an asset, depreciation should be recorded for the partial period up to the date of the disposal. This brings the asset's Accumulated Depreciation account up to that date. For example, when a machine is discarded (thrown out), Accumulated Depreciation, Machinery is debited and Machinery is credited for the present balance in the Accumulated Depreciation account. If the machine has not been fully depreciated, then to balance the entry, Loss on Disposal of Machinery must be debited for the carrying value.

20. When a machine is sold for cash, both the Cash and the Accumulated Depreciation, Machinery accounts are debited, and the Machinery account is credited. If the cash received is less than the carrying value of the machine, then Loss on Sale of Machinery is debited. If the cash received is greater than the carrying value, Gain on Sale of Machinery is credited to balance the entry.

21. Exchanges (trade-ins) of plant assets may involve similar assets or dissimilar ones. In either case, the purchase price is reduced by the amount of the trade-in allowance. Further, if the trade-in allowance is greater than the asset's carrying value, the company realizes a gain. If the allowance is less, it realizes a loss.

Objective 5: Identify the issues related to accounting for natural resources, and compute depletion.

22. *Depletion* refers both to the exhaustion of a natural resource and to the allocation of its cost to accounting periods, which is based on the amount of the resource extracted in each period. Depletion for each period is computed as follows:

$$\frac{\text{Cost} - \text{Residual Value}}{\substack{\text{Estimated Units} \\ \text{Available}}} \times \substack{\text{Units Extracted} \\ \text{and Sold} \\ \text{During Period}}$$

Units extracted but not sold within an accounting period are recorded as inventory, to be charged as an expense in the period in which they are sold.

23. Assets acquired in conjunction with a natural resource that have no useful purpose after the natural resource is depleted (e.g., drills and pumps) should be depreciated on the same basis as the depletion.

24. Two methods are used to account for the exploration and development of oil and gas resources. Under the **successful efforts method,** the cost of a dry well is written off immediately as a loss. The **full-costing method,** on the other hand, capitalizes and depletes the costs of both productive and dry wells. Both methods are in accordance with GAAP.

Objective 6: Identify the issues related to accounting for intangible assets, including research and development costs and goodwill.

25. Intangible assets acquired from others should initially be recorded as assets. Those with determinable useful lives (such as patents, copyrights, and leaseholds) should be written off over their useful lives through periodic amortization. This is normally accomplished by a direct reduction of the asset account and an increase in amortization expense. Any substantial and permanent decline (impairment) in value must also be recognized. However, a business must expense the costs of *developing* its intangible assets.

    a. **Goodwill** is the excess of the cost of a group of assets (usually a business) over the fair market value of the individual assets.

    b. A **trademark** or **brand name** is a registered symbol or name that gives the owner the exclusive right to use it to identify a product or service.

    c. A **copyright** is an exclusive right granted by the federal government to reproduce and sell literary, musical, and other artistic materials and computer programs for a period of the author's life plus 70 years.

    d. A **patent** is an exclusive right granted by the federal government for a period of 20 years (14 years for a design) to make a particular product or use a specific process.

    e. A **license** or **franchise** is the right to an exclusive territory or market, or the right to use a formula, technique, process, or design.

    f. A **leasehold** is a right to occupy land or buildings under a long-term rental contract.

    g. **Software** is the capitalized cost of computer programs developed for sale or lease or for use within the firm.

    h. A **noncompete covenant** is a contract that limits the rights of others to compete in a specific industry or line of business for a specified time.

    i. Customer lists are lists of customers or of subscribers.

26. *Research and development* (*R&D*) refers to developing new products, testing existing ones, and doing pure research. The costs associated with these activities should be charged as expenses in the period in which they are incurred.

27. The costs of developing computer software should be treated as R&D costs until the product is deemed technologically feasible (i.e., when a detailed working program has been designed). At that point, the costs should be recorded as assets and amortized over the estimated economic life of the product using the straight-line method.

28. *Goodwill,* as the term is used in accounting, equals the excess of the purchase cost of a business over the fair market value of the net assets purchased. It should be recorded only when a controlling interest in another company has been acquired. Goodwill is reported as a separate line item on the balance sheet. Once recorded, it is subject to annual impairment reviews. When its fair value drops below its carrying value, an impairment loss is reported on the income statement, and goodwill is reduced on the balance sheet.

Summary of Journal Entries Introduced in Chapter 9

A. (LO 3) Depreciation Expense, Asset Name   XX (amount allocated)
         Accumulated Depreciation, Asset Name   XX (amount allocated)
             To record depreciation for the period (review of
             entry introduced in Chapter 3)

B. (LO 4) Accumulated Depreciation, Machinery   XX (existing balance)
         Loss on Disposal of Machinery   XX (carrying value)
             Machinery   XX (purchase price)
                 Discarded machine no longer used in the business

C. (LO 4) Cash   XX (proceeds on sale)
         Accumulated Depreciation, Machinery   XX (existing balance)
             Machinery   XX (purchase price)
                 Sale of machine for carrying value; no gain or loss

D. (LO 4) Cash   XX (proceeds on sale)
         Accumulated Depreciation, Machinery   XX (existing balance)
         Loss on Sale of Machinery   XX (CV minus cash)
             Machinery   XX (purchase price)
                 Sale of machine at less than carrying value (CV);
                 loss recorded

E. (LO 4) Cash   XX (proceeds on sale)
         Accumulated Depreciation, Machinery   XX (existing balance)
             Gain on Sale of Machinery   XX (cash minus CV)
             Machinery   XX (purchase price)
                 Sale of machine at more than carrying value (CV);
                 gain recorded

F. (LO 5) Depletion Expense, Coal Deposits   XX (amount allocated)
         Accumulated Depletion, Coal Deposits   XX (amount allocated)
             To record depletion of coal mine

SELF-TEST

Test your knowledge of the chapter by choosing the best answer for each item below.

1. Which of the following does *not* characterize all long-term assets?

    a. Used in the operation of a business
    b. Possess physical substance
    c. Have a useful life of more than one year
    d. Are not for resale

2. Which of the following would *not* be included in the cost of land?

    a. The cost of paving the land for parking
    b. An assessment from the local government for installing a sewer
    c. The cost of tearing down an old building on the land
    d. A commission to the real estate agent involved in the purchase of the land

3. Which of the following most appropriately describes *depreciation,* as the term is used in accounting?

    a. Allocation of the cost of a plant asset
    b. Decline in the value of a plant asset
    c. Gradual obsolescence of a plant asset
    d. Physical deterioration of a plant asset

4. Which of the following intangible assets has a legal life of 20 years?

    a. Goodwill
    b. Copyright
    c. Customer list
    d. Patent

5. The sale of equipment costing $16,000, with accumulated depreciation of $13,400 and a sale price of $4,000, would result in a

    a. gain of $4,000.
    b. gain of $1,400.
    c. loss of $1,400.
    d. loss of $12,000.

6. A business's net cash flows from operating activities is $50,000, it sold plant assets for $12,000, it purchased plant assets for $20,000, and it paid dividends of $15,000. Its free cash flow equals

    a. $43,000.
    b. $57,000.
    c. $27,000.
    d. $33,000.

7. Which of the following is *not* classified as a natural resource?

    a. Timberland
    b. Gas reserve
    c. Goodwill
    d. Oil well

8. Which of the following intangible assets would grant its owner the exclusive right to publish and sell sheet music?

    a. Copyright
    b. Noncompete covenant
    c. Patent
    d. Trademark

9. According to generally accepted accounting principles, the proper accounting treatment of the cost of research and development is to

    a.   amortize the cost over a period not to exceed 20 years.
    b.   amortize the cost over five years.
    c.   carry the cost as an asset indefinitely.
    d.   write the cost off immediately as an expense.

10. Reliable Insurance Company has many items of office equipment in its home office. Rather than compute depreciation on each item individually, the company may combine like items in one account and use

    a.   income tax depreciation.
    b.   combined depreciation.
    c.   group depreciation.
    d.   aggregate depreciation.

TESTING YOUR KNOWLEDGE

Matching*

Match each term with its definition by writing the appropriate letter in the blank.

1. _____ Long-term assets
2. _____ Depreciation
3. _____ Obsolescence
4. _____ Franchise
5. _____ Residual value (salvage or disposal value)
6. _____ Accelerated method
7. _____ Straight-line method
8. _____ Production method
9. _____ Full-costing method
10. _____ Double-declining-balance method
11. _____ Group depreciation
12. _____ Natural resources
13. _____ Depletion
14. _____ Amortization
15. _____ Software
16. _____ Capital expenditure
17. _____ Revenue expenditure
18. _____ Patent
19. _____ Copyright

a. The exclusive right to make a particular product or use a specific process for 20 years

b. Using one depreciation rate for several similar items

c. The allocation of an intangible asset's cost to the periods benefited by the asset

d. The right to occupy property under a long-term rental contract

e. Assets to be used in the business for more than one year

f. The allocation of the cost of a tangible asset to the periods benefited by the asset

g. An expenditure for services needed to maintain and operate plant assets (an expense)

h. The depreciation method under which cost allocation is based on units, not time

i. The exclusive right to publish literary, musical, and other artistic materials and computer programs for the author's life plus 70 years

20. _____Leasehold
21. _____Trademark
22. _____Successful efforts method

j. The accelerated depreciation method based on twice the straight-line rate

k. Capitalized costs associated with computer programs

l. The estimated value of an asset on the disposal date

m. An expenditure for the purchase or expansion of long-term assets (an asset)

n. One reason for an asset's limited useful life

o. Assets in the form of valuable substances that can be extracted and sold

p. An identifying symbol or name for a product or service that can be used only by its owner

q. The method of accounting for oil and gas that immediately writes off the cost of dry wells

r. The depreciation method that charges equal depreciation each year

s. The exclusive right to sell a product within a certain territory

t. The practice of charging the highest depreciation in the first year and decreasing depreciation each year thereafter

u. The allocation of a natural resource's cost to the periods over which the resource is consumed

v. The method of accounting for oil and gas that capitalizes the cost of dry wells

Note to student: The matching quiz might be completed more efficiently by starting with the definition and searching for the corresponding term.

Short Answer

Use the lines provided to answer each item.

1. Distinguish between an addition and a betterment.

_____

_____

_____

_____

2. When a plant asset is sold for cash, under what unique circumstance would no gain or loss be recorded?

_____

_____

3. List four pieces of information necessary to compute the depletion expense of an oil well for a given year.

_____

_____

_____

_____

4. Distinguish between ordinary and extraordinary repairs.

_____

_____

_____

_____

5. For each asset category listed below, provide the accounting term for the allocation of its cost to the periods benefited.

Category	Term for Cost Allocation
Intangible assets	_____
Plant and equipment	_____
Natural resources	_____

6. Plant assets have limited useful lives for two reasons. What are they?

_____

_____

True-False

Circle T if the statement is true, and F if it is false. Provide explanations for the false answers, using the blank lines at the end of the section.

1.   T   F   Net income or loss is a component in the calculation of free cash flow.

2.   T   F   The loss recorded on a discarded asset is equal to the carrying value of the asset at the time it is discarded.

3.   T   F   Land held for speculative reasons is not classified as property, plant, and equipment.

4.   T   F   Depreciation is a process of valuation, not allocation.

5.   T   F   Depreciation for a machine can be calculated by having an appraiser determine the extent of the machine's deterioration.

6.   T   F   When land is purchased for use as a plant site, its cost should include the cost of clearing and draining the land.

7.   T   F   Each type of depreciable asset should have its own accumulated depreciation account.

8.   T   F   Estimated useful life in years is irrelevant when applying the production method of depreciation.

9.   T   F   If depreciation expense under the straight-line method is $1,000 in the first year, it will be $2,000 in the second year.

10.   T   F   When the estimated useful life of an asset is revised after some depreciation has been taken, the accountant should not go back to previous years to make corrections.

11.   T   F   The double-declining-balance method initially disregards the asset's residual value.

12.   T   F   In an asset's last year of depreciation, accelerated depreciation generally results in less net income than does straight-line depreciation.

13.   T   F   Depreciable cost equals cost minus accumulated depreciation.

14.   T   F   Estimated useful life and residual value are ignored when applying income tax depreciation.

15.   T   F   A copyright is a name or symbol that can be used only by its owner.

16.   T   F   If ordinary maintenance is mistakenly capitalized instead of being charged as an expense, net income for the period will be overstated.

17.   T   F   A betterment is an example of a revenue expenditure.

18.   T   F   Recording an extraordinary repair leaves the carrying value of the asset unchanged.

19.   T   F   When a machine is sold for less than its carrying value, one of the debits is to Loss on Sale of Machinery and one of the credits is to Accumulated Depreciation, Machinery.

20.   T   F   *Capital expenditure* is another term for *expense.*

21.   T   F   Interest charges incurred in purchasing an asset are normally treated as an operating expense.

22.   T   F   When a plant asset is sold, depreciation expense need not be recorded for the partial period up to the date of the sale.

23. T   F   In determining the number of years over which to amortize copyrights and patents, useful life is more important than the period legally covered by these assets.

24. T   F   As accumulated depreciation increases, carrying value decreases.

25. T   F   Goodwill may be recorded when management feels the business is worth more than its balance sheet indicates.

26. T   F   The full-costing method capitalizes the cost of both successful and dry wells.

27. T   F   A long-term asset's carrying value should be reduced when its value is impaired.

Multiple Choice

Circle the letter of the best answer.

1. A building and land are purchased for a lump-sum payment of $66,000. How much should be allocated to land if the land is appraised at $20,000 and the building is appraised at $60,000?

   a. $22,000
   b. $20,000
   c. $16,500
   d. $13,750

2. The expired cost of a plant asset is called its

   a. accumulated depreciation.
   b. carrying value.
   c. depreciable cost.
   d. residual value.

3. When applied to an asset in its first year of use, which depreciation method results in the greatest depreciation charge?

   a. Declining-balance
   b. Production
   c. Straight-line
   d. Impossible to determine without more data

4. When a machine was purchased, its estimated useful life was 20 years. However, after it had been depreciated for 5 years, the company decided that it originally had overestimated the machine's useful life by 3 years. What should be done?

   a. Go back and adjust depreciation for the first 5 years.
   b. Depreciate the remainder of the depreciable cost over the next 15 years.
   c. Depreciate the remainder of the depreciable cost over the next 12 years.
   d. Both **a** and **b** should be done.

5. According to GAAP, goodwill should

   a. be expensed when acquired.
   b. be amortized over its useful life.
   c. be written down when an impairment occurs.
   d. never be expensed, amortized, or written down.

6. The costs of land improvements

   a. should be included in the cost of the land.
   b. are subject to depreciation.
   c. should be deducted from the cost of the land.
   d. should be charged as expenses in the year they are incurred.

7. A machine that cost $9,000 has a carrying value of $2,000 and is sold for $1,700. Which of the following is true about the entry made to record the sale?

   a. Accumulated Depreciation is debited for $2,000.
   b. Machinery is credited for $2,000.
   c. Loss on Sale of Machinery is credited for $300.
   d. Accumulated Depreciation is debited for $7,000.

8. Which of the following items is *not* a revenue expenditure?

   a. Ordinary maintenance of a machine
   b. Replacing an old roof with a new one
   c. The installation of new light bulbs
   d. Repair of a tire on a company truck

9. Charging a depreciable item as an expense instead of capitalizing it results in

    a. overstated total assets.
    b. understated net income in the next period.
    c. overstated depreciation expense in the next period.
    d. understated net income in the current period.

10. Overestimating the number of barrels that can be pumped from an oil well over its lifetime results in

    a. understated net income each year.
    b. understated depletion cost per unit each year.
    c. overstated depletion expense each year.
    d. understated total assets each year.

11. The cost of developing computer software should be

    a. expensed up to the point that the product is technologically feasible.
    b. capitalized in its entirety and amortized over 14 years.
    c. expensed after the product is deemed to be technologically feasible.
    d. expensed in its entirety when incurred.

12. Which of the following normally is charged as an expense in the period of expenditure?

    a. Goodwill
    b. Leaseholds
    c. Leasehold improvements
    d. Research and development costs

APPLYING YOUR KNOWLEDGE

Exercises

1. A machine that cost $26,000 had an estimated useful life of five years and a residual value of $2,000 when purchased on January 2, 20x4. Fill in the amount of depreciation expense for 20x5, as well as the accumulated depreciation and carrying value of the machine as of December 31, 20x5, under both of the methods listed below.

	Depreciation Expense for 20x5	Accumulated Depreciation as of 12/31/x5	Carrying Value as of 12/31/x5
a. Straight-line	$ _____	$ _____	$ _____
b. Double-declining-balance	$ _____	$ _____	$ _____

2. A machine that was to produce a certain type of toy was purchased for $35,000 on April 30, 20x6. The machine was expected to produce 100,000 toys during the ten years that the company expected to keep the machine. The company estimated that it then could sell the machine for $5,000. Using the production method, calculate the depreciation expense in 20x6, when the machine produced 7,500 toys.

3. Classify each of the following as a capital expenditure or a revenue expenditure by placing a *C* or an *R* next to each item.

    _____ a. Replacement of a roof

    _____ b. Replacement of the battery in a company vehicle

    _____ c. Painting of a firm's executive offices

    _____ d. Installation of aluminum siding

    _____ e. Replacement of the motor in a machine

    _____ f. Repair of an air-conditioning unit

    _____ g. Installation of a piece of machinery

    _____ h. Addition of a building wing

    _____ i. Tune-up of a company vehicle

4. Kiner Manufacturing is investigating the purchase of a piece of equipment that would cost $22,000. It is estimated that the equipment would be used for six years, have a residual value of $3,000, and generate positive net cash flows of $4,000 in each of its six years of use. Using Tables 3 and 4 in the text's appendix on future and present value tables, calculate the equipment's net present value, and state whether Kiner should make the purchase. Assume an interest rate of 8 percent.

5. In 20xx, Valley Coal Company purchased a coal mine for $800,000. It is estimated that 2 million tons of coal can be extracted from the mine. In the journal provided below, prepare Valley's adjusting entry for December 31, 20xx, to reflect the extraction and sale of 100,000 tons during the year.

General Journal			
Date	**Description**	**Debit**	**Credit**

CHAPTER 10

Long-Term Liabilities

REVIEWING THE CHAPTER

Objective 1: Identify the management issues related to long-term debt.

1. To foster growth, companies often invest in long-term assets and in research and development and other activities that will benefit the business in the long run. To finance these investments, they must obtain long-term funding. They commonly do so by issuing stock and long-term debt in the form of bonds, notes, mortgages, and leases. Long-term debt consists of liabilities to be settled beyond one year or the normal operating cycle, whichever is longer. The management issues related to issuing long-term debt are whether to issue it, how much of it to carry, and what types of it to incur.

2. In considering whether to issue long-term debt, management must weigh the advantages of this method of obtaining funds against the advantages of relying solely on stockholders' equity.

   a. One advantage of issuing long-term debt is that bondholders and other creditors do not have voting rights, and common stockholders therefore retain their level of control. Another advantage is that interest on debt is tax-deductible, which lowers the company's tax burden. A third advantage of issuing long-term debt is that it may give the company **financial leverage**—that is, if earnings on the funds obtained exceed the interest incurred, then stockholders' earnings will increase (this is also called *trading on equity*).

   b. One disadvantage of issuing long-term debt is that the more of it a company issues, the more periodic interest it must pay. Failure to pay either periodic interest or the principal at maturity can force a company into bankruptcy. Another disadvantage is that financial leverage can work against a company if the earnings from its investments do not exceed its interest payments. Thus, when a business issues long-term debt, it assumes financial risk, as well as the possibility of negative financial leverage.

3. Managers can determine how much debt to carry by computing the debt to equity ratio. It is expressed in "times" and is calculated as follows:

$$\frac{\text{Total Liabilities}}{\text{Total Stockholders' Equity}}$$

4. When a business structures its long-term debts in such a way that they do not appear as liabilities on the balance sheet (as for certain leases), that business is engaging in **off-balance-sheet financing**. However, because the business is committed to cash payments in the long-run, off-balance-sheet financing has the same effect as long-term liabilities. The practice is perfectly legal.

5. Financial leverage is advantageous as long as a business is able to make timely interest payments and to settle the debt at maturity. A common measure of how much risk a company undertakes in issuing debt is the **interest coverage ratio.** It is expressed in "times" and is calculated as follows:

$$\frac{\text{Income Before Income Taxes} + \text{Interest Expense}}{\text{Interest Expense}}$$

The higher the interest coverage ratio, the lower the company's risk will be of defaulting on interest payments.

6. The most common types of long-term debt are bonds payable, notes payable, mortgages payable, long-term leases, pension liabilities, other postretirement benefits, and deferred income taxes.

    a. Long-term bonds are the most common type of long-term debt. They can have many different characteristics, and will be covered in much detail below.

    b. A long-term note is a written promise to pay, resulting from a loan from a bank or other creditor. A bond, however, is a more complex financial instrument that usually involves debt to many creditors. Notes and bonds produce similar effects on the financial statements.

    c. A **mortgage** is a long-term debt secured by real property. It is usually paid in equal monthly installments. When a payment is made, both Mortgage Payable and Mortgage Interest Expense are debited, and Cash is credited. Each month, the interest portion of the payment decreases, while the principal portion of the payment increases.

    d. A lease is a contract that allows a business or individual to use an asset for a specific length of time in return for periodic payments. The parties involved in a lease are the lessor, who owns the lease asset, and the lessee, who pays rent to the lessor for use of the leased asset. A **capital lease** is a long-term lease in which the risks of ownership lie with the lessee and whose terms resemble those of a purchase on installment. It is, in fact, so much like a purchase that the lessee should record it as an asset (to be depreciated) and a related liability. An **operating lease** is a short-term lease in which the risks of ownership remain with the lessor; each monthly lease payment should be charged to Rent Expense.

    e. A **pension plan** is a contract under which a company agrees to pay benefits to its employees after they retire. Benefits to retirees are usually paid out of a **pension fund.** Pension plans are classified as *defined contribution plans* or *defined benefit plans*. **Other postretirement benefits,** such as health care, should be estimated and accrued while the employee is still working (in accordance with the matching rule).

    f. A liability for **deferred income taxes** arises from the use of different accounting methods for financial reporting purposes than for tax-return purposes. It represents an amount that is currently expensed on the income statement (based on GAAP), but which need not be paid to the government until a later time (as allowed by income tax laws).

Objective 2: Describe the features of a bond issue and the major characteristics of bonds.

7. A **bond** is a security representing money borrowed from the investing public. The holders of bonds are creditors of the issuing organizations. They are entitled to periodic interest and to the principal of the debt on some specified date. Their claims to a corporation's assets, like the claims of all creditors, have priority over stockholders' claims.

8. When a corporation issues bonds, it enters into a contract, called a **bond indenture,** with the bondholders. It may also give each bondholder a **bond certificate** as evidence of the corporation's debt. A **bond issue** is the total value of bonds issued at one time. Bonds are usually issued with a face value that is some multiple of $1,000. Bond prices are expressed as a percentage of face value; for example, when bonds with a face value of $100,000 are issued at 97, the corporation receives $97,000.

9. The **face interest rate** is the rate paid to bondholders based on the face value, or principal, of the bonds. The **market interest rate** (also called the *effective interest rate*) is the rate paid in the market on bonds of similar risk.

a. When the face interest rate is less than the market interest rate for similar bonds on the issue date, the bonds will probably sell at a **discount** (less than face value).

b. When the face interest rate is greater than the market interest rate for similar bonds on the issue date, the bonds usually sell at a **premium** (greater than face value).

10. A corporation can issue several types of bonds, each having different features.

a. **Unsecured bonds** (also called *debenture bonds*) are issued on the general credit of the corporation. **Secured bonds** give the bondholders a pledge of certain of the corporation's assets as a guarantee of repayment.

b. When all the bonds in an issue mature on the same date, they are called **term bonds.** When the bonds in an issue mature on different dates, they are called **serial bonds.**

c. **Callable bonds** give the issuer the right to buy back and retire the bonds at a specified **call price** before the maturity date. The retirement of a bond issue before its maturity date is called **early extinguishment of debt.** A company may decide to retire its callable bonds for a number of reasons—for example, because it wants to restructure its debt to equity ratio or, if the market interest rate drops, because it wants to issue new debt at a lower interest rate.

d. **Convertible bonds** give the bondholder the option of converting them to the common stock of the issuing corporation. Because of this feature, the interest rate the corporation pays is usually lower than the rate it pays on other types of bonds.

e. **Registered bonds** are those for which the corporation maintains a record of bondholders and pays them interest by check on the interest payment date. **Coupon bonds** have detachable coupons stating the amount of interest due and the payment date, which the bondholders remove and present at a bank for collection of the interest due.

Objective 3: Record bonds issued at face value and at a discount or premium.

11. It is not necessary to make a journal entry to record the authorization of a bond issue. However, most companies disclose the authorization in the notes to their financial statements. The bonds will eventually be sold at face value, at a discount, or at a premium.

a. When the face interest rate equals the market interest rate on the issue date, the corporation will probably receive face value for the bonds. The journal entry consists of a debit to Cash and a credit to Bonds Payable for the face amount of the bond. When periodic interest is paid or accrued, the journal entry consists of a debit to Bond Interest Expense and a credit to Cash or Interest Payable. The formula for calculating interest for a period is as follows:

$$\text{Interest} = \text{Principal} \times \text{Rate} \times \text{Time}$$

b. When bonds are issued at a discount, the journal entry consists of a debit to Cash, a debit to Unamortized Bond Discount, and a credit to Bonds Payable. Unamortized Bond Discount appears on the balance sheet as a contra-liability to Bonds Payable. The difference between the two amounts is the carrying value, or present value, of the bonds. The carrying value increases as the discount is amortized and equals the face value of the bonds at maturity.

c. When bonds are issued at a premium, the journal entry consists of a debit to Cash, a credit to Unamortized Bond Premium, and a credit to Bonds Payable. Unamortized Bond Premium is added to Bonds Payable on the balance sheet to produce the carrying value. The carrying value decreases as the premium is amortized and equals the face value of the bonds at maturity.

12. The costs involved in issuing bonds (such as underwriters' fees) benefit the entire life of a bond issue. The usual way of treating these costs is to establish a separate account for them and to spread them out over the life of the bonds, often through the amortization of a discount or premium.

Objective 4: Use present values to determine the value of bonds.

13. Theoretically, the value of a bond is equal to the sum of the present values of (a) the periodic interest payments and (b) the single payment of the principal at maturity. The present value of an ordinary annuity table is used for the interest payment component, and the present value of a single sum table is used for the principal payment component. The discount rate used is based on the current market rate of interest.

14. When semiannual interest is assumed, cut the discount rate in half and double the number of periods when referring to the tables. If the present value of the bond is less than its face value, then a discount applies. However, if the present value of the bond is *greater* than its face value, a premium applies.

Objective 5: Amortize bond discounts and bond premiums using the straight-line and effective interest methods.

15. When a company issues bonds at a discount or premium, the interest payments it makes do *not* equal the actual total interest cost. Instead, total interest cost equals the interest payments over the life of the bond plus the original discount amount or minus the original premium amount.

16. A discount on bonds payable is considered an interest charge that must be amortized (spread out) over the life of the bond. Amortization is usually recorded on the interest payment dates, using either the straight-line method or the effective interest method.

    a. The **straight-line method** allocates a bond discount equally over each interest period in the life of the bond. The amount to be amortized each period is calculated by dividing the bond discount by the total number of interest payments.

    b. The **effective interest method** is more difficult to apply than the straight-line method, but it must be used when the results of the two methods differ significantly. To apply the effective interest method to the amortization of a discount, it is first necessary to determine the market interest rate for similar securities on the issue date. This rate (halved for semiannual interest) is multiplied by the carrying value of the bonds for each interest period to obtain the bond interest expense to be recorded. The actual interest paid is then subtracted from the recorded bond interest expense to obtain the discount amortization for the period. Because the unamortized discount is now less, the carrying value is greater. The new carrying value is applied to the next period, and the same procedure is repeated.

    c. A **zero coupon bond** is a promise to pay a fixed amount at maturity, with no periodic interest payments. Investors' earnings consist of the large discount given when the bond is issued, which the issuing organization then amortizes over the life of the bond.

17. Amortization of a premium acts as an offset against interest paid in determining the interest expense to be recorded.

    a. Under the straight-line method, the premium to be amortized in each period equals the bond premium divided by the number of interest payments during the life of the bond.

b. The effective interest method is applied to the amortization of bond premiums in almost exactly the same way as it is applied to the amortization of bond discounts. The only difference is that the amortization for the period is computed by subtracting the bond interest expense recorded from the actual interest paid (rather than by subtracting actual interest paid from the bond interest expense recorded).

Objective 6: Account for the retirement of bonds and the conversion of bonds into stock.

18. Whenever bonds are called, an entry is needed to eliminate Bonds Payable and any unamortized premium or discount and to record the payment of cash at the call price. In addition, a gain or loss on the retirement of the bonds must be recorded.

19. When a bondholder converts his or her bonds into common stock, the company records the common stock at the carrying value of the bonds. The entry eliminates Bonds Payable and any unamortized discount or premium and records common stock and additional paid-in capital. No gain or loss is recorded.

Supplemental Objective 7: Record bonds issued between interest dates and year-end adjustments.

20. When an organization issues bonds between interest payment dates, it collects from investors the interest that has accrued since the last interest payment date. The journal entry consists of a debit to Cash, a credit to Bond Interest Expense, and a credit to Bonds Payable. At the end of the first interest period, the investors are reimbursed for the payment described above, and are paid for the rest of the interest earned during the period.

21. When an accounting period ends between interest payment dates, the accrued interest and the proportionate discount or premium amortization must be recorded. On the subsequent interest payment date, the journal entry must eliminate the liability for interest that was previously established.

Summary of Journal Entries Introduced in Chapter 10

A. (LO 1) Mortgage Payable   XX (principal)
             Mortgage Interest Expense   XX (interest)
                 Cash   XX (monthly payment)
                     Made monthly mortgage payment

B. (LO 1) Capital Lease Equipment   XX (present value)
                 Capital Lease Obligations   XX (present value)
                     To record capital lease

C. (LO 1) Depreciation Expense, Capital Lease Equipment   XX (amount allocated)
                 Accumulated Depreciation, Capital Lease Equipment   XX (amount allocated)
                     To record depreciation expense on capital lease

D. (LO 1) Interest Expense   XX (amount incurred)
             Capital Lease Obligations   XX (amount reduced)
                 Cash   XX (amount paid)
                     Made payment on capital lease

E.   (LO 3)   Cash   XX (amount received)

                    Bonds Payable   XX (face value)

                    Sold bonds at face value

F.   (LO 3)   Bond Interest Expense   XX (amount incurred)

                    Cash (or Interest Payable)   XX (amount paid or due)

                    Paid (or accrued) interest to bondholders

G.   (LO 3)   Cash   XX (amount received)

               Unamortized Bond Discount   XX (amount of discount)

                    Bonds Payable   XX (face value)

                    Sold bonds at a discount

H.   (LO 3)   Cash   XX (amount received)

                    Unamortized Bond Premium   XX (amount of premium)

                    Bonds Payable   XX (face value)

                    Sold bonds at a premium

I.   (LO 5)   Bond Interest Expense   XX (amount incurred)

               Unamortized Bond Discount   XX (amount amortized)

               Cash (or Interest Payable)   XX (amount paid or due)

                    Paid (or accrued) interest to bondholders and

                    amortized the discount

J.   (LO 5)   Bond Interest Expense   XX (amount incurred)

               Unamortized Bond Premium   XX (amount amortized)

               Cash (or Interest Payable)   XX (amount paid or due)

                    Paid (or accrued) interest to bondholders and

                    amortized the premium

K.   (LO 6)   Bonds Payable   XX (face value)

           Unamortized Bond Premium   XX (current credit balance)

           Loss on Retirement of Bonds   XX (see explanation)

                    Cash   XX (amount paid)

                    Retired bonds at a loss (the loss equals the excess

                    of the call price over the carrying value)

L.   (LO 6)   Bonds Payable   XX (face value)

           Unamortized Bond Premium   XX (current credit balance)

                    Cash   XX (amount paid)

                    Gain on Retirement of Bonds   XX (see explanation)

                    Retired bonds at a gain (the gain equals

                    the excess of the carrying value over the

                    call price)

M. (LO 6)   Bonds Payable   XX (face value)
             Unamortized Bond Premium   XX (current credit balance)
                Common Stock   XX (par value)
                Additional Paid-in Capital   XX (excess of par)
                   Converted bonds payable into common stock
                   (Note: No gain or loss is recorded; also, when
                   appropriate, an unamortized bond discount would
                   be credited in the entry.)

N. (SO 7)   Cash   XX (amount received)
                Bonds Interest Expense   XX (accrued amount)
                Bonds Payable   XX (face value)
                   Sold bonds at face value plus accrued interest
                   (see entry O)

O. (SO 7)   Bond Interest Expense   XX (six months' amount)
                Cash (or Interest Payable)   XX (amount paid or due)
                   Paid (or accrued) semiannual interest on bonds
                   issued in entry N

P. (SO 7)   The year-end accrual for bond interest expense is identical
             to entry I for discounts and entry J for premiums, except
             that in both cases Interest Payable is credited instead of
             Cash.

Q. (SO 7)   Bond Interest Expense   XX (amount incurred)
             Bond Interest Payable   XX (amount accrued)
             Unamortized Bond Premium   XX (amount amortized)
                Cash   XX (amount paid)
                   Paid semiannual interest including interest
                   previously accrued, and amortized the
                   premium for the period since the end of
                   the fiscal year

SELF-TEST

Test your knowledge of the chapter by choosing the best answer for each item below.

1. It is advantageous for a company to use financial leverage when
    a. its investments in assets earn more than the interest it pays to finance the investments.
    b. it wants to promote its serial bonds.
    c. its debt to equity ratio is very high.
    d. it needs to conserve cash.
2. A bond indenture is a(n)
    a. bond on which interest is past due.
    b. bond secured by corporate assets.
    c. agreement between the issuing corporation and the bondholders.
    d. unsecured bond.

3.   If the market interest rate is lower than the face interest rate on the date on which bonds are issued, the bonds will

    a.   sell at a discount.
    b.   sell at a premium.
    c.   sell at face value.
    d.   not sell until the face interest rate is adjusted.

4.   The current value of a bond can be determined by calculating the present value of the

    a.   face value of the bond.
    b.   interest payments.
    c.   interest payments plus any discount or minus any premium.
    d.   interest payments and of the single payment of principal at maturity.

5.   When the straight-line method is used to amortize a bond discount, the interest expense for an interest period is calculated by

    a.   deducting the amount of discount amortized for the period from the amount of cash paid for interest during the period.
    b.   adding the amount of discount amortized for the period to the amount of cash paid for interest during the period.
    c.   multiplying the face value of the bonds by the face interest rate.
    d.   multiplying the carrying value of the bonds by the market interest rate.

6.   The total interest cost on a 9 percent, ten-year, $1,000 bond that is issued at 95 is

    a. $50.
    b. $140.
    c. $900.
    d. $950.

7.   Hoey Corporation issued a ten-year, 10 percent bond payable in 20x5 at a premium. During 20x6, the corporation's accountant failed to amortize any of the bond premium. The omission of the premium amortization

    a.   does not affect the net income reported for 20x6.
    b.   causes the net income for 20x6 to be overstated.
    c.   causes the net income for 20x6 to be understated.
    d.   causes retained earnings at the end of 20x6 to be overstated.

8.   Timmons Corporation has authorized a bond issue with interest payment dates of January 1 and July 1. If the bonds are sold at the face amount on March 1, the cash Timmons receives is equal to the face amount of the bonds

    a.   plus the interest accrued from March 1 to July 1.
    b.   plus the interest accrued from January 1 to March 1.
    c.   minus the interest accrued from March 1 to July 1.
    d.   minus the interest accrued from January 1 to March 1.

9.   Bonds that allow the holders to exchange them for other securities of the issuing corporation are called

    a.   secured bonds.
    b.   callable bonds.
    c.   debenture bonds.
    d.   convertible bonds.

10. Which of the following is most likely a capital lease?

    a. A five-year lease on a new building
    b. A two-year lease on a truck with an option to renew for one more year
    c. A five-year lease on a computer with an option to buy it for a small amount at the end of the lease
    d. A monthly lease on a building that can be canceled with 90 days' notice

TESTING YOUR KNOWLEDGE

Matching*

Match each term with its definition by writing the appropriate letter in the blank.

1. _____ Bonds
2. _____ Bond indenture
3. _____ Secured bonds
4. _____ Debentures
5. _____ Term bonds
6. _____ Serial bonds
7. _____ Registered bonds
8. _____ Coupon bonds
9. _____ Callable bonds
10. _____ Bond discount
11. _____ Bond premium
12. _____ Effective interest method
13. _____ Capital lease
14. _____ Operating lease
15. _____ Convertible bonds
16. _____ Pension plan
17. _____ Pension fund
18. _____ Bond certificate
19. _____ Early extinguishment of debt
20. _____ Zero coupon bonds
21. _____ Financial leverage

a. Unsecured bonds
b. A lease that amounts to a purchase
c. Bonds that the issuing corporation can retire before their maturity date
d. A method of borrowing that can increase stockholders' earnings
e. The amount by which the face value of a bond exceeds its issue price
f. Bonds with detachable forms that are redeemed for interest
g. A short-term lease that is recorded with debits to Rent Expense
h. Proof of a company's debt to a bondholder
i. Long-term debt instruments
j. Bonds whose owners receive interest by check directly from the company
k. The retirement of a bond issue before its maturity date
l. The amortization method based on carrying value
m. The amount by which the issue price of a bond exceeds its face value
n. A contract under which a company agrees to pay benefits to its employees after they retire
o. Bonds that mature on the same date
p. The source of benefits paid to retirees

q. Bonds backed by certain corporate assets

r. Bonds that may be exchanged for common stock

s. Bonds that mature in installments

t. Bonds that pay no periodic interest but that are issued at a large discount

u. A contract between bondholders and the issuing corporation

Note to student: The matching quiz might be completed more efficiently by starting with the definition and searching for the corresponding term.

Short Answer

Use the lines provided to answer each item.

1. Distinguish between *debenture* and *indenture* as these terms apply to bonds.

2. Under what circumstances would a bond issue be likely to sell at a premium?

3. What is the formula for computing interest for a time period?

4. When valuing a bond, what two components are added together to determine the present value of the bond?

5. Describe three advantages of issuing long-term debt rather than common stock.

True-False

Circle T if the statement is true, and F if it is false. Provide explanations for the false answers, using the blank lines at the end of the section.

1. T F Bondholders are owners of a corporation.

2. T F A liability is not reported when off-balance-sheet financing is conducted.

3. T F Bond interest can be paid only when declared by the board of directors.

4. T F Bonds with a lower interest rate than the market rate for similar bonds will probably sell at a discount.

5. T F When a bond premium is amortized, the bond interest expense recorded is greater than the cash paid.

6. T F When the effective interest method is used to amortize a bond discount, the amount amortized increases each year.

7. T F When bonds are issued between interest dates, Bond Interest Expense is debited for interest accrued since the last interest date.

8. T F As a bond premium is amortized, the carrying value of bonds payable decreases.

9. T F When bonds are issued at a discount, the total interest cost to the issuing corporation equals the interest payments minus the bond discount.

10. T F When bonds are retired, all of the premium or discount associated with the bonds must be canceled.

11. T F When the effective interest method is used to amortize a premium on bonds payable, the premium amortized decreases each year.

12. T F When bonds are issued at a premium, the total interest cost to the issuing corporation equals the interest payments minus the bond premium.

13. T F For operating leases, assets should be recorded at the present value of future lease payments.

14. T F Pension expense is usually difficult to measure because it is based on estimates of many factors, such as employees' life expectancy and employee turnover.

15. T F When bonds are converted into stock, a gain or loss should be recorded.

16. T F Bond issue costs should be amortized over the life of the bonds.

17. T F Postretirement health care benefits should be expensed while the employee is still working.

18. T F A disadvantage of issuing long-term debt is the increased risk of default.

19. T F A low interest coverage ratio indicates a low risk of default on interest payments.

20. T F Deferred income taxes arise when a different method is used for financial reporting purposes than for tax return purposes.

_____
_____
_____

_____

_____

_____

_____

_____

_____

_____

_____

_____

_____

_____

_____

_____

_____

_____

_____

Multiple Choice

Circle the letter of the best answer.

1. Assume that $900,000 of 5 percent bonds are issued at face value two months before the next semiannual interest payment date. Which of the following statements correctly describes the related journal entry?

    a. Cash is debited for $900,000.
    b. Cash is debited for $907,500.
    c. Bond Interest Expense is credited for $7,500.
    d. Bond Interest Expense is credited for $15,000.

2. As a mortgage is paid off, the

    a. principal portion of a fixed payment increases.
    b. interest portion of a fixed payment increases.
    c. principal and interest portions do not change.
    d. monthly payments increase.

3. Unamortized Bond Premium is presented on the balance sheet as a(n)

    a. long-term asset.
    b. stockholders' equity account.
    c. deduction from Bonds Payable.
    d. addition to Bonds Payable.

4.   When the interest dates on a bond issue are May 1 and November 1, the adjusting entry to record bond interest expense on December 31 might include a

   a.   debit to Interest Payable.
   b.   credit to Cash.
   c.   credit to Unamortized Bond Discount.
   d.   credit to Bond Interest Expense.

5.   Under the effective interest method, as a discount is amortized each period, the

   a.   amount amortized decreases.
   b.   interest expense recorded increases.
   c.   interest paid to bondholders increases.
   d.   bonds' carrying value decreases.

6.   Which of the following would most likely be considered an operating lease?

   a.   A 6-year lease on equipment with an option to renew for another 6 years
   b.   A 5-year lease on machinery, which the lessor can cancel at the end of the lease
   c.   A 40-year lease on a building, which covers the building's useful life
   d.   A 7-year lease on a company vehicle with an option to buy the vehicle for $1 at the end of the lease

7.   A $200,000 bond issue with a carrying value of $195,000 is called at 102 and retired. Which of the following statements about the journal entry for this transaction is *true*?

   a.   A gain of $5,000 is recorded.
   b.   A loss of $4,000 is recorded.
   c.   A loss of $9,000 is recorded.
   d.   No gain or loss is recorded.

8.   A company has $600,000 in bonds payable with an unamortized premium of $12,000. If one-third of the bonds are converted to common stock, the carrying value of the bonds payable will decrease by

   a. $196,000.
   b. $200,000.
   c. $204,000.
   d. $208,000.

APPLYING YOUR KNOWLEDGE

Exercises

1.   A corporation issues $600,000 of 7 percent, 10-year bonds at 98 1/2 on one of its semiannual interest dates. Assuming straight-line amortization, answer each of the following questions:

   a.   What is the amount of the bond discount? $_____

   b.   How much interest is paid on the next interest date? $_____

   c.   How much bond interest expense is recorded on the next interest date? $_____

   d.   After three years, what is the carrying value of the bonds? $_____

2.   A corporation issues $500,000 of 7 percent, 20-year bonds at 110. Interest is paid semiannually, and the effective interest method is used for amortization. Assume that the market rate for similar investments is 6 percent and that the bonds are issued on an interest date.

   a.   What amount was received for the bonds? $_____

   b.   How much interest is paid each interest period? $_____

    c.   How much bond interest expense is recorded on the first interest date? $_____

    d.   How much of the premium is amortized on the first interest date? $_____

    e.   What is the carrying value of the bonds after the first interest date? $_____

3.   A corporation issued $600,000 of 8 percent, 10-year bonds at 106. Calculate the total interest cost.

Crossword Puzzle: Chapters 9 and 10

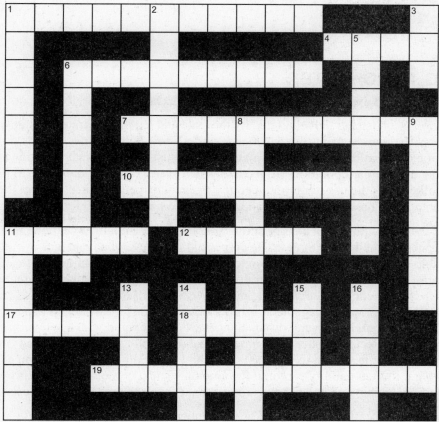

ACROSS

- **1** Arrangement for retirement income (2 words)
- **4** Estimated useful _____
- **6** Registered symbol or name
- **7** Periodic loan payment
- **10** Exclusive right to a market
- **11** Buys back bonds before maturity
- **12** Residual _____
- **17** Sale of bonds
- **18** Use another's property for a fee
- **19** Bonds, e.g. (3 words, first 2 hyphenated)

DOWN

- **1** Opposite of bond discount
- **2** Type of repair
- **3** _____ present value
- **5** _____ coverage ratio
- **6** Possessing physical substance
- **8** Type of depreciation method
- **9** Exchange (2 words)
- **11** _____ expenditure
- **13** _____ coupon bonds
- **14** Long-term asset account (abbr.)
- **15** Bonds with one maturity date
- **16** Older term for long-term assets

CHAPTER 11

Contributed Capital

REVIEWING THE CHAPTER

Objective 1: Identify and explain the management issues related to contributed capital.

1. A *corporation* is a business unit chartered by the state and legally separate from its owners—the stockholders. The management of *contributed capital* (stockholders' investments) is critical to the financing of a corporation. Specifically, management must fully understand (a) the advantages and disadvantages of incorporation, (b) the issues involved in equity financing, (c) the business's dividend policies, (d) the use of return on equity to evaluate performance, and (d) the company's stock option plans. These topics will be addressed in the paragraphs to follow.

2. Because of the ease with which a corporation can raise large amounts of capital, it is the dominant form of business in the United States. The corporation has several advantages over the sole proprietorship and partnership. In addition to its ability to raise large amounts of capital, it is a separate legal entity, offers its owners limited liability, lacks the mutual agency that characterizes a partnership, has a continuous existence, and allows for centralized authority and responsibility, as well as for professional management. It is also easy to transfer ownership in a corporation. However, a corporation has several disadvantages when compared with a sole proprietorship or partnership. It is subject to greater government regulation and to **double taxation** (i.e., the corporation's income is subject to income taxes, and its stockholders are taxed on any dividends), and the owners' limited liability can limit the amount a small corporation can borrow. Moreover, separation of ownership and control may allow management to make harmful decisions.

3. Ownership in a corporation is evidenced by a document called a **stock certificate,** which shows the number of shares the stockholder owns. A stockholder sells stock by endorsing the stock certificate and sending it to the corporation's secretary. The secretary—or in many instances, an independent registrar or transfer agent—is responsible not only for transferring the stock, but also for maintaining stockholders' records, preparing a list of stockholders for stockholders' meetings, and paying dividends. **Par value** is an arbitrary amount assigned to each share of stock, and it constitutes a corporation's legal capital. **Legal capital** equals the number of shares issued times the par value; it is the minimum amount that can be reported as contributed capital. Par value bears little if any relationship to the market value or book value of the shares.

4. Corporations often hire an **underwriter,** an intermediary between the corporation and the investing public, to help in their **initial public offering (IPO)** of capital stock. A corporation in this instance is said to be "going public." The underwriter guarantees the sale of the stock and charges a fee for this service.

5. The costs of forming a corporation are called **start-up and organization costs.** Incurred before a corporation starts operations, they include state incorporation fees, attorneys' fees, accountants' fees, and the cost of printing stock certificates. Such costs are expensed when incurred.

6. Equity financing, or financing a business by issuing common stock, has the following advantages: (a) The risk of default is lower than when financing with bonds, (b) earnings can be plowed back into operations by withholding dividend payments, and (c) the debt to equity ratio will be improved.

7. Equity financing, on the other hand, has the following disadvantages: (a) Unlike interest on bonds, dividends paid on stock are not tax-deductible to the issuing corporation, and (b) when a corporation issues more stock, the current stockholders must, therefore, yield some control to the new stockholders.

8. A **dividend** is a distribution of assets to stockholders, based on past earnings. Although a board of directors has the sole authority to declare dividends, senior managers, who usually serve on the board, influence dividend policies. A **liquidating dividend** is a dividend that exceeds retained earnings. It represents a return of contributed capital to the stockholders and is usually issued when a corporation is going out of business or reducing its operations.

9. A corporation's board of directors decides on the timing of dividend payments, which may be quarterly, semiannually, annually, or at other times. In addition, most states do not allow a corporation to declare a dividend that exceeds its retained earnings. The **declaration date** is the date on which the board formally declares a dividend, specifying that the owners of the stock on the **record date** will receive their dividends on the **date of payment.** Between the record date and the date of payment, the stock is said to be **ex-dividend** (without dividend rights). The liability for payment of cash dividends arises on the date of declaration. The declaration is recorded with a debit to Dividends and a credit to Dividends Payable. No journal entry is made on the record date. On the date of payment, Dividends Payable is debited, and Cash is credited. The Dividends account is closed to Retained Earnings at the end of the accounting period.

10. Investors evaluate the amount of the dividends they receive by looking at the **dividends yield,** which is calculated as follows:

$$\frac{\text{Dividends per Share}}{\text{Market Price per Share}}$$

Expressed as a percentage, the dividends yield measures the return, in terms of dividends, per share of stock.

11. Among the factors that affect a company's decision to pay dividends are the level of profitable operations, the dividend policy that prevails among other companies in the same industry, the expected volatility of earnings, and the actual amount of cash available for dividend payments.

12. Management's decisions about a variety of matters, including the issuance of stock, affect **return on equity.** Return on equity is therefore commonly used as a measure of management's performance. Expressed as a percentage, it is calculated as follows:

$$\frac{\text{Net Income}}{\text{Average Stockholders' Equity}}$$

One way to increase return on equity (other than increasing net income) is to reduce average stockholders' equity. This can be accomplished by buying back some of the company's stock on the open market. These shares are then described as **treasury stock.**

13. The **price/earnings (P/E) ratio,** on the other hand, measures investors' confidence in a company's future. The P/E ratio is calculated as follows:

$$\frac{\text{Market Price per Share}}{\text{Earnings per Share}}$$

A P/E ratio of 15 times, for example, means that investors are confident enough in a company to pay $15 per share for every dollar of earnings accruing to one share.

14. A **stock option plan** allows a corporation's employees to purchase a certain quantity of the corporation's stock at a certain price over a certain period of time. Sometimes, stock options are offered only to management personnel. On the date on which the options are granted, their fair value must first be estimated. Then, the amount by which the fair value exceeds the option price must be recorded as compensation expense (a tax-deductible expense) over the grant period. If the market price of the stock increases above the fixed option price during the option period, the employee can purchase the stock and then sell it for a gain.

Objective 2: Identify the components of stockholders' equity.

15. On a corporation's balance sheet, the owners' claims to the business are called *stockholders' equity.* The stockholders' equity section is divided into at least three parts: contributed capital (the stockholders' investments in the corporation), retained earnings (earnings that have remained in the business), and treasury stock (issued stock that has been bought back by the issuing corporation).

16. If a corporation issues only one type of stock, it is called **common stock.** A second type of stock, called **preferred stock,** can also be issued. Because common stockholders' claims to corporate assets rank behind the claims of creditors and preferred stockholders in the case of liquidation, common stock is considered a corporation's **residual equity.**

17. **Authorized shares** are the maximum number of shares that a corporation's state charter allows it to issue. **Issued shares** consist of stock that a corporation has sold or otherwise transferred to stockholders. **Outstanding shares** consist of issued stock that is still in circulation.

Objective 3: Identify the characteristics of preferred stock.

18. Each share of preferred stock entitles its owner to a dividend each year. Although holders of preferred stock usually lack the voting rights that common stockholders enjoy, they have preference over common stockholders in terms of the receipt of dividends; that is, when a board of directors declares dividends, holders of preferred stock must receive a certain amount of dividends before common stockholders receive anything. The amount they receive is a specific dollar amount or a percentage of the par value of the preferred shares.

19. If a board of directors fails to declare an annual dividend to preferred stockholders, the consequences vary according to the terms under which the shares were issued. If the stock is **cumulative preferred stock**, the unpaid amount is carried over to the next year. Unpaid back dividends are called **dividends in arrears.** They become a liability only when the board declares a dividend, and they should then be disclosed in the financial statements or in a note to the financial statements. If the stock is **noncumulative preferred stock,** the corporation is under no obligation to make up the missed dividends.

20. In addition to having preference over common stockholders in terms of receipt of dividends, holders of preferred stock have preference in terms of assets when a corporation is liquidated. In this case, preferred stockholders must receive the par value of their shares or a larger stated liquidation per share before common stockholders receive any share of the corporation's assets.

21. An owner of **convertible preferred stock** has the option of exchanging each share of preferred stock for a specified number of shares of common stock. However, once the stockholder has converted to common, he or she cannot convert back to preferred.

22. Most preferred stock is **callable preferred stock,** which means that the corporation has the right to buy the stock back at a specified price (called the *call price*, or redemption price), which is usually higher than the par value of the stock. If the stock is nonconvertible, the holder must surrender it to the corporation when asked to do so. If it is convertible preferred stock, the holder has the option of converting it to common stock. When preferred stock is called and surrendered, the stockholder is entitled to (a) the par value of the stock, (b) the call premium, (c) any dividends in arrears, and (d) a prorated portion of the current period's dividend.

Objective 4: Account for the issuance of stock for cash and other assets.

23. Capital stock may or may not have a par value, depending on the specifications in the corporate charter. When par value stock is issued, the Capital Stock account (that is, Common Stock or Preferred Stock) is credited for the legal capital (par value), and any excess is recorded as Additional Paid-in Capital. The entire amount is labeled *total contributed capital* in the stockholders' equity section of the balance sheet. On the rare occasions that stock is issued at a discount (less than par value), Discount on Capital Stock is debited.

24. **No-par stock** is stock for which a par value has not been established. It can be issued with or without a **stated value.** The stated value can be any value assigned by the board of directors unless state law specifies a minimum amount. The total stated value is recorded in the Capital Stock account. Any amount received in excess of the stated value is part of the corporation's contributed capital; it is recorded as Additional Paid-in Capital. When a corporation issues no-par stock without a stated value, the entire amount received is credited to Capital Stock. Unless state law specifies a different amount, that amount is designated as legal capital, which can be withdrawn only if the corporation is being liquidated.

25. Stock is sometimes issued in exchange for noncash assets or for services received. This kind of transaction should be recorded at the fair market value of the stock. If the stock's fair market value cannot be determined, the fair market value of the assets or services received should be used.

Objective 5: Account for treasury stock.

26. **Treasury stock** is stock that the issuing corporation has reacquired (i.e., the stock is issued but is no longer outstanding). Companies may purchase their own stock for several reasons: to distribute it to employees through stock option plans, to maintain a favorable market for the stock, to increase earnings per share, to use in purchasing other companies, or to prevent a hostile takeover by another company. Treasury stock can be held indefinitely, reissued, or retired. It has no rights until it is reissued. It appears as the last item in the stockholders' equity section of the balance sheet as a deduction from the total of contributed capital and retained earnings.

27. When treasury stock is acquired, its account is debited for the purchase cost, and Cash is credited. The par value, stated value, or original issue price of the stock is disregarded.

28. Treasury stock may be reissued at the purchase cost, above that cost, or below it. When cash received from a reissue exceeds the purchase cost, the difference is credited to Paid-in Capital, Treasury Stock. When cash received is less than the purchase cost, the difference is debited to Paid-in Capital, Treasury Stock. If Paid-In Capital, Treasury Stock does not exist or if the balance in that account is insufficient to cover the difference, Retained Earnings should be debited. In no case should a gain or loss on the reissuance of treasury stock be recorded.

29. When treasury stock is retired (stockholder approval is required), all the contributed capital associated with the retired shares must be removed from the accounts. If less was paid to acquire the stock than was contributed originally, the difference is credited to Paid-in Capital, Retirement of Stock. If more was paid, the difference is debited to Retained Earnings.

Summary of Journal Entries Introduced in Chapter 11

A. (LO 1)   Dividends   XX (amount declared)
        Dividends Payable   XX (amount to be paid)
           Declared cash dividend to common
           stockholders

B. (LO 1)   Dividends Payable   XX (amount paid)
        Cash   XX (amount paid)
           Paid cash dividends declared in Entry A

C. (LO 4)   Cash   XX (amount invested)
        Common Stock   XX (legal capital amount)
        Additional Paid-in Capital   XX (excess of par value)
           Issued par value common stock for amount in
           excess of par value

D. (LO 4)   Cash   XX (amount invested)
        Common Stock   XX (legal capital amount)
           Issued no-par common stock (no stated value
           established)

E. (LO 4)   Cash   XX (amount invested)
        Common Stock   XX (legal capital amount)
        Additional Paid-in Capital   XX (excess of stated value)
           Issued no-par common stock with stated value
           for amount in excess of stated value

F. (LO 4)   Start-Up and Organization Costs   XX (fair market value of
                                services)
        Common Stock   XX (par value)
        Additional Paid-in Capital   XX (excess of par value)
           Issued par value common stock for
           incorporation services

G. (LO 4)   Land   XX (fair market value of stock)
        Common Stock   XX (par value)
        Additional Paid-in Capital   XX (excess of par value)
           Issued par value common stock with a market
           value in excess of par value for a piece of land

H. (LO 5)   Treasury Stock, Common   XX (cost)
        Cash   XX (amount paid)
           Acquired shares of the company's common
           stock

I. (LO 5)   Cash   XX (amount received)
        Treasury Stock, Common   XX (cost)
           Reissued shares of treasury stock at cost

J.   (LO 5)   Cash   XX (amount received)
             Treasury Stock, Common   XX (cost)
             Paid-in Capital, Treasury Stock   XX ("gain")
                Sold shares of treasury stock at amount above
                cost

K.   (LO 5)   Cash   XX (amount received)
             Paid-in Capital, Treasury Stock   XX ("loss")
             Retained Earnings (only if needed)   XX ("loss")
                Treasury Stock, Common   XX (cost)
                Sold shares of treasury stock at amount below
                cost

L.   (LO 5)   Common Stock   XX (par value)
             Additional Paid-in Capital   XX (excess of par value)
             Retained Earnings (only if needed)   XX (premium paid)
                Treasury Stock, Common   XX (cost)
                Retired treasury stock; cost exceeded original
                investment amount

M.   (LO 5)   If the treasury stock in Entry L were retired for an amount less than the original investment, then instead of Retained Earnings being debited for the excess paid, Paid-in Capital, Retirement of Stock would be credited for the difference.

SELF-TEST

Test your knowledge of the chapter by choosing the best answer for each item below.

1. One disadvantage of the corporate form of business is
   a. government regulation.
   b. centralized authority and responsibility.
   c. the corporation's status as a separate legal entity.
   d. continuous existence.
2. The start-up and organization costs of a corporation should
   a. be recorded and maintained as an intangible asset for the life of the corporation.
   b. be recorded as an intangible asset and amortized over a reasonable length of time.
   c. be written off as an expense when incurred.
   d. not be incurred before the state grants the corporation its charter.
3. All of the following normally are found in the stockholders' equity section of a corporate balance sheet *except*
   a. additional paid-in capital.
   b. retained earnings.
   c. dividends payable.
   d. common stock.

4. The board of directors of Bryant Corporation declared a cash dividend on January 18, 20x8, to be paid on February 18, 20x8, to shareholders holding stock on February 2, 20x8. February 2, 20x8, is the

    a. declaration date.
    b. record date.
    c. date of payment.
    d. ex-dividend date.

5. The journal entry to record the declaration of a cash dividend

    a. reduces assets.
    b. increases liabilities.
    c. increases total stockholders' equity.
    d. does not affect total stockholders' equity.

6. Dividends in arrears are dividends on

    a. noncumulative preferred stock that have not been declared for a specific period.
    b. cumulative preferred stock that have been declared but not paid.
    c. cumulative preferred stock that have not been declared for a specific period.
    d. common stock that can never be declared.

7. The par value of common stock represents the

    a. amount entered in a corporation's Common Stock account when the shares are issued.
    b. exact amount a corporation receives when it issues the stock.
    c. liquidation value of the stock.
    d. stock's market value.

8. The Additional Paid-in Capital account is used when

    a. the par value of capital stock is greater than the stated value.
    b. capital stock is sold at an amount greater than stated value.
    c. the market value of the stock rises above its stated value.
    d. the number of shares issued exceeds the stock's stated value.

9. Which of the following is properly deducted from stockholders' equity?

    a. Treasury stock
    b. Retained earnings
    c. Dividends in arrears
    d. Additional paid-in capital

10. A plan under which employees are allowed to purchase shares of stock in a company at a specified price is called a stock

    a. option plan.
    b. subscription plan.
    c. dividend plan.
    d. compensation plan.

TESTING YOUR KNOWLEDGE

Matching*

Match each term with its definition by writing the appropriate letter in the blank.

1. _____Corporation

2. _____Start-up and organization costs

3. _____Issued stock

    a. Unpaid back dividends

    b. The common stock of a corporation

    c. Without dividend rights

4. _____Authorized shares

5. _____Outstanding shares

6. _____Common stock

7. _____Preferred stock

8. _____Dividends in arrears

9. _____Par value

10. _____No-par stock

11. _____Stated value

12. _____Treasury stock

13. _____Ex-dividend

14. _____Liquidating dividend

15. _____Convertible preferred stock

16. _____Callable preferred stock

17. _____Cumulative preferred stock

18. _____Stock option plan

19. _____Stock certificate

20. _____Residual equity

d. The amount of legal capital of a share of no-par stock

e. Stock currently held by stockholders

f. The dominant form of business in the United States

g. The type of stock whose holders have prior claim to dividends over common stockholders

h. Stock that the issuing corporation has reacquired

i. Stock whose unpaid dividends carry over to future years

j. Proof of ownership in a corporation

k. · Expenditures necessary to form a corporation

l. The maximum amount of stock that a corporation may issue

m. The name of the stock when only one type of stock is issued

n. Stock that may or may not have a stated value

o. The legal value of a share of stock

p. Stock that has been sold to stockholders and may or may not have been bought back by the corporation

q. Stock that may be bought back at the option of the issuing corporation

r. An agreement whereby a corporation allows certain employees to purchase its stock at a fixed price

s. The return of contributed capital to a corporation's stockholders

t. Preferred stock that the holder may exchange for common stock

Note to students: The matching quiz might be completed more efficiently by starting with the definition and searching for the corresponding term.

Short Answer

Use the lines provided to answer each item.

1.   List eight advantages of the corporate form of business.

_____

_____

_____

_____

_____

_____

_____

_____

2.   List four disadvantages of the corporate form of business.

_____

_____

_____

_____

3.   Name the three major components of the stockholders' equity section of a balance sheet.

_____

_____

4.   Under what two circumstances are preferred shareholders given preference over common shareholders?

_____

_____

5.   Under what circumstance would a corporation have more shares of stock issued than outstanding?

_____

_____

_____

6.   What is the difference between treasury stock and unissued stock?

_____

_____

_____

_____

True False

Circle T if the statement is true, and F if it is false. Provide explanation for the false answers, using the blank lines below.

1. T F   Corporate earnings are taxed twice: once as corporate income and once as stockholders' income from dividend payments.

2. T F   The concept of legal capital was designed to protect a corporation's stockholders.

3. T F   Creditors cannot attach the personal assets of a corporation's stockholders.

4. T F   Start-up and organization costs should be charged as expenses in the year the corporation is formed.

5. T F   Contributed capital consists of capital stock plus additional paid-in capital.

6. T F   A transfer agent keeps records of stock transactions.

7. T F   Preferred stock cannot be both convertible and cumulative.

8. T F   Dividends in arrears do not exist when preferred stock is noncumulative.

9. T F   The worth of a share of stock can be measured by its par value.

10. T F   The purchase of treasury stock reduces total assets and total stockholders' equity.

11. T F   Preferred stockholders are guaranteed annual dividends; common stockholders are not.

12. T F   Preferred stock is considered the residual equity of a corporation.

13. T F   The amount of compensation in connection with a stock option plan is measured on the date the option is exercised.

14. T F   On the date a dividend is paid, total assets and total stockholders' equity decrease.

15. T F   Dividends in arrears should appear as a liability on the balance sheet.

16. T F   Treasury Stock is listed on the balance sheet as an asset.

17. T F   When corporations initially sell their stock to the public, they often engage the services of an underwriter.

18. T F   When treasury stock is sold at more than its cost, Gain on Sale of Treasury Stock is credited.

19. T F   The higher the market price per share of stock, the lower the dividends yield is.

20. T F   A corporation's purchase of treasury stock will decrease its return on equity.

21. T F   The higher the price/earnings ratio, the higher investors' confidence in a firm's future is.

_____

_____

_____

_____

_____

_____

_____

_____

_____

_____

_____

_____

_____

_____

_____

_____

_____

_____

_____

_____

Multiple Choice

Circle the letter of the best answer.

1. When treasury stock is reissued below cost, all of the following may be true *except*

    a. Retained Earnings is debited.
    b. Treasury Stock is credited.
    c. Paid-in Capital, Treasury Stock is debited.
    d. Loss on Reissue of Treasury Stock is debited.

2. The purchase of treasury stock does *not* affect

    a. the amount of stock outstanding.
    b. the amount of stock issued.
    c. total assets.
    d. total stockholders' equity.

3. Which of the following statements is *true*?

    a. Outstanding shares plus issued shares equal authorized shares.
    b. Unissued shares plus outstanding shares equal authorized shares.
    c. Authorized shares minus unissued shares equal issued shares.
    d. Unissued shares minus issued shares equal outstanding shares.

4. Royer Corporation has outstanding 20,000 shares of $10 par value common stock and 1,000 shares of $100 par value, 7 percent noncumulative preferred stock. Last year, the company paid no dividends; this year, it paid $40,000 in dividends. What portion of this $40,000 should common stockholders receive?

    a. $0
    b. $2,800
    c. $26,000
    d. $33,000

5.   Which of the following is *not* a characteristic of corporations?

   a.   Separation of ownership and management

   b.   Ease of transfer of ownership

   c.   Double taxation

   d.   Unlimited liability of stockholders

6.   On which of the following dates is a journal entry made?

   a.   Record date

   b.   Date of payment

   c.   Declaration date

   d.   Both **b** and **c**

7.   Stock is said to be "ex-dividend" after

   a.   it has been sold to another party.

   b.   the record date.

   c.   the date of payment.

   d.   the declaration date.

8.   When callable preferred stock is called and surrendered to a corporation, the stockholder is *not* entitled to

   a.   a call premium.

   b.   the par value of the stock.

   c.   any dividends in arrears.

   d.   the market value of the stock.

APPLYING YOUR KNOWLEDGE

Excerises

1.   In the journal provided below, prepare entries for the following transactions:

Jan.   1   Paid $8,000 in legal and incorporation fees to form EHJ Corporation.

Feb.   9   Issued 5,000 shares of $100 par value common stock at $115 per share.

Apr.   12   Exchanged 2,000 shares of 4 percent, no-par preferred stock, which had a stated value of $100 per share, for a building with a market value of $240,000. The market value of the stock cannot be determined.

June   23   Declared a $4 per share dividend on the preferred stock, to be paid on July 8. The date of record is July 1.

July   8   Paid the dividend declared on June 23.

General Journal

Date	Description	Debit	Credit

2. Mavis Corporation began operations on August 10, 20x5, by issuing 50,000 shares of $10 par value common stock at $50 per share. As of January 1, 20x6, its capital structure was the same. During January 20x6, Mavis Corporation engaged in the transactions described below. Prepare the proper entry for each transaction in the journal that follows. In all cases, assume sufficient cash and retained earnings.

Jan.   12   Purchased 5,000 shares of stock from its stockholders at $60 per share.

20   Reissued 2,000 shares of treasury stock at $65 per share.

27   Reissued another 2,000 shares of treasury stock at $58 per share.

31   Retired the remaining 1,000 treasury shares.

General Journal

Date		Description	Debit	Credit

3. Oringer Corporation paid no dividends in its first two years of operations. In its third year, it paid $51,000 in dividends. In all three years, it has had outstanding 5,000 shares of $10 par value common stock and 1,000 shares of 6 percent, $100 par value cumulative preferred stock. How much of the $51,000 in dividends goes to

a. preferred stockholders? $ _____

b. common stockholders? $ _____

4. Assume the same facts as in Exercise **3** except that Oringer's preferred stock is *noncumulative*. How much of the $51,000 in dividends goes to

a. preferred stockholders? $ _____

b. common stockholders? $ _____

CHAPTER 12

The Corporate Income Statement and the Statement of Stockholders' Equity

REVIEWING THE CHAPTER

Objective 1: Define *quality of earnings*, and identify the components of a corporate income statement.

1. The most commonly used predictors of a company's performance are expected changes in earnings per share and expected return on equity. Net income is a key component of both measures.

2. Because net income is so important in measuring a company's prospects, it is equally important to evaluate the quality of the net income figure, or the **quality of earnings.** The quality of earnings refers to the substance of earnings and their sustainability into future accounting periods. It is affected by the accounting methods and estimates that management chooses and by the gains and losses, write-downs and restructurings, and nature of the nonoperating items reported on the income statement. Management also has choices about the content and positioning of these income-statement categories.

3. Net income or loss for a period includes all revenues, expenses, gains, and losses. A corporate income statement may therefore contain many line items and subtotals. On the income statement of a corporation that has both continuing and discontinued operations, the operating income section is called **income from continuing operations.** This section, which includes revenues, costs and expenses, gains and losses on the sale of assets, write-downs of assets, and restructurings, is followed by a section on income taxes. Appearing below that are nonoperating items, such as discontinued operations, extraordinary gains and losses, and the write-off of goodwill that has been impaired. Earnings per share data appear at the bottom of the statement.

4. The different estimates and methods that management can choose for dealing with such matters as uncollectible accounts, inventory, and depreciation produce different net income figures. In general, an accounting method or estimate that produces a lower, or more conservative, figure produces a more reliable quality of earnings. Management's choices about how nonoperating and nonrecurring items are reported on the income statement also affect the "bottom line." Financial analysts should therefore look beyond the net income figure to the notes to the financial statements, where generally accepted accounting principles require full disclosure of the significant accounting methods used in preparing the statements and any changes in those methods.

5. Although gains or losses on the sale of assets appear in the operating section of the income statement, they usually represent one-time events. They are not sustainable, ongoing operations, and management often has some choice as to their timing. Analysts should therefore ignore them when considering operating income.

6. A **write-down** (also known as a *write-off*) is recorded when the value of an asset drops below its carrying value. (Write-downs are reflected on both the balance sheet and the income statement.) A **restructuring** is the estimated cost of altering a company's operations, often involving plant closures and layoffs. Write-downs and restructurings are frequently an indication of bad management decisions in the past. Both reduce current operating income; however, because they shift future costs to the current period, they make it more likely that future earnings will show improvement. They are therefore often taken when a company is having a bad year anyway or when there is a change in management.

7. Generally speaking, gains and losses, asset write-downs, restructurings, and nonoperating items have no effect on cash flows; the cash expenditures for these items were made in previous periods. However, sustainable earnings generally *do* have a relationship to future cash flows.

Objective 2: Show the relationships among income taxes expense, deferred income taxes, and net of taxes.

8. A corporation's taxable income is determined by subtracting allowable business deductions from includable gross income. Tax rates currently range from a 15 percent to a 39 percent marginal rate.

9. Income taxes expense is the expense recognized in the accounting records on an accrual basis that applies to income from continuing operations. It may or may not equal the amount of taxes actually paid and recorded as income taxes payable in the current period. The difference arises because generally accepted accounting principles govern how income taxes are computed for financial reporting purposes, whereas the Internal Revenue Code dictates methods of computing income taxes owed to the federal government.

10. When income computed for financial reporting purposes differs from taxable income, the **income tax allocation** method should be used. Under this method, the difference between the income taxes expense and income taxes payable is debited or credited to an account called **Deferred Income Taxes.** This account is evaluated yearly to determine whether changes in income tax laws and regulations have made adjustments necessary.

11. Deferred income taxes are the result of temporary differences in the treatment of certain items (such as depreciation) for tax and financial reporting purposes. They are classified as current or noncurrent, depending on the classification of the asset or liability that created the difference.

12. To avoid distorting net operating income on the income statement, certain items must be reported **net of taxes**—that is, after considering applicable tax effects. These items are discontinued operations and extraordinary gains and losses.

Objective 3: Describe the disclosure on the income statement of discontinued operations and extraordinary items.

13. **Segments** are distinct parts of a company, such as a separate major line of business or class of customer. Any gain or loss on the **discontinued operations** of a segment must be disclosed on the income statement separately from continuing operations and net of taxes.

14. **Extraordinary items** are events that are both unusual in nature and infrequent. Gains and losses arise from such extraordinary events as natural disasters, theft, the passage of a new law, and a foreign government's takeover of property. Extraordinary gains and losses that are material in amount should be disclosed separately on the income statement (net of taxes) after discontinued operations.

Objective 4: Compute earnings per share.

15. Readers of financial statements use earnings per share of common stock to judge a company's performance and to compare it with the performance of other companies. Appearing on the income statement just below net income, the earnings per share section always shows (a) income from continuing operations, (b) income before extraordinary items and the cumulative effect of accounting changes, (c) the cumulative effect of accounting changes, and (d) net income.

16. A company that has issued no securities that are convertible to common stock has a **simple capital structure.** In this case, the income statement presents only **basic earnings per share,** which is calculated as follows:

$$\frac{\text{Net Income} - \text{Nonconvertible Preferred Dividends}}{\text{Weighted-Average Common Shares Outstanding}}$$

17. A company that has issued securities that can be converted to common stock has a **complex capital structure.** Potentially dilutive securities, such as stock options and convertible preferred stocks or bonds, are so called because they have the potential to decrease earnings per share. When a company has a complex capital structure, its income statement must present both basic and **diluted earnings per share.** Diluted earnings per share shows the maximum potential effect of dilution on the ownership position of common stockholders.

Objective 5: Define *comprehensive income,* and describe the statement of stockholders' equity.

18. Corporate financial statements should report **comprehensive income**—that is, the change in a company's equity from sources other than stockholders during an accounting period. Comprehensive income includes net income, changes in unrealized investment gains and losses, and other items affecting equity. Although sometimes reported in a separate statement or in the income statement, comprehensive income is most often reported in the statement of stockholders' equity.

19. The **statement of stockholders' equity** (also called the *statement of changes in stockholders' equity*) is often used in place of the statement of retained earnings. It is a labeled computation of the changes in stockholders' equity accounts during an accounting period. It contains all the components of the statement of retained earnings, a summary of the period's stock transactions, and accumulated other comprehensive income, such as adjustments for foreign currency translations.

20. **Retained earnings** are the profits a corporation has earned since its beginning, minus any losses, dividends declared, or transfers to contributed capital. Ordinarily, Retained Earnings has a credit balance. When a debit balance exists, the corporation is said to have a **deficit.** Retained earnings are not the same as cash or any other asset; they are simply an intangible representation of earnings "plowed back into the business."

Objective 6: Account for stock dividends and stock splits.

21. A **stock dividend** is a proportional distribution of shares among stockholders. A board of directors may declare a stock dividend to (a) give evidence of the company's success without paying a cash dividend, (b) reduce the stock's market price by increasing the number of shares outstanding, (c) make a nontaxable distribution to stockholders, or (d) increase the company's permanent capital. A stock dividend results in the transfer of a part of retained earnings to contributed capital. For a small stock dividend (less than 20 to 25 percent of outstanding common stock), the market value of the shares distributed is transferred from retained earnings; for a large stock dividend (greater than 20 to 25 percent), the par or stated value is transferred. A stock

dividend does not change total stockholders' equity or any individual's proportionate equity in the company.

22. A **stock split** is an increase in the number of shares of stock outstanding, with a corresponding decrease in the par or stated value of the stock. For example, a 3-for-1 split on 40,000 shares of $30 par value would result in the distribution of 80,000 additional shares (i.e., someone who owned one share would now own three shares). The par value would be reduced to $10. A stock split does not change the number of shares authorized or the balances in stockholders' equity. Its main purpose is to improve a stock's marketability by pushing its market price down. In our example, if the stock was selling for $180 per share, a 3-for-1 split would probably cause its market price to fall to about $60 per share. Although a stock split does not have to be journalized, it is appropriate to document it with a memorandum entry in the general journal.

Objective 7: Calculate book value per share.

23. The **book value** of a company's stock represents the company's total assets less its liabilities. It is simply the stockholders' equity or, to put it another way, the company's net assets. If a company has common stock only, the **book value per share** is computed by dividing total stockholders' equity by the number of outstanding and distributable shares. If the company also has preferred stock, the call or par value of the preferred stock, plus any dividends in arrears, is deducted from stockholders' equity in computing the book value per share of common stock.

Summary of Journal Entries Introduced in Chapter 12

A. (LO 2)   Income Taxes Expense   XX (amount per GAAP)
                  Income Taxes Payable   XX (currently payable)
                  Deferred Income Taxes   XX (eventually payable)
                      To record estimated current and deferred income
                      taxes

B. (LO 6)   Stock Dividends   XX (amount transferred)
                  Common Stock Distributable   XX (par value amount)
                  Additional Paid-in Capital   XX (excess of par)
                      Declared a stock dividend on common stock

C. (LO 6)   Common Stock Distributable   XX (par value amount)
                  Common Stock   XX (par value amount)
                    Distributed a stock dividend

SELF-TEST

Test your knowledge of the chapter by choosing the best answer for each item below.

1. The balance of the Retained Earnings account represents
    a. an excess of revenues over expenses for the most current operating period.
    b. the profits of a company since its inception, less any losses, dividends to stockholders, or transfers to contributed capital.
    c. cash set aside for specific future uses.
    d. cash available for daily operations.

2. A corporation should account for the declaration of a 3 percent stock dividend by

   a. transferring from retained earnings to contributed capital an amount equal to the market value of the dividend shares.

   b. transferring from retained earnings to contributed capital an amount equal to the legal capital represented by the dividend shares.

   c. making only a memorandum entry in the general journal.

   d. transferring from retained earnings to contributed capital whatever amount the board of directors deems appropriate.

3. Which of the following increases the number of shares of common stock outstanding?

   a. Stock split

   b. Restructuring

   c. Purchase of treasury stock

   d. Cash dividend

4. Which of the following items should be reported "net of taxes" in the income statement?

   a. Sales

   b. Net income

   c. Discontinued operations

   d. Write-down of assets

5. The primary purpose of a statement of stockholders' equity is to

   a. summarize the changes in the components of stockholders' equity over the accounting period.

   b. disclose the computation of book value per share of stock.

   c. budget for the transactions expected to occur during the forthcoming period.

   d. replace the statement of retained earnings.

6. All of the following elements of a corporation's common stock can be determined from the accounting records *except*

   a. par value.

   b. stated value.

   c. book value.

   d. market value.

7. Which of the following items appears on the corporate income statement before income from continuing operations?

   a. Income from operations of a discontinued segment

   b. Income taxes expense

   c. Comprehensive income

   d. Extraordinary gain

8. When there is a difference in the timing of revenues and expenses for financial reporting and income tax purposes, it is usually necessary to

   a. prepare an adjusting entry.

   b. adjust figures on the corporate tax return.

   c. use the income tax allocation method.

   d. do nothing because the difference is a result of two different sets of rules.

9. Comprehensive income includes all of the following *except*

   a. net income.

   b. certain unrealized investment gains and losses.

   c. dividends declared.

   d. foreign currency translation adjustments.

10. Which of the following would be involved in the computation of earnings per common share for a company with a simple capital structure?
    a. Common shares authorized
    b. Dividends declared on nonconvertible preferred stock
    c. The shares of nonconvertible preferred stock outstanding
    d. Treasury shares

TESTING YOUR KNOWLEDGE

Matching*

Match each term with its definition by writing the appropriate letter in the blank.

1. _____ Retained earnings
2. _____ Deficit
3. _____ Statement of stockholders' equity
4. _____ Income tax allocation
5. _____ Simple capital structure
6. _____ Complex capital structure
7. _____ Discontinued operations
8. _____ Comprehensive income
9. _____ Stock dividend
10. _____ Stock split
11. _____ Book value per share
12. _____ Segments
13. _____ Potentially dilutive securities
14. _____ Extraordinary item
15. _____ Earnings per share
16. _____ Restructuring

a. An event resulting in an unusual and infrequent gain or loss

b. The make-up of a corporation that has issued convertible securities or stock options

c. A negative figure for retained earnings

d. Distinct parts of a business

e. A summary of the changes in stockholders' equity accounts during an accounting period

f. The net assets represented by one share of a corporation's stock

g. The change in a company's equity during a period from sources other than owners, including net income, changes in unrealized investment gains and losses, and other items affecting equity

h. Options and convertible securities that can lower earnings per share

i. A proportional distribution of shares among stockholders

j. The profits that a corporation has earned since its inception, minus any losses, dividends declared, or transfers to contributed capital

k. A measure of the net income earned by each share of common stock

l. The estimated cost of plant closings and layoffs

m. The makeup of a corporation that has not issued convertible securities or stock options

n. The income statement section immediately before extraordinary gains or losses

o. The method used to reconcile accounting income and taxable income

p. A corporate stock maneuver that results in a change in par or stated value

Note to students: The matching quiz might be completed more efficiently by starting with the definition and searching for the corresponding term.

Short Answer

Use the lines provided to answer each item.

1. List three ways in which the Retained Earnings account can be reduced.

_____

_____

_____

2. What are the two major distinctions between a stock dividend and a stock split?

_____

_____

_____

3. What two conditions must be met for an item to qualify as extraordinary?

_____

_____

4. Number the following items to indicate the order of their appearance on an income statement:

_____ Revenues

_____ Extraordinary gains and losses

_____ Net income

_____ Discontinued operations

_____ Income from continuing operations

5.   What are the three ways in which corporations report comprehensive income?

_____

_____

_____

True-False

Circle T if the statement is true, and F if it is false. Provide explanations for the false answers, using the blank lines at the end of the section.

1.   T   F   If an extraordinary gain of $20,000 has occurred, it should be reported net of taxes at more than $20,000.

2.   T   F   The book value of a share of common stock decreases when dividends are declared.

3.   T   F   After a stock dividend is distributed, each stockholder owns a greater percentage of the corporation.

4.   T   F   The market value of a stock on the date a small stock dividend is declared has no bearing on the journal entry.

5.   T   F   The main purpose of a stock split is to reduce the stock's par value.

6.   T   F   A gain on the sale of a plant asset qualifies as an extraordinary item.

7.   T   F   Extraordinary items should appear on the statement of stockholders' equity.

8.   T   F   Common Stock Distributable is a current liability on the balance sheet.

9.   T   F   The income statement of a corporation with a complex capital structure should present both basic and diluted earnings per share.

10.   T   F   If taxable income always equaled accounting income, there would be no need for income tax allocation.

11.   T   F   The quality of earnings is affected by the existence of an extraordinary item on the income statement.

12.   T   F   Potentially dilutive securities are included in the calculation of basic earnings per share.

13.   T   F   The account Stock Dividends is closed to Retained Earnings at the end of an accounting period.

14.   T   F   Write-downs often are an indication that management has made bad decisions in the past.

_____

_____

_____

_____

_____

_____

_____

_____

_____

_____

_____

_____

Multiple Choice

Circle the letter of the best answer.

1. Which of the following has no effect on retained earnings?

   a. Stock split
   b. Stock dividend
   c. Cash dividend
   d. Net loss

2. A company with 10,000 shares of common stock outstanding has distributed a 10 percent stock dividend and then split its stock 4 for 1. How many shares are now outstanding?

   a. 2,750
   b. 41,000
   c. 44,000
   d. 55,000

3. On the date that a stock dividend is declared,

   a. Common Stock Distributable is debited.
   b. Additional Paid-in Capital is debited.
   c. Stock Dividends is debited.
   d. no entry is made.

4. Chiu Corporation had 60,000 shares of common stock outstanding from January 1 to October 1; from October 1 to December 31, it had 40,000 shares outstanding. What is the weighted-average number of shares used to calculate earnings per share?

   a. 45,000 shares
   b. 50,000 shares
   c. 55,000 shares
   d. 100,000 shares

5. If retained earnings were $70,000 on January 1, 20xx, and $100,000 on December 31, 20xx, and if cash dividends of $15,000 were declared and paid during the year, net income for the year must have been

   a. $30,000.
   b. $45,000.
   c. $55,000.
   d. $85,000.

6. Which of the following would *not* appear on a statement of stockholders' equity?

   a. Conversion of preferred stock into common stock
   b. Dividends declared
   c. Discontinued operations
   d. Accumulated other comprehensive income

7. A corporation has issued only one type of stock and wants to compute book value per share. It needs all of the following information *except*

  a. retained earnings.
  b. the current year's dividends.
  c. total contributed capital.
  d. total shares outstanding and distributable.

8. Retained earnings

  a. are the same as cash.
  b. are the amount invested by stockholders in a corporation.
  c. equal cumulative profits, less any losses, dividends declared, or transfers to contributed capital.
  d. are not affected by revenues and expenses.

9. The quality of a company's earnings may be affected by the

  a. countries in which the company operates.
  b. choice of independent auditors.
  c. industry in which the company operates.
  d. accounting methods used by the company.

APPLYING YOUR KNOWLEDGE

Exercises

1. In the journal provided below, prepare the proper entry, where appropriate, for each of the following:

  Sept. 1 Mettler Corporation begins operations by issuing 10,000 shares of $100 par value common stock at $120 per share.

  Mar. 7 A 5 percent stock dividend is declared. The market price of the stock is $130 per share on March 7.

  30 This is the date of record for the stock dividend declared on March 7.

  Apr. 13 The stock dividend is distributed.

General Journal			
Date	Description	Debit	Credit

2. A company has $100,000 in operating income before taxes. It had an extraordinary loss of $30,000 when lightning struck one of its warehouses. The company must pay a 40 percent tax on all items. Complete the partial income statement below in good form.

Operating income before taxes $100,000
_____
_____
_____
_____
_____
_____
_____
_____

3. Dillon Corporation had taxable income of $40,000, $40,000, and $80,000 in 20x3, 20x4, and 20x5, respectively. Its income for accounting purposes was $60,000, $30,000, and $70,000 in 20x3, 20x4, and 20x5, respectively. The difference between taxable income and accounting income was due to $30,000 in expenses that were deductible in full for tax purposes in 20x3 but were expensed one-third per year for accounting purposes. Make the correct journal entry to record income taxes expense in each of the three years. Assume a 40 percent tax rate.

General Journal			
Date	Description	Debit	Credit

4. Zimms Corporation's balance sheet as of December 31, 20xx, includes the following information about stockholders' equity:

    Contributed capital
        Preferred stock, $50 par value, $50 call
            price, 7% cumulative, 4,000 shares
            authorized, issued, and outstanding $200,000
        Additional paid-in capital,
            preferred   40,000
        Common stock, no-par, 30,000 shares
            authorized, issued, and outstanding   360,000
        Total contributed capital $600,000
    Retained earnings   80,000
    Total stockholders' equity $680,000
    Dividends in arrears total $28,000.

    Compute the book value per share of both the preferred stock and the common stock.

5. Throughout 20xx, Tate Corporation had 10,000 shares of common stock and 30,000 shares of nonconvertible preferred stock outstanding. Tate's net income for the year was $50,000, dividends on preferred stock totaled $20,000, and dividends on common stock totaled $5,000. Calculate basic earnings per share.

Crossword Puzzle: Chapters 11 and 12

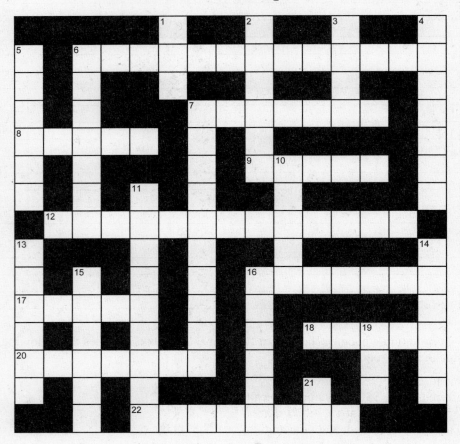

ACROSS

6 All-inclusive income
7 Dividends in _____
8 Legal capital designation (hyphenated)
9 Corporate stock maneuver
12 Unusual and infrequent (event)
16 Portion of business operations
17 Buy and sell investments
18 _____ earnings per share
20 Cancelled, as treasury stock
22 Ex-_____

DOWN

1 First-time public stock issue, for short
2 Stock units
3 Financial statement reader
4 Negative retained earnings
5 Mutual _____
6 Capital structure type
7 Maximum number of shares allowed to be issued
10 _____/earnings ratio
11 Type of stock
13 _____ on equity
14 Equity securities
15 _____, first-out
16 Stock value for 8-Across
19 Overseer of publicly-owned corporations (abbr.)
21 Additional paid-_____ capital

CHAPTER 13

The Statement of Cash Flows

REVIEWING THE CHAPTER

Objective 1: Describe the principal purposes and uses of the statement of cash flows, and identify its components.

1. The **statement of cash flows** focuses on a company's liquidity and contains much information not found in the income statement, balance sheet, or statement of stockholders' equity. It explains the changes in cash and cash equivalents from one accounting period to the next by showing the cash inflows and outflows from a company's operating, investing, and financing activities during an accounting period. For the statement of cash flows, **cash** is defined as including both cash and cash equivalents. **Cash equivalents** are short-term, highly liquid investments, such as money market accounts, commercial paper (short-term notes), and U.S. Treasury bills. Marketable securities are not considered cash equivalents.

2. The principal purpose of the statement of cash flows is to provide information about a company's cash receipts and cash payments during an accounting period. A secondary purpose is to provide information about a company's operating, investing, and financing activities.

3. Management uses the statement of cash flows to assess the company's debt-paying ability, to determine dividend policy, and to plan for investing and financing needs. Investors and creditors use the statement to assess such things as the company's ability to manage cash flows, to generate positive future cash flows, to pay its liabilities, to pay dividends and interest, and to anticipate its need for additional financing.

4. The statement of cash flows classifies cash receipts (inflows) and cash payments (outflows) as stemming from operating, investing, and financing activities. The statement may be accompanied by a schedule of significant noncash transactions.

    a. **Operating activities** include receiving cash from the sale of goods and services, receiving interest and dividends on loans and investments, receiving cash from the sale of trading securities, and making cash payments for wages, goods and services, interest, taxes, and purchases of trading securities.

    b. **Investing activities** include purchasing and selling property, plant, and equipment and other long-term assets; purchasing and selling long- or short-term held-to-maturity and available-for-sale securities; and making and collecting on loans to other entities.

    c. **Financing activities** include issuing and buying back stock, as well as borrowing and repaying loans on a short- or long-term basis (i.e., issuing bonds and notes). Dividend payments are also included in this category, but payments of accounts payable and accrued liabilities are not (they are classified as operating activities).

    d. Settling a debt by issuing stock and purchasing land by taking out a mortgage are significant financing and investing activities, but they do not involve cash inflows and outflows and are therefore not reflected on the statement of cash flows. However, because they will affect future cash flows, they should be disclosed in a separate schedule of **noncash investing and**

financing transactions that accompanies the statement of cash flows. These transactions involve only long-term assets, long-term liabilities, and stockholders' equity.

5.   The three main sections of a statement of cash flows are operating activities, investing activities, and financing activities. A reconciliation of the beginning and ending balances of cash appears near the bottom of the statement, tying into the cash balances of the balance sheets.

6.   Because users often focus on cash flows from operations to gauge performance, an incentive exists to overstate these cash flows. For example, a business could boost net cash flows from operating activities by classifying outflows for operations as investing activities or by classifying inflows that are really financing activities as operating activities. Such practices are unethical, and possibly in violation of GAAP, when they obscure the company's true performance.

Objective 2: Analyze the statement of cash flows.

7.   Two areas that analysts focus on when evaluating a firm's statement of cash flows are cash-generating efficiency and free cash flow. Because cash flows can vary from year to year, it is best to look at trends in these areas over several years.

8.   **Cash-generating efficiency** is a company's ability to generate cash from its current or continuing operations. It can be expressed in terms of three ratios: cash flow yield, cash flows to sales, and cash flows to assets.

   a.   **Cash flow yield** equals net cash flows from operating activities divided by net income (or by income from continuing operations). A cash flow yield of 2.0 times, for example, means that operating activities have generated twice as much cash flow as net income.

   b.   **Cash flows to sales** equals net cash flows from operating activities divided by sales. A ratio of 5.7 percent, for example, means that operating cash flows of 5.7 cents have been generated for every dollar of sales.

   c.   **Cash flows to assets** equals net cash flows from operating activities divided by average total assets. A ratio of 4.8 percent, for example, means that operating cash flows of 4.8 cents have been generated for every dollar of average total assets.

9.   **Free cash flow** is the cash that remains from operating activities after deducting the funds a company must commit to continue operating at its planned level. It equals net cash flows from operating activities minus dividends minus purchases of plant assets plus sales of plant assets. A *positive* free cash flow means that the company has met its cash commitments and has cash remaining to reduce debt or expand further. A *negative* free cash flow means that the company will have to sell investments, borrow money, or issue stock to continue at its planned level.

Objective 3: Use the indirect method to determine cash flows from operating activities.

10.   To determine cash flows from operating activities, the figures on the income statement must be converted from an accrual basis to a cash basis using either the **direct method** or the **indirect method.** The direct and indirect methods produce the same net figure, and both conform to GAAP, but the indirect method is far more widely used.

11.   Under the indirect method, the net cash flows from operating activities are determined by adding to or deducting from net income items that do not affect cash flows from operations. Items that are added include depreciation expense, amortization expense, depletion expense, losses, decreases in certain current assets (accounts receivable, inventory, and prepaid expenses), and increases in certain current liabilities (accounts payable, accrued liabilities, and income taxes payable). Items that are deducted include gains, increases in certain current assets (see above), and decreases in certain current liabilities (see above).

Objective 4: Determine cash flows from investing activities.

12. To determine cash flows from investing activities, each account involving cash receipts and cash payments from investing activities is examined. The objective is to explain the change in each account balance from one year to the next.

13. Investing activities center on long-term assets shown on the balance sheet, but they also include transactions affecting short-term investments from the current assets section of the balance sheet and investment gains and losses from the income statement.

Objective 5: Determine cash flows from financing activities.

14. The procedure for determining cash flows from financing activities is similar to the procedure for determining cash flows from investing activities. The difference is that the accounts to be analyzed involve short-term borrowings, long-term liabilities, and stockholders' equity. Cash dividends from the statement of stockholders' equity are also considered.

15. Exhibit 5 in the text shows a statement of cash flows that was prepared using the indirect method. As already noted, the essence of the indirect approach is the conversion of net income to net cash flows from operating activities.

SELF-TEST

Test your knowledge of the chapter by choosing the best answer for each item below.

1. Cash equivalents include
   a. three-month U.S. Treasury bills.
   b. marketable securities.
   c. accounts receivable.
   d. long-term investments.

2. The primary purpose of the statement of cash flows is to provide information about
   a. the results of a company's operations in an accounting period.
   b. a company's financial position at the end of an accounting period.
   c. a company's operating, investing, and financing activities during an accounting period.
   d. a company's cash receipts and cash payments during an accounting period.

3. Which of the following would appear at the bottom of the statement of cash flows, within a supplementary schedule?
   a. Operating activities
   b. Investing activities
   c. Significant noncash transactions
   d. Financing activities

4. Which of the following would be classified as an operating activity on the statement of cash flows?
   a. Paying a cash dividend
   b. Issuing long-term notes for plant assets
   c. Paying interest on a long-term note
   d. Purchasing a patent with cash

5. Which of the following would be classified as an investing activity on the statement of cash flows?
   a. Paying a cash dividend
   b. Issuing long-term notes for plant assets
   c. Paying interest on a long-term note
   d. Purchasing land with cash

6. Which of the following would be classified as a financing activity on the statement of cash flows?

    a. Paying a cash dividend
    b. Purchasing a trading security with cash
    c. Paying interest on a long-term note
    d. Purchasing a machinery with cash

7. On the statement of cash flows, the net amount of the major components of cash flow will equal the increase or decrease in

    a. cash and accounts receivable.
    b. working capital.
    c. cash and cash equivalents.
    d. short-term investments.

8. Cash flow yield is expressed in terms of

    a. dollars.
    b. times.
    c. a percentage.
    d. days.

9. In a statement of cash flows, all of the following would be classified as operating activities *except*

    a. paying wages.
    b. purchasing inventory with cash.
    c. selling trading securities.
    d. purchasing treasury stock with cash.

10. The calculation of free cash flow contains a subtraction for

    a. the sale of plant assets.
    b. interest.
    c. dividends.
    d. net cash flows from operating activities.

TESTING YOUR KNOWLEDGE

Matching*

Match each term with its definition by writing the appropriate letter in the blank.

1. _____Statement of cash flows

2. _____Cash equivalents

3. _____Operating activities

4. _____Investing activities

5. _____Financing activities

6. _____Noncash investing and financing transactions

7. _____Direct method

8. _____Indirect method

9. _____Cash-generating efficiency

10. _____Free cash flow

a. The items in a separate schedule that may accompany the statement of cash flows

b. Net cash flows from operating activities minus dividends minus purchases of plant assets plus sales of plant assets

c. The procedure for determining cash flows from operations that starts with the net income figure

d. A company's ability to produce cash flows from its current or continuing operations

e.   The section in a statement of cash flows that deals mainly with stockholders' equity accounts and borrowing

f.   A financial report that explains the change in a company's cash during an accounting period

g.   The section in a statement of cash flows that deals mainly with long-term assets and marketable securities other than trading securities or cash equivalents

h.   The procedure for determining cash flows from operations that adjusts each income statement item from an accrual basis to a cash basis

i.   The section in a statement of cash flows that most closely relates to net income (loss)

j.   Short-term, highly liquid investments

Note to student: The matching quiz might be completed more efficiently by starting with the definition and searching for the corresponding term.

Short Answer

Use the lines provided to answer each item.

1.   Give two examples of noncash investing and financing transactions.

_____

_____

2.   When the statement of cash flows is prepared under the indirect method, why are depreciation, amortization, and depletion expenses added back to net income to determine cash flows from operating activities?

_____

_____

_____

3.   List three examples of cash equivalents.

_____

_____

_____

True-False

Circle T if the statement is true, and F if it is false. Provide explanations for the false answers, using the blank lines below.

1.   T   F   Much of the information presented in the statement of cash flows cannot be found in the other major financial statements.

2.   T   F   Payment on an account payable is considered a financing activity.

3.   T   F   Proceeds from the sale of available-for-sale securities, whether the securities are short-term or long-term, are considered cash inflows from investing activities.

4.   T   F   Under the indirect method, a decrease in prepaid expenses is added to net income in determining net cash flows from operating activities.

5.   T   F   The schedule of noncash investing and financing transactions may contain line items for depreciation, depletion, and amortization recorded during the period.

6.   T   F   A net positive figure for cash flows from investing activities implies that the business is generally expanding.

7.   T   F   The issuance of common stock for cash is disclosed in the financing activities section of the statement of cash flows.

8.   T   F   Under the indirect method, a loss on the sale of buildings is deducted from net income in the operating activities section of the statement of cash flows.

9.   T   F   Cash obtained by borrowing, whether the debt is short-term or long-term, is considered a financing activity.

10.   T   F   The purchase of land in exchange for common stock represents both an investing and a financing activity.

11.   T   F   Free cash flow does not include a deduction for dividends because a dividend payment is never required.

12.   T   F   Both the direct method and the indirect method convert the figures on the income statement from an accrual basis to a cash basis.

13.   T   F   The purchase of treasury stock is disclosed in the investing activities section of the statement of cash flows.

_____

_____

_____

_____

_____

_____

_____

_____

_____

_____

Multiple Choice

Circle the letter of the best answer.

1. On a statement of cash flows that employs the indirect method, interest and dividends received would be

    a. included as components of net income in the operating activities section.
    b. deducted from net income in the operating activities section.
    c. included in the investing activities section.
    d. included in the financing activities section.
    e. included in the schedule of noncash investing and financing transactions.

2. On a statement of cash flows that employs the indirect method, a gain on the sale of investments would be

    a. added to net income in the operating activities section.
    b. deducted from net income in the operating activities section.
    c. included in the investing activities section.
    d. included in the financing activities section.
    e. included in the schedule of noncash investing and financing transactions.

3. On a statement of cash flows that employs the indirect method, an increase in accounts payable would be

    a. added to net income in the operating activities section.
    b. deducted from net income in the operating activities section.
    c. included in the investing activities section.
    d. included in the financing activities section.
    e. included in the schedule of noncash investing and financing transactions.

4. On a statement of cash flows that employs the indirect method, the purchase of a building by incurring a mortgage payable would be

    a. added to net income in the operating activities section.
    b. deducted from net income in the operating activities section.
    c. included in the investing activities section.
    d. included in the financing activities section.
    e. included in the schedule of noncash investing and financing transactions.

5. On a statement of cash flows that employs the indirect method, dividends paid would be

    a. added to net income in the operating activities section.
    b. deducted from net income in the operating activities section.
    c. included in the investing activities section.
    d. included in the financing activities section.
    e. included in the schedule of noncash investing and financing transactions.

6. On a statement of cash flows that employs the indirect method, an increase in inventory would be

    a. added to net income in the operating activities section.
    b. deducted from net income in the operating activities section.
    c. included in the investing activities section.
    d. included in the financing activities section.
    e. included in the schedule of noncash investing and financing transactions.

7.   All of the following represent cash flows from operating activities *except* cash

    a.   payments for income taxes.
    b.   receipts from sales.
    c.   receipts from the issuance of stock.
    d.   payments for purchases of inventory.

8.   The calculations of cash flow yield, cash flows to sales, and cash flows to assets are all based on

    a.   net cash flows from financing activities.
    b.   net increase or decrease in cash.
    c.   net cash flows from operating activities.
    d.   net cash flows from investing activities.

APPLYING YOUR KNOWLEDGE

Exercises

1.   For 20x7, Madsen Corporation had average total assets of $800,000, sales of $900,000, net income of $60,000, net cash flows from operating activities of $120,000, dividend payments of $30,000, purchases of plant assets of $75,000, and sales of plant assets of $40,000. Using this information, compute the following cash flow measures.

    a.   Cash flow yield = _____ times

    b.   Cash flows to sales = _____ %

    c.   Cash flows to assets = _____ %

    d.   Free cash flow = $_____

2. Harding Corporation's comparative balance sheets as of December 31, 20x5, and 20x4, and its income statement for the year ended December 31, 20x5, are as follows:

Harding Corporation
Comparative Balance Sheets
December 31, 20x5 and 20x4

	20x5	20x4
Assets		
Cash	$108,000	$103,000
Accounts receivable (net)	96,000	72,000
Merchandise inventory	61,000	75,000
Equipment	77,000	70,000
Accumulated depreciation, equipment	(28,000)	(19,000)
Total assets	$314,000	$301,000

Liabilities and Stockholders' Equity

	20x5	20x4
Accounts payable	$ 50,000	$ 46,000
Income taxes payable	2,500	1,800
Notes payable (long-term)	30,000	25,000
Bonds payable	45,000	60,000
Common stock, $10 par value	95,000	80,000
Additional paid-in capital	35,000	35,000
Retained earnings	56,500	53,200
Total liabilities and stockholders' equity	$314,000	$301,000

Harding Corporation
Income Statement
For the Year Ended December 31, 20x5

Sales	$842,000
Cost of goods sold	333,000
Gross margin	$509,000
Operating expenses (including depreciation expense of $14,000)	412,000
Income from operations	$97,000
Loss on sale of equipment ($4,000)	
Interest expense (9,000)	(13,000)
Income before income taxes	$ 84,000
Income taxes	29,000
Net income	$ 55,000

During 20x5, Harding sold for $11,000 equipment that cost $20,000 and that had accumulated depreciation of $5,000. It also purchased equipment for $27,000, paid a $10,000 note and borrowed $15,000 on a new note, converted bonds with a face value of $15,000 into 1,500 shares of common stock, and paid $51,700 in cash dividends. Using the indirect method, complete the statement of cash flows that appears below.

Harding Corporation
Statement of Cash Flows
For the Year Ended December 31, 20x5

Cash flows from operating activities

Cash flows from investing activities

Cash flows from financing activities

Net increase (decrease) in cash
Cash at beginning of year
Cash at end of year

Schedule of Noncash Investing and Financing Transactions

CHAPTER 14

Financial Performance Measurement

REVIEWING THE CHAPTER

Objective 1: Describe the objectives, standards of comparison, sources of information, and compensation issues in measuring financial performance.

1. **Financial performance measurement,** or *financial statement analysis,* comprises all the techniques users of financial statements employ to show important relationships in an organization's financial statements and to relate them to important financial objectives. Internal users of financial statements include top managers, who set and strive to achieve financial performance objectives; middle-level managers of business processes; and lower-level employee stockholders. External users are creditors and investors who want to assess how well management has accomplished its financial objectives, as well as customers who have cooperative agreements with the company.

2. Management is responsible for devising, executing, monitoring, and reporting on a complete financial plan for the business. Such a plan should focus on the financial objectives of *liquidity,* or the ability to pay bills when due and to meet unexpected needs for cash; *profitability,* the ability to earn a satisfactory net income; *long-term solvency,* the ability to survive for many years; *cash flow adequacy,* the ability to generate sufficient cash through operating, investing, and financing activities; and *market strength,* the ability to increase the wealth of owners.

3. Investors and creditors use financial performance to judge a company's past performance, present position, and future potential. They also use it to assess the risk connected with acting on that potential.

   a. In judging a company's past performance and current status, investors and creditors look at trends in past sales, expenses, net income, cash flows, and return on investment. They also look at a company's assets and liabilities, its debt in relation to equity, and its levels of inventories and receivables.

   b. Information about a company's past and present enables creditors and investors to make more accurate projections about its future—and the more accurate their projections are, the lower their risk of realizing a loss will be. In return for assuming a higher risk, creditors may charge higher interest rates or demand security on their loans; stock investors look for a higher return in the form of dividends or an increase in market price.

4. When analyzing financial statements, decision makers commonly use three standards of comparison: rule-of-thumb measures, past performance of the company, and industry norms.

   a. Rule-of-thumb measures for key financial ratios are helpful but should not be the only basis for making a decision. For example, a company may report high earnings per share but lack the assets needed to pay current debts.

   b. Analysis of a company's past performance is helpful in showing current trends and may also indicate future trends. However, trends reverse at times, so projections based on past performance should be made with care.

c.   Using industry norms to compare a company's performance with the performance of other companies in the same industry has advantages, but it also has three limitations. First, the operations of two companies in the same industry may be so different that the companies cannot be compared. Second, **diversified companies,** or *conglomerates,* operate in many unrelated industries, which makes it difficult if not impossible to use industry norms as standards. (The FASB requirement that financial information be reported by segments has provided a partial solution to this problem.) Third, companies may use different acceptable accounting procedures for recording similar items.

5.   The major sources of information about publicly held corporations are reports published by the company, SEC reports, business periodicals, and credit and investment advisory services.

a.   A corporation's annual report provides much useful financial information. Its main sections are management's analysis of the past year's operations; the financial statements; the notes to the financial statements, which include a summary of significant accounting policies; the auditors' report; and financial highlights for a five- or ten-year period. Most public companies also publish **interim financial statements** each quarter. These reports present limited financial information in the form of condensed financial statements and may indicate significant trends in a company's earnings.

b.   Publicly held corporations must file an annual report with the SEC on Form 10-K, a quarterly report on Form 10-Q, and a current report of significant events on Form 8-K. These reports are available to the public and are a valuable source of financial information.

c.   Financial analysts obtain information from such sources as *The Wall Street Journal, Forbes, Barron's, Fortune,* the *Financial Times,* Moody's, Standard & Poor's, and Dun & Bradstreet.

6.   Under the Sarbanes-Oxley Act of 2002, a public corporation's board of directors must establish a **compensation committee** comprised of independent directors to determine how the company's top executives will be compensated. Companies must disclose the components of compensation (such as a base salary, incentive bonuses, and stock option awards) and the criteria they use to remunerate top executives in documents they file with the SEC.

Objective 2: Apply horizontal analysis, trend analysis, vertical analysis, and ratio analysis to financial statements.

7.   The most widely used tools of financial analysis are horizontal analysis, trend analysis, vertical analysis, and ratio analysis.

a.   **Horizontal analysis** is commonly used to study comparative financial statements, which present data for the current year and previous year side by side. Horizontal analysis computes both dollar and percentage changes in specific items from one year to the next. The first year is called the **base year,** and the percentage change is computed by dividing the amount of the change by the base year amount.

b.   **Trend analysis** is like horizontal analysis, except that it calculates percentage changes for several consecutive years. To show changes in related items over time, trend analysis uses an **index number,** which is calculated by setting the base year equal to 100 percent.

c.   **Vertical analysis** uses percentages to show the relationship of individual items on a statement to a total within the statement (e.g., cost of goods sold as a percentage of net sales). The result is a **common-size statement.** On a common-size balance sheet, total assets are set at 100 percent, as are total liabilities and stockholders' equity; on a common-size income statement, net sales or net revenues are set at 100 percent. Comparative common-size statements enable analysts to identify changes both within a period and between periods. They also make it easier to compare companies.

d.   **Ratio analysis** identifies meaningful relationships between the components of the financial statements. The primary purpose of ratios is to identify areas needing further investigation.

Objective 3: Apply ratio analysis to financial statements in a comprehensive evaluation of a company's financial performance.

8.   The ratios used in ratio analysis provide information about a company's liquidity, profitability, long-term solvency, cash flow adequacy, and market strength. The most common ratios are shown in the table that follows.

Ratio	Components	Use
Liquidity Ratios		
Current ratio	Current Assets / Current Liabilities	Measure of short-term debt-paying ability
Quick ratio	Cash + Marketable Securities + Receivables / Current Liabilities	Measure of short-term debt-paying ability
Receivable turnover	Net Sales / Average Accounts Receivable	Measure of relative size of accounts receivable and effectiveness of credit policies
Days' sales uncollected	Days in Year / Receivable Turnover	Measure of average days taken to collect receivables
Inventory turnover	Cost of Goods Sold / Average Inventory	Measure of relative size of inventory
Days' inventory on hand	Days in Year / Inventory Turnover	Measure of average days taken to sell inventory
Payables turnover	Cost of Goods Sold+/−Change in Inventory / Average Accounts Payable	Measure of relative size of accounts payable
Days' payable	Days in Year / Payables Turnover	Measure of average days taken to pay accounts payable

(**Note:** The **operating cycle** is the time taken to sell and collect for products sold. It equals days' inventory on hand plus days' sales uncollected.)

Ratio	Components	Use
Profitability Ratios		
Profit margin	Net Income / Net Sales	Measure of net income produced by each dollar of sales
Asset turnover	Net Sales / Average Total Assets	Measure of how efficiently assets are used to produce sales

Return on assets	Net Income / Average Total Assets	Measure of overall earning power or profitability
Return on equity	Net Income / Average Stockholders' Equity	Measure of the profitability of stockholders' investments

Long-Term Solvency Ratios

Debt to equity ratio	Total Liabilities / Stockholders' Equity	Measure of capital structure and leverage
Interest coverage ratio	Income Before Inc. Taxes + Int. Expense / Interest Expense	Measure of creditors' protection from default on interest payments

Cash Flow Adequacy Ratios

Cash flow yield	Net Cash Flows from Operating Activities / Net Income	Measure of the ability to generate operating cash flows in relation to net income
Cash flows to sales	Net Cash Flows from Operating Activities / Net Sales	Measure of the ability of sales to generate operating cash flows
Cash flows to assets	Net Cash Flows from Operating Activities / Average Total Assets	Measure of the ability of assets to generate operating cash flows
Free cash flow	Net Cash Flows from Operating Activities − Dividends − Net Capital Expenditures	Measure of cash generated or cash deficiency after providing for commitments

Market Strength Ratios

Price/earnings (P/E) ratio	Market Price per Share / Earnings per Share	Measure of investor confidence in a company
Dividends yield	Dividends per Share / Market Price per Share	Measure of a stock's current return to an investor

SELF-TEST

Test your knowledge of the chapter by choosing the best answer for each of the following items.

1. A general rule in choosing among alternative investments is that the higher the risk involved, the
    a. greater the return expected.
    b. lower the profits expected.
    c. lower the potential expected.
    d. greater the price of the investment.

2. Which of the following is the most useful in evaluating whether a company has improved its position in relation to its competitors?

    a.   Rule-of-thumb measures
    b.   A company's past performance
    c.   A company's past performance and current financial position
    d.   Industry averages

3. One of the best places to look for early signals of change in a firm's profitability is the firm's

    a.   interim financial statements.
    b.   year-end financial statements.
    c.   annual report sent to stockholders.
    d.   annual report sent to the SEC.

4. Cash flow yield equals net cash flows from operating activities divided by

    a.   average stockholders' equity.
    b.   net income.
    c.   average total assets.
    d.   net sales.

5. In trend analysis, each item is expressed as a percentage of the

    a.   net income figure.
    b.   retained earnings figure.
    c.   base year figure.
    d.   total assets figure.

6. In a common-size balance sheet for a wholesale company, which of the following could represent the 100 percent figure?

    a.   Merchandise inventory
    b.   Total current assets
    c.   Total property, plant, and equipment
    d.   Total assets

7. The best way to study the changes in financial statements between two years is to prepare

    a.   common-size statements.
    b.   a trend analysis.
    c.   a horizontal analysis.
    d.   a ratio analysis.

8. A common measure of liquidity is

    a.   return on assets.
    b.   profit margin.
    c.   inventory turnover.
    d.   interest coverage ratio.

9. Asset turnover is most closely related to

    a.   profit margin and return on assets.
    b.   profit margin and debt to equity ratio.
    c.   interest coverage ratio and debt to equity ratio.
    d.   earnings per share and profit margin.

10. Which of the following describes the computation of the interest coverage ratio?

    a.   Net income minus interest expense divided by interest expense
    b.   Net income plus interest expense divided by interest expense
    c.   Income before income taxes plus interest expense divided by interest expense
    d.   Net income divided by interest expense

TESTING YOUR KNOWLEDGE

Matching*

Match each term with its definition by writing the appropriate letter in the blank.

1. _____ Financial performance measurement

2. _____ Compensation committee

3. _____ Diversified companies

4. _____ Interim financial statements

5. _____ Horizontal analysis

6. _____ Base year

7. _____ Trend analysis

8. _____ Index number

9. _____ Vertical analysis

10. _____ Common-size statement

11. _____ Ratio analysis

12. _____ Operating cycle

a. The time it takes to sell and collect for products sold

b. The group that determines how the top executives of a public corporation will be paid

c. A means of identifying significant relationships between the components of financial statements

d. A statement produced by vertical analysis in which components of a total figure are stated as percentages of that total

e. Statements presenting financial information for periods of less than a year

f. The first year considered in horizontal analysis

g. All the techniques used to show important relationships in financial statements and to relate them to important financial objectives

h. A technique for showing percentage changes in specific items over several years

i. A number used in trend analysis to show changes in related items over time

j. A technique for showing dollar and percentage changes in specific items between two years

k. A technique that uses percentages to show the relationships of individual items on a financial statement to a total within the statement

l. Large companies that operate in many unrelated industries

Note to student: The matching quiz might be completed more efficiently by starting with the definition and searching for the corresponding term.

Short Answer

Use the lines provided to answer each item.

1. List four ratios that measure profitability.

    _____

    _____

    _____

    _____

2. Briefly distinguish between horizontal analysis and vertical analysis.

    _____

    _____

    _____

3. List the three standards that decision makers use in assessing a company's performance.

    _____

    _____

    _____

4. List four measures of cash flow adequacy.

    _____

    _____

    _____

    _____

True-False

Circle T if the statement is true, and F if it is false. Provide explanations for the false answers, using the blank lines below.

1. T   F   Horizontal analysis is applicable to both an income statement and a balance sheet.

2. T   F   Common-size statements show the dollar amount of changes in specific items from one year to the next.

3. T   F   A company with a 2.0 current ratio experiences a decline in the current ratio when it pays a short-term liability.

4. T   F   Inventory is not a component in the computation of the quick ratio.

5. T   F   Inventory turnover equals average inventory divided by cost of goods sold.

6. T   F   The price/earnings ratio must be computed before earnings per share can be determined.

7. T   F   In computing return on equity, interest expense is added back to net income.

8. T   F   When a company has no debt, its return on assets equals its return on equity.

9. T   F   A company with a low debt to equity ratio is a high-risk investment.

10.   T   F   Receivable turnover measures the time taken to collect an average receivable.

11.   T   F   A low interest coverage ratio would be of concern to a company's bondholders.

12.   T   F   Days' inventory on hand is a liquidity ratio.

13.   T   F   Dividends yield is a profitability ratio.

14.   T   F   On a common-size income statement, net income is set at 100 percent.

15.   T   F   Interim financial statements may provide early signals of significant changes in a company's earnings trend.

16.   T   F   *The Wall Street Journal* is the most complete financial newspaper in America.

17.   T   F   Return on assets equals the profit margin times asset turnover.

18.   T   F   The higher the payables turnover is, the longer the days' payable is.

19.   T   F   Market strength refers to the ability of a company to increase stockholders' wealth.

Multiple Choice

Circle the letter of the best answer.

1. Which of the following is a measure of long-term solvency?

   a. Current ratio
   b. Interest coverage ratio
   c. Asset turnover
   d. Profit margin

2. Short-term creditors would probably be *most* interested in which of the following ratios?

   a. Current ratio
   b. Days' inventory on hand
   c. Debt to equity ratio
   d. Quick ratio

3. Net income is irrelevant in computing which of the following ratios?

   a. Cash flow yield
   b. Return on assets
   c. Asset turnover
   d. Return on equity

4. A high price/earnings ratio indicates

   a. investor confidence in future earnings.
   b. that the stock is probably overvalued.
   c. that the stock is probably undervalued.
   d. lack of investor confidence in future earnings.

5. Index numbers are used in

   a. trend analysis.
   b. ratio analysis.
   c. vertical analysis.
   d. common-size statements.

6. The principal internal users of financial statements are

   a. SEC administrators.
   b. managers.
   c. investors.
   d. creditors.

7. Using industry norms to evaluate a company's financial performance is complicated by

   a. the existence of diversified companies.
   b. the use of different accounting procedures by different companies.
   c. the fact that companies in the same industry usually differ in some respect.
   d. all of the above.

8. A low receivable turnover indicates that

   a. few customers are defaulting on their debts.
   b. the company's inventory is moving slowly.
   c. the company is slow in making collections from its customers.
   d. a small proportion of the company's sales are credit sales.

9. In a common-size income statement, net income is set at

    a.   0 percent.

    b.   the percentage that it is in relation to net sales.

    c.   the percentage that it is in relation to operating expenses.

    d.   100 percent.

10. Which of the following is a measure of cash generated or cash deficiency after providing for commitments?

    a.   Cash flows to assets

    b.   Cash flow yield

    c.   Free cash flow

    d.   Cash flows to sales

APPLYING YOUR KNOWLEDGE

Exercises

1. Complete the horizontal analysis for the comparative income statements shown below. Round percentages to the nearest tenth of a percent.

	20x6	20x5	Increase (Decrease) Amount	Percentage
Sales	$250,000	$200,000		
Cost of goods sold	144,000	120,000		
Gross margin	$106,000	$ 80,000		
Operating expenses	62,000	50,000		
Income before income taxes	$ 44,000	$ 30,000		
Income taxes	16,000	8,000		
Net income	$ 28,000	$ 22,000		

2. The following is financial information for Norton Corporation for 20xx. Current assets consist of cash, accounts receivable, marketable securities, and inventory.

Average accounts receivable	$100,000
Average (and ending) inventory	180,000
Cost of goods sold	350,000
Current assets, Dec. 31	500,000
Current liabilities, Dec. 31	250,000
Market price, Dec. 31, on 21,200 shares	40/ share
Net income	106,000
Net sales	600,000
Average stockholders' equity	480,000
Average total assets	880,000
Net cash flows from operating activities	75,000

Compute the following ratios as of December 31. Round off to the nearest tenth of a whole number.

a. Current ratio = _____

b. Quick ratio = _____

c. Inventory turnover = _____

d. Days' inventory on hand = _____

e. Return on assets = _____

f. Return on equity = _____

g. Receivable turnover = _____

h. Days' sales uncollected = _____

i. Profit margin = _____

j. Cash flow yield = _____

k. Cash flows to sales = _____

l. Cash flows to assets = _____

m. Asset turnover = _____

n. Price/earnings ratio = _____

CHAPTER 15

Investments

REVIEWING THE CHAPTER

Objective 1: Identify and explain the management issues related to investments.

1. In making investments, management must address the issues of recognition, valuation, classification, disclosure, and ethics. Each will be discussed below.

2. The purchases and sales of investments, as well as the realization of investment income and gains and losses, are recognized in the accounting records as they occur. The cash amounts of purchases and sales of investments appear in the investing activities section of the statement of cash flows.

3. Investments are recorded at cost, which would include any commissions or fees paid. However, their valuation on the balance sheet should reflect (depending upon the type of investment) changes in their fair value, amortization, or changes in the operations of the investee companies. In addition, long-term investments must be evaluated annually for any impairment that appears to be permanent (whereby a loss would be recognized).

4. Investments in debt and equity securities are classified as either short-term or long-term. **Short-term investments** (also called **marketable securities**) have a maturity of more than 90 days but are intended to be held only until cash is needed for current operations. *Long-term investments* are intended to be held for more than one year, and are reported in the investments section of the balance sheet. Short- and long-term investments are further classified as trading, available-for-sale, and held-to-maturity securities.

    a. **Trading securities** are debt or equity securities expected to be held for only a short period of time, in hopes of generating short-term gains. They are classified on the balance sheet as current assets.

    b. **Available-for-sale securities** are debt or equity securities that do not qualify as either trading securities or held-to-maturity securities. They are classified as current assets or long-term investments, depending on management's intent.

    c. **Held-to-maturity securities** are debt securities that management intends to hold until their maturity date. They are classified as current assets or long-term investments, depending upon the proximity of the maturity date.

5. The percentage ownership in another company can be described as noninfluential and controlling, influential but noncontrolling, and controlling.

    a. A *noninfluential and noncontrolling investment* exists when a company owns less than 20 percent of another company's voting stock.

    b. An *influential but noncontrolling investment* exists when a company owns 20 to 50 percent of another company's voting stock. With that degree of ownership, the investor company can normally exercise **significant influence** over (i.e., affect) the investee's operating and financial policies.

    c.   A *controlling investment* exists when a company owns more than 50 percent of another company's voting stock. With that level of ownership, the investor company can normally exercise **control** over (i.e., decide) the investee's operating and financial policies.

6.   Companies provide detailed information about their investments and the manner in which they account for them in the notes to their financial statements.

7.   In the United States, **insider trading,** or making use of inside information for personal gain, is both unethical and illegal. Specifically, before a publicly held corporation releases significant information about an investment, its officers and employees are not allowed to buy or sell stock in that company. Offenders are vigorously prosecuted by the Securities and Exchange Commission.

Objective 2: Explain the financial reporting implications of short-term investments.

8.   As stated above, trading securities consist of both debt and equity securities expected to be held for just a short period of time. These securities, which serve to generate profits on short-term price increases, are valued on the balance sheet at their fair value (normally, market value). Also, dollar increases or decreases in the total trading portfolio during the period are reflected on that period's income statement.

    a.   Upon the purchase of trading securities, Short-Term Investments is debited and Cash is credited.

    b.   At the end of the accounting period, the cost and market (fair) value of the securities are compared, and an adjustment is made. When a decline in value has been suffered, Unrealized Loss on Investments (an income statement account) is debited and Allowance to Adjust Short-Term Investments to Market (a contra-asset account) is credited. When, on the other hand, an increase in value is experienced, Allowance to Adjust Short-Term Investments to Market is debited and Unrealized Gain on Investments (an income statement account) is credited. In either case, the investments are reported on the balance sheet at market value.

    c.   When an investment is sold, Cash is debited for the proceeds, Short-Term Investments is credited for the original cost, and Realized Gain (or Realized Loss) on Investments is credited (or debited) for the difference.

9.   As stated above, available-for-sale securities are debt and equity securities that do not qualify as trading or held-to-maturity securities. These securities are accounted for in the same way as trading securities, except that (a) an unrealized gain or loss is reported as a special item in the stockholders' equity section of the balance sheet, and (b) if a decline in the value of a security is considered permanent, it is charged as a loss in the income statement.

Objective 3: Explain the financial reporting implications of long-term investments in stock and the cost-adjusted-to-market and equity methods used to account for them.

10.   The cost-adjusted-to-market method should be used in accounting for noninfluential and noncontrolling available-for-sale investments. The equity method, on the other hand, should be used in accounting for all other (that is, influential or controlling) investments. In addition, consolidated financial statements should usually be prepared when a controlling relationship exists.

    a.   Under the **cost-adjusted-to-market method,** the securities are initially recorded at cost. As dividends are received, Dividend Income is recorded. At the end of the accounting period, an adjustment is made for the difference between total cost and total market value. If total cost exceeds total market value, Unrealized Loss on Long-Term Investments is debited and Allowance to Adjust Long-Term Investments to Market is credited for the decline in value. The Unrealized Loss account appears as a special item within stockholders' equity (assuming the loss is temporary), as well as a component of comprehensive income. The Allowance account appears as a contra account to the investment. An adjusting entry opposite to the one described above would be made when market value relative to cost has increased. When the investment is sold, any realized gain or loss would be reported in the income statement.

b. Under the **equity method,** the investor records investment income as a debit to the Investment account and a credit to an Investment Income account. The amount recorded is the investee's periodic net income times the investor's ownership percentage. When the investor receives a cash dividend, the Cash account is debited and the Investment account is credited. All long-term investments in stock are initially recorded at cost, regardless of the method used to account for subsequent transactions.

11. When a company has a controlling interest in another company, the investor is called the **parent company** and the investee is called the **subsidiary.** Companies in such a relationship must prepare **consolidated financial statements** (combined statements of the parent and its subsidiaries).

Objective 4: Explain the financial reporting implications of consolidated financial statements.

12. Consolidated financial statements are useful because they present a financial picture of the entire economic entity (parent and subsidiaries). Preparing consolidated statements under the **purchase method** involves combining similar accounts from the separate statements of the affiliated companies.

13. When consolidated financial statements are prepared, **eliminations** must be made on the consolidating work sheet for intercompany items. Among those items that must be eliminated are intercompany receivables, payables, sales, purchases, interest income, and interest expense, as well as the investment in the subsidiary company. In addition, under the purchase method, the entire stockholders' equity section of the subsidiary is eliminated. These eliminations appear only on the work sheet and not in the accounting records or on the consolidated financial statements.

14. Under the purchase method of preparing a consolidated balance sheet, the parent records the investment at the purchase cost.

a. When the book value of the net assets purchased equals their purchase cost, the assets and liabilities acquired should appear at cost on the consolidated balance sheet. No goodwill should be recorded.

b. The stockholders' equity section of the subsidiary at acquisition is not included on the consolidated balance sheet.

c. When less than 100 percent of the subsidiary has been purchased, the **minority interest** (outside ownership) must be disclosed on the consolidated balance sheet, either as a component of stockholders' equity or by itself between long-term liabilities and stockholders' equity.

15. If the purchase cost exceeds the book value of the net assets purchased, the extra amount should be allocated to the assets and liabilities acquired when consolidated financial statements are being prepared. The allocation should be based on fair market values at the date of acquisition. Any unassigned excess should be recorded as **goodwill** (or *goodwill from consolidation*) in the consolidated balance sheet, subject to an annual impairment test.

16. When the book value of the net assets purchased exceeds their purchase cost, the book value of the subsidiary's long-term assets (other than marketable securities) should be reduced proportionately until the extra amount is eliminate.

17. When preparing a consolidated income statement, intercompany items must be eliminated. They include (a) intercompany purchases and sales, (b) intercompany income and expenses on loans, receivables, or bond indebtedness, and (c) other intercompany income and expenses.

18. Businesses that expand internationally are called **multinational or transnational corporations.** When such a business prepares consolidated financial statements, it must include the financial information of any foreign subsidiaries it controls. However, before consolidation can take place, the subsidiary's financial statements—most likely presented in a foreign currency—must be **restated** into the parent's **reporting currency** (usually the U.S. dollar for U.S. companies).

Objective 5: Explain the financial reporting implications of debt investments.

19. As mentioned above, held-to-maturity securities are debt securities that management intends to hold until their maturity date. Such securities are recorded at cost and valued on the balance sheet at amortized cost (that is, at cost adjusted for the effects of interest). When held-to-maturity securities are purchased, Short-Term Investments is debited and Cash credited. At year-end, accrued interest is recognized with a debit to Short-Term Investments and a credit to Interest Income. At maturity, Cash is debited for the maturity amount, and Short-Term Investments and Interest Income are credited.

20. Long-term investments in bonds are recorded at cost (including commissions). When the bonds are purchased between interest dates, the investor must also pay for the accrued interest (which will be returned to the investor on the next interest payment date).

21. Most long-term bond investments are classified as available-for-sale securities because investors usually sell before the securities mature. Such securities are value at fair (market) value. Long-term bond investments are classified as held-to-maturity securities when an early sale is *not* intended. Such securities are valued at cost, adjusted by discount or premium amortization.

Summary of Journal Entries Introduced in Chapter 15

A. (LO 2) Short-Term Investments   XX (purchase price)
            Cash   XX (amount paid)
                Investment in stocks for trading

B. (LO 2) Unrealized Loss on Investments   XX (market decline)
            Allowance to Adjust Short-Term Investments to   XX (market decline)
            Market
                Recognition of unrealized loss on trading portfolio

C. (LO 2) Cash   XX (proceeds on sale)
            Short-Term Investments   XX (purchase price)
            Realized Gain on Investments   XX (the difference)
                Sale of trading securities

D. (LO 2) Allowance to Adjust Short-Term Investments to Market   XX (market increase)
            Unrealized Gain on Investments   XX (market increase)
                Recognition of unrealized gain on trading portfolio

E. (LO 3) Long-Term Investments   XX (purchase price)
            Cash   XX (purchase price)
                Made long-term investment in stock

F.   (LO 3)   Unrealized Loss on Long-Term Investments   XX (market decline)
                     Allowance to Adjust Long-Term Investments to   XX (market decline
                     Market
                           To record reduction of long-term investment to
                           market

G.   (LO 3)   Cash   XX (amount received)
                   Loss on Sale of Investments   XX (the difference)
                     Long-Term Investments   XX (purchase price)
                         Sale of long-term investment in stock

H.   (LO 3)   Cash   XX (amount received)
                     Dividend Income   XX (amount received)
                         Receipt of cash dividend on stock investment

I.   (LO 3)   Allowance to Adjust Long-Term Investments to Market   XX (amount of recovery)
                     Unrealized Loss on Long-Term Investments   XX (amount of recovery)
                         To record adjustment in long-term investment so it
                           is reported at market

J.   (LO 3)   Investment in Quay Corporation   XX (purchase price)
                     Cash   XX (amount paid)
                         Investment in Quay Corporation common stock (equity
                           method to be used)

K.   (LO 3)   Investment in Quay Corporation   XX (equity percentage of income)
                     Income, Quay Corporation Investment   XX (equity percentage of
                           income)

                         Recognition of 40% of income reported by Quay
                         Corporation.

L.   (LO 3)   Cash   XX (amount received)
                     Investment in Quay Corporation   XX (amount received)
                         Cash dividend from Quay Corporation

M.   (LO 4)   Investment in Subsidiary Company   XX (book value)
                     Cash   XX (amount paid)
                         Purchase of 100 percent of Subsidiary Company at
                         book value

N.   (LO 4)   Common Stock (subsidiary)   XX (current balance)
               Retained Earnings (subsidiary)   XX (current balance)
                     Investment in Subsidiary Company   XX (current balance)
                         Work sheet entry to eliminate intercompany
                         investment at acquisition date; subsidiary wholly
                         owned

O.	(LO 4)	Common Stock (subsidiary)	XX (current balance)
		Retained Earnings (subsidiary)	XX (current balance)
		Investment in Subsidiary Company	XX (current balance)
		Minority Interest	XX (equity percentage)

                Work sheet entry to eliminate intercompany
                investment at acquisition date; subsidiary less than
                100 percent owned

P.	(LO 4)	Other Assets	XX (excess allocated)
		Goodwill	XX (excess allocated)
		Common Stock (subsidiary)	XX (current balance)
		Retained Earnings (subsidiary)	XX (current balance)
		Investment in Subsidiary Company	XX (current balance)

                Work sheet entry to eliminate intercompany investment
                at acquisition date; cost exceeds book value

Q.	(LO 4)	Sales	XX (intercompany amount)
		Cost of Goods Sold	XX (intercompany amount)

                Work sheet entry to eliminate intercompany sales
                and purchases

R.	(LO 4)	Other Revenues	XX (intercompany amount)
		Other Expenses	XX (intercompany amount)

                Work sheet entry to eliminate intercompany
                interest

S.	(LO 5)	Short-Term Investments	XX (purchase price)
		Cash	XX (amount paid)

                Purchase of U.S. Treasury bills (held-to-maturity
                securities) that mature in 120 days

T.	(LO 5)	Short-Term Investments	XX (accrued interest)
		Interest Income	XX (accrued amount)

                Accrual of interest on U.S. Treasury bills

U.	(LO 5)	Cash	XX (maturity amount)
		Short-Term Investments	XX (debit balance)
		Interest Income	XX (interest this period)

                Receipt of cash at maturity of U.S. Treasury bills
                and recognition of related income

SELF-TEST

Test your knowledge of the chapter by choosing the best answer for each item below.

1. An unrealized loss on trading securities appears on the
   a. balance sheet within stockholders' equity
   b. income statement.
   c. balance sheet as a liability.
   d. balance sheet as an asset.

2. U.S. Treasury bills due in 180 days are purchased for $97,000. When the maturity amount of $100,000 is received (assuming no year-end adjustment has been made), the journal entry would contain a

   a. credit to Interest Income for $3,000.
   b. debit to Gain on Investment for $3,000.
   c. credit to the Investment account for $100,000.
   d. credit to Gain on Investment for $3,000.

3. In preparing consolidated financial statements, all of the following commonly require eliminating entries *except*

   a. intercompany sales and purchases.
   b. intercompany interest expense and income.
   c. stockholders' equity of parent.
   d. stockholders' equity of subsidiary.

4. B Company buys all the stock of C Company for $634,000. C Company has contributed capital of $404,000 and retained earnings of $160,000, and assets are fairly valued. The consolidated financial statements would contain

   a. minority interest and goodwill.
   b. goodwill but not minority interest.
   c. minority interest but not goodwill.
   d. neither minority interest nor goodwill.

5. The ability to affect the operating and financial policies of a company whose shares are owned, even if the investor company holds less than 50 percent of the investee's voting stock, is referred to as

   a. noninfluential.
   b. noncontrolling.
   c. controlling.
   d. significant influence.

6. When the equity method is used to account for a long-term investment in stock of another company, the carrying value of the investment is affected by

   a. an excess of market price over cost.
   b. neither earnings nor dividends of the investee.
   c. both earnings and dividends of the investee.
   d. a decline in the market value of the stock.

7. Which of the following items would *not* require an elimination during the preparation of consolidated financial statements?

   a. Amount owed by subsidiary to parent
   b. Amount owed by parent to subsidiary
   c. Sales made to outside parties
   d. Investment in subsidiary

8. Which of the following can be both a debt security and an equity security?

   a. Trading securities
   b. Available-for-sale securities
   c. Held-to-maturity securities
   d. Both **a** and **b** above

9. A controlling interest is defined as having what level of ownership in another company?

   a. 100 percent
   b. 75 percent
   c. Greater than 50 percent
   d. 20 to 50 percent

10. Held-to-maturity securities are valued on the balance sheet at
    a. original cost.
    b. fair value.
    c. lower-of-cost-or-market.
    d. amortized cost.

TESTING YOUR KNOWLEDGE

Matching*

Match each term with its definition by writing the appropriate letter in the blank.

1. _____Cost-adjusted-to-market method
2. _____Equity method
3. _____Parent company
4. _____Subsidiary
5. _____Consolidated financial statements
6. _____Purchase method
7. _____Significant influence
8. _____Minority interest
9. _____Control
10. _____Eliminations
11. _____Restatement
12. _____Reporting currency
13. _____Multinational corporation
14. _____Goodwill
15. _____Insider trading
16. _____Marketable securities

a. A business that operates in more than one country

b. The method used to account for noninfluential and noncontrolling investments

c. The excess paid for a subsidiary over the fair value of its net assets

d. The method used when the parent owns more than 50 percent of the subsidiary's voting stock

e. The denomination in which a given set of consolidated financial statements is presented

f. The method used to account for influential but noncontrolling investments

g. A company that is controlled by another company

h. A company that has a controlling interest in another company

i. Combined statements of the parent and its subsidiaries

j. Usually, ownership of 20 to 50 percent of another company's voting stock

k. Ownership of more than 50 percent of the voting stock of another company

l. Entries that appear on a consolidated work sheet

m. Another term for short-term investments

n. Outside ownership of a subsidiary

o.   The expression of one currency in
      terms of another

p.   Using knowledge not yet public for
      personal financial gain

Note to students: The matching quiz might be completed more efficiently by starting with the
definition and searching for the corresponding term.

Short Answer

Use the lines provided to answer each item.

1. List the three classifications for long-term investments in stocks (in terms of level of ownership),
    as well as the ownership percentage that defines each classification.

    _____

    _____

    _____

2. List and briefly define the three types of investments in terms of the intended length of time they
    will be held.

    _____

    _____

    _____

3. Briefly explain the accounting treatment for dividends received under the cost-adjusted-to-market
    method and under the equity method.

    _____

    _____

    _____

    _____

4. Under what circumstance should goodwill be presented on a consolidated balance sheet?

    _____

    _____

    _____

    _____

5. Why must certain items be eliminated when consolidated financial statements are prepared?

    _____

    _____

    _____

    _____

    _____

True-False

Circle T if the statement is true, and F if it is false. Provide explanations for the false answers, using the blank lines at the end of the section.

1.   T   F   When one company has an influential but noncontrolling interest in another company, it would use the equity method to account for the investment.

2.   T   F   Under the cost-adjusted-to-market method, the investor records investment income for a percentage (based on percentage ownership) of the investee's periodic net income.

3.   T   F   When one company owns at least 20 percent of another company, consolidated financial statements should be prepared.

4.   T   F   When consolidated financial statements are prepared, the parent's investment of the subsidiary must be eliminated.

5.   T   F   Unrealized gains and losses on trading securities are reported on the income statement.

6.   T   F   Under the equity method, the investor records a cash dividend by debiting Cash and crediting Dividend Income.

7.   T   F   Minority interest should be reported as an asset on the consolidated balance sheet.

8.   T   F   Goodwill from consolidation does not appear on the unconsolidated balance sheet of the parent or subsidiary, but may appear on the consolidated balance sheet.

9.   T   F   When preparing consolidated financial statements, purchases of goods and services from outside parties should be eliminated.

10. T   F   When the book value of the net assets purchased equals their purchase cost, the assets and liabilities purchased should appear at cost on the consolidated balance sheet.

11. T   F   Long-term bonds treated as held-to-maturity investments are accounted for at fair (market) value.

12. T   F   An unrealized gain or loss on available-for-sale securities is reported as a special item within stockholders' equity.

13. T   F   Insider trading is illegal worldwide.

14. T   F   The account Allowance to Adjust Short-Term Investments to Market is a contra-asset account when it has a credit balance.

15. T   F   The entry to eliminate intercompany purchases and sales is debit Cost of Goods Sold and credit Sales.

_____

_____

_____

_____

_____

_____

_____

_____

_____

_____

_____

_____

_____

_____

_____

Multiple Choice

Circle the letter of the best answer.

1. The journal entry to record the receipt of a dividend under the cost-adjusted-to-market method would include a

    a.   debit to the Investment account.
    b.   credit to Dividend Income.
    c.   debit to Goodwill.
    d.   credit to the Investment account.

2. The elimination of an intercompany investment cannot include a

    a.   debit to the investment account.
    b.   debit to Goodwill.
    c.   debit to Retained Earnings.
    d.   credit to Minority Interest.

3. The unconsolidated financial statements of a parent company may *not* include

    a.   purchases from its subsidiary.
    b.   goodwill.
    c.   an account reflecting the investment in its subsidiary.
    d.   purchases from outside parties.

4. Which of the following items would *not* be eliminated when consolidated financial statements are prepared, assuming that the subsidiary is 100 percent owned?

    a.   The subsidiary's common stock
    b.   The parent's investment in the subsidiary
    c.   Interest owed to the subsidiary from the parent
    d.   Profit on goods sold by the subsidiary to outside parties

5. Mann Company uses the cost-adjusted-to-market method to account for its three long-term investments. The total cost of the investments is $95,000, and the total market value of the investments at the end of 20xx is $60,000. The account Allowance to Adjust Long-Term Investments to Market has a credit balance of $10,000 before the 20xx adjusting entry is made. The year-end adjusting entry for 20xx would include a

    a.   debit to Unrealized Loss on Long-Term Investments for $35,000.
    b.   debit to Allowance to Adjust Long-Term Investments to Market for $10,000.
    c.   credit to Allowance to Adjust Long-Term Investments to Market for $60,000.
    d.   debit to Unrealized Loss on Long-Term Investments for $25,000.

6. Which of the following investments could be classified as short-term, but never long-term?

    a.   Trading securities
    b.   Available-for-sale securities
    c.   Held-to-maturity securities
    d.   Both **b** and **c** above

7. Under the equity method, the investor's entry to recognize its portion of the investee's earnings would contain a

    a.   debit to cash.
    b.   debit to the Investment account.
    c.   debit to the Investment Income account.
    d.   credit to the Realized Gain account.

8. The adjusting entry to accrue interest at year-end on held-to-maturity securities would contain a

    a.   debit to Cash.
    b.   debit to Interest Income.
    c.   debit to the Investment account.
    d.   credit to Interest Receivable.

APPLYING YOUR KNOWLEDGE

Exercises

1. Graham Corporation purchased 80 percent of the common stock of Day Corporation for $165,000. Day's stockholders' equity contained common stock of $60,000 and retained earnings of $90,000. In the journal provided, prepare the eliminating entry that would be entered on the work sheet for consolidating the balance sheets of Graham and Day. Assume that up to $10,000 of any excess of cost over carrying value is allocated to the building purchased. (*Hint:* Your entry should contain four debits and two credits.)

General Journal				
Date		**Description**	**Debit**	**Credit**
				·

2. Bryant Corporation owns 15 percent of the common stock of Ray Company and 30 percent of the common stock of Marsh Company. Both are long-term investments. During a given year, Ray paid total dividends of $80,000 and earned $110,000, and Marsh paid total dividends of $50,000 and earned $65,000. In the journal provided, prepared Bryant's entries to reflect the above facts. Leave the date column empty, as no dates have been specified.

General Journal

Date	Description	Debit	Credit

3. On November 17, 20x1, Valdez Corporation purchased 2,000 shares of Welu Corporation stock for $30 per share. The purchase was made for trading purposes. At December 31, 20x1, the stock had a market value of $28 per share. On January 12, 20x2, Valdez sold all 2,000 shares for $66,000. In the journal provided, prepare the entries for November 17, December 31, and January 12.

General Journal

Date	Description	Debit	Credit

Crossword Puzzle: Chapters 13, 14, and 15

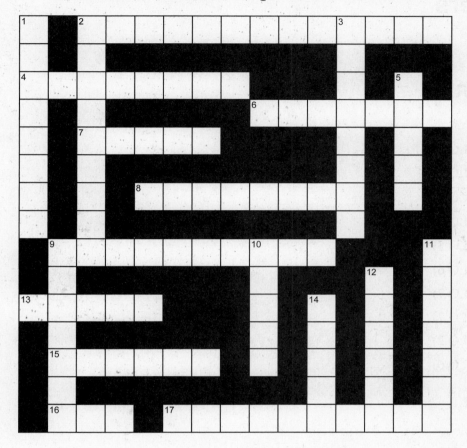

ACROSS

2 Ratio indicating investor confidence in a company (2 words)

4 Analysis resulting in 9-Across

6 Quarterly financial statement, e.g.

7 Statement of cash _____

8 Financial statement examination

9 Statement showing percentage relationships (hyphenated)

13 _____ analysis, a variation of horizontal analysis

15 Method to account for long-term investments

16 An operating-activity outflow

17 Analysis involving dollar and percentage changes

DOWN

1 Interest _____ ratio

2 Group of investments or loans

3 An operating-activity inflow or outflow

5 Dividends _____

9 With 14-Down, a measure of liquidity

10 Number used in 13-Across

11 Majority ownership of voting stock

12 Method for 7-Across

14 See 9-Down

Answers

CHAPTER 1

Self-Test

1. a   (LO 3)
2. a   (LO 2)
3. b   (LO 3)
4. b   (LO 4)
5. c   (LO 5)
6. d   (LO 6)
7. a   (LO 7)
8. c   (LO 7)
9. d   (LO 2)
10. b   (LO 6)

Matching

1. h
2. f
3. o
4. r
5. w
6. n
7. s
8. c
9. j
10. v
11. i
12. b
13. u
14. e
15. l

16. q

17. m

18. t

19. d

20. g

21. y

22. p

23. k

24. x

25. a

Short Answer

1. (LO 6)

   Tolan Corporation

   Income Statement

   For the Year Ended July 31, 20xx

2. (LO 1) *Bookkeeping* deals only with the mechanical and repetitive recordkeeping process. *Accounting* involves bookkeeping as well as the design of an accounting system, its use, and the analysis of its output.

3. (LO 7)

   a. *Integrity*—The accountant is honest, regardless of consequences.

   b. *Objectivity*—The accountant is impartial in performing his or her job.

   c. *Independence*—The accountant avoids all relationships or situations that could impair or appear to impair his or her objectivity.

   d. *Due care*—The accountant carries out his or her responsibilities with competence and diligence.

4. (LO 2) Management, outsiders with a direct financial interest, and outsiders with an indirect financial interest

5. (LO 1) Profitability (earning enough income to attract and hold investment capital) and liquidity (keeping sufficient funds on hand to pay debts as they fall due)

6. (LO 6)

   Statement

   a. Income statement

   b. Statement of retained earnings

   c. Balance sheet

   d. Statement of cash flows

Purpose

a. Measures net income during a certain period

b. Shows how retained earnings changed during the period

c. Shows financial position at a point in time

d. Discloses the cash flows that result from the business's operating, investing, and financing activities during the period

True-False

1. T (LO 6)

2. F (LO 7) The IRS interprets and enforces tax laws.

3. T (LO 5)

4. T (LO 5)

5. F (LO 5) It indicates that the company has one or more debtors.

6. T (LO 5)

7. T (LO 3)

8. F (LO 6) Dividends are a deduction on the statement of retained earnings.

9. F (LO 7) The FASB dictates accounting practice.

10. T (LO 4)

11. T (LO 6)

12. T (LO 6)

13. F (LO 7) That is the GASB's responsibility.

14. F (LO 4) A corporation is managed by its board of directors.

15. T (LO 7)

16. F (LO 5) Net assets equal assets *minus* liabilities.

17. F (LO 6) Balance sheets do not list revenues and expenses.

18. F (LO 3) Nonexchange transactions, such as the accumulation of interest, do exist.

19. T (LO 1)

20. T (LO 6)

21. T (LO 3)

22. F (LO 2) Economic planners have an indirect financial interest in accounting information.

23. T (LO 5)

24. F (LO 1) Cash flow is a measure of liquidity.

25. T (LO 1)

26. F (LO 6) They appear as financing activities.

27. F (LO 7) It is expressed as a percentage.
28. T (LO 5)

Multiple Choice

1. a (LO 6) The income statement reports revenues and expenses. Utilities Expense would therefore appear on that statement rather than on the balance sheet.

2. c (LO 7) Public corporations must file various reports containing specific financial information with the SEC (Securities and Exchange Commission), the agency that regulates the issuance and trading of stock in the United States. The SEC makes these reports available to the public, thus helping to ensure that investors have complete and accurate information on which to base their decisions.

3. b (LO 4) The owners of a corporation—the stockholders—can easily transfer their shares to other investors.

4. b (LO 6) The balance sheet is in a sense a "snapshot" of a business on a given date. The account balances on the statement are a report of the ultimate effect of financial transactions during an accounting period, not a report of the actual transactions.

5. a (LO 7) The principal purpose of an audit is to verify the quality of the information that a company's management presents in its financial statements. *Fairness* refers to the ability of users of the financial statements to rely on the information as presented.

6. c (LO 1) Recording an expense when incurred is actually in accordance with GAAP. The other three choices are listed in the text as examples of fraudulent financial reporting.

7. d (LO 4) The partners *are* the partnership (i.e., there is no separate legal entity in this form of business organization). When a partner leaves the partnership, the original partnership is dissolved, although a new partnership may then be formed by replacing the exiting partner.

8. a (LO 6) "Assets" is a major heading found on the balance sheet; Accounts Receivable is a type of asset.

9. b (LO 6) The statement of cash flows does not list any "funding" activities.

10. c (LO 3) The wear and tear on an asset does not create an exchange of anything tangible. The other choices, however, do involve a physical exchange.

Exercises

1. (LO 2)

   a. Potential investors need all recent financial statements to assess the future profitability of a company to determine whether they should invest in it.

   b. The principal goal of the SEC is to protect the investing public. Insisting that Atlantic make its statements public as well as examining the statements for propriety certainly will help the public make decisions regarding Atlantic.

   c. The bank would have difficulty in determining Atlantic's ability to repay the loan if it does not have access to Atlantic's most recent financial statements.

   d. Present stockholders will wish to see the statements in order to decide whether to sell, maintain, or increase their investments.

e.   Management will want to see the statements because the statements should help them pinpoint the weaknesses that caused the year's loss.

2.   (LO 5) $55,000

3.   (LO 6)

Philo's TV Repair Corporation
Balance Sheet
December 31, 20xx

Assets

Cash	$ 2,950
Accounts receivable	1,500
Equipment	850
Land	1,000
Building	8,000
Truck	4,500
Total assets	$18,800

Liabilities

Accounts payable	$ 1,300

Stockholders' Equity

Common stock	14,500
Retained earnings	3,000
Total liabilities and stockholders' equity	$18,800

Solution to
Crossword Puzzle: Chapter 1

CHAPTER 2

Self-Test

1.	a	(LO 1)
2.	b	(SO 6)
3.	d	(LO 2)
4.	b	(LO 2)
5.	c	(LO 2)
6.	a	(LO 3)
7.	c	(LO 3)
8.	c	(SO 6)
9.	a	(SO 6)
10.	a	(LO 4)

Matching

1. k
2. f
3. q
4. o
5. b
6. g
7. a
8. m
9. l
10. s
11. j
12. r
13. e
14. t
15. p
16. h
17. c
18. i
19. d
20. k

Short Answer

1. (LO 1)

    a. Apr. 22

    b. 200

    c. Cash and Accounts Receivable

2. (LO 3) One example is the purchase of an asset for cash. Another example is the collection of an account receivable.

3. (LO 3) One example is the payment of an account payable.

4. (LO 2) Revenues, expenses, and dividends

5. (LO 2) Liabilities, stockholders' equity, and revenues are credited when increased.

True-False

1. F (LO 1) A sale should be recorded when it takes place.

2. F (LO 1) The hiring of a new employee would not be entered into the accounting records.

3. T (SO 6)

4. F (LO 2) The credit side of an account does not imply anything favorable or unfavorable.

5. F (LO 2) Only accounts with zero balances have equal debits and credits.

6. F (SO 6) One can quickly determine cash on hand by referring to the ledger.

7. T (SO 6)

8. F (SO 6) Notes Payable is the proper account title; the liability is evidenced by the existence of a promissory note.

9. T (LO 1)

10. T (LO 2)

11. F (LO 2) It is possible to have only increases or only decreases in a journal entry.

12. F (SO 6) Journal entries are made before transactions are posted to the ledger.

13. F (SO 6) Liabilities and stockholders' equity accounts are indented only when credited.

14. T (SO 6)

15. T (SO 6)

16. T (SO 6)

17. T (SO 6)

18. F (SO 6) It is a table of contents to the general ledger.

19. F (LO 2) Unearned Revenue has a normal credit balance.

20. F (LO 2) Retained earnings is not cash and should be shown in the stockholders' equity section.

21. T (LO 2)

22. T (LO 4)

23.   T   (LO 4)

24.   F   (LO 1) It is not a recordable transaction because the product has not been received.

Multiple Choice

1.   c   (LO 1) Summarization of accounting data occurs at the end of the accounting cycle.

2.   d   (LO 3) When a liability is paid, each side of the accounting equation is reduced by the same amount. The transaction results in a reduction in an asset and a corresponding reduction in a liability.

3.   c   (SO 6) The explanation accompanying a journal entry is a brief statement about the entire transaction. Debits and credits are elements of the recorded transaction. The explanation is entered after all debit and credit entries have been made.

4.   d   (SO 7) The final step in the posting process is the transfer of the ledger account number to the Post. Ref. column of the general journal. It is an indication that all other steps in the process are complete.

5.   c   (LO 4) If only part of a journal entry has been posted, the information omitted would usually be either a debit or a credit. As a result, total debits would not equal total credits in the general ledger accounts. The trial balance would therefore be out of balance.

6.   b   (LO 3) When cash is received in payment of an account receivable, one asset is being exchanged for another. Total assets would therefore remain unchanged.

7.   a   (LO 2) Increasing the Dividends account ultimately causes a reduction in Retained Earnings, a stockholders' equity account. A decrease in stockholders' equity is recorded with a debit.

8.   b   (LO 2) Of the accounts listed, Prepaid Rent is the only one that is classified as an asset. Unearned Revenue is a liability account, Retained Earnings is a stockholders' equity account, and Service Revenue is a revenue account.

9.   a   (LO 2) Of the accounts listed, only Interest Payable would represent an amount owed.

10.   b   (LO 3) Unearned Rent would represent a liability on the accounting records of the *lessor*. The question refers to the possible entries of the *lessee,* which include entries for Prepaid Rent, Rent Payable, and Rent Expense.

11.   c   (LO 4) Fees Earned is a revenue account. Revenues increase with a credit entry, and therefore Fees Earned is referred to as having a *normal credit balance.* Revenues ultimately cause an increase in Retained Earnings, which also has a normal credit balance.

12.   d   (LO 4) The use of an incorrect account will not cause a trial balance to be out of balance. However, in this case, both Accounts Receivable and Accounts Payable will be overstated.

Exercises

1. (SO 6)

		General Journal		
Date		**Description**	**Debit**	**Credit**
May	2	Cash	28,000	
		Common Stock		28,000
		Recorded the stockholders' original investment		
	3	Prepaid Rent	900	
		Cash		900
		Paid three months' rent in advance		
	5	Printing Equipment	10,000	
		Photographic Equipment	3,000	
		Cash		2,000
		Accounts Payable		11,000
		Purchased a press and equipment from Irvine Press, Inc.		
	8	No entry		
	9	Cash	1,200	
		Unearned Revenue		1,200
		Received payment in advance from Raymond's Department Store for brochures to be printed		
	11	Printing Supplies	800	
		Notes Payable		800
		Purchased paper from Pacific Paper Company		
	14	Cash	250	
		Accounts Receivable	250	
		Revenue from Services		500
		Completed job for Sunrise Shoes		
	14	Salaries Expense	200	
		Cash		200
		Paid the pressman his weekly salary		
	15	Accounts Payable	1,000	
		Cash		1,000
		Paid on account amount owed to Irvine Press, Inc.		
	18	Cash	250	
		Accounts Receivable		250
		Sunrise Shoes paid its debt in full		

	20	Dividends		700	
		Cash			700
		The board of directors declared and paid a $700 cash dividend			
	24	Utilities Expense		45	
		Accounts Payable			45
		Recorded electric bill			
	30	Accounts Payable		45	
		Cash			45
		Recorded payment of electric bill			

2. (LO 2)

  a.   debit balance of $2,250

  b.   credit balance of $1,000

  c.   debit balance of $14,600

3. (SO 6)

General Journal					Page 4
Date		**Description**	**Post. Ref.**	**Debit**	**Credit**
May	3	Cash	11	2,000	
		Revenue from Services	41		2,000
		Received payment from Rodgers Company for services			
	5	Accounts Payable	21	700	
		Cash	11		700
		Paid Grant Supply Company for supplies purchased on March 31 on credit			

Cash							Account No. 11
						Balance	
Date		**Item**	**Post. Ref.**	**Debit**	**Credit**	**Debit**	**Credit**
May	3		J4	2,000		2,000	
	5		J4		700	1,300	

Accounts Payable | | | | | | | **Account No. 21**

			Post. Ref.	Debit	Credit	Balance*	
Date		Item				Debit	Credit
May	5		J4	700		700	

Revenue from Services | | | | | | | **Account No. 41**

			Post. Ref.	Debit	Credit	Balance*	
Date		Item				Debit	Credit
May	3		J4		2,000		2,000

*Previous postings have been omitted, resulting in an improbable debit balance in Accounts Payable.

CHAPTER 3

Self-Test

1. c (LO 5)
2. d (LO 3)
3. d (LO 1)
4. b (LO 5)
5. a (LO 2)
6. c (LO 3)
7. b (LO 3)
8. b (LO 5)
9. d (LO 6)
10. c (LO 4)

Matching

1. i
2. v
3. w
4. r
5. c
6. q
7. f
8. t

9. e

10. o

11. s

12. h

13. m

14. p

15. l

16. j

17. b

18. g

19. d

20. a

21. k

22. n

23. u

Short Answer

1. (LO 3) Dividing recorded expenses between two or more accounting periods; dividing recorded revenues between two or more accounting periods; recording unrecorded expenses; and recording unrecorded revenues

2. (LO 1) The matching rule means that revenues should be recorded in the period in which they are earned and that all expenses related to those revenues also should be recorded in that period.

3. (LO 2) Depreciation is the allocation of the cost of a long-lived asset to the periods benefiting from the asset.

4. (LO 2) Prepaid expenses are expenses paid in advance; they initially are recorded as assets. Unearned revenues represent payments received in advance of providing goods or services; they initially are recorded as liabilities.

5. (LO 2)

   a. A purchase or sale arrangement exists.

   b. Goods have been delivered or services rendered.

   c. The price is fixed or determinable.

   d. Collectibility is reasonably assured.

6. (LO 5) Revenue accounts, expense accounts, Income Summary, Dividends

True-False

1. T   (LO 3)

2. T   (LO 1)

3. F   (LO 1) The calendar year is the period from January 1 to December 31.

4.   T   (LO 1)

5.   F   (LO 2) Under accrual accounting, the timing of cash exchanges is irrelevant in recording revenues and expenses.

6.   F   (LO 4) Adjusting entries are made before the financial statements are prepared.

7.   T   (LO 3)

8.   F   (LO 3) It is debited for the amount consumed during the period (the amount available during the period less ending inventory).

9.   F   (LO 3) Accumulated Depreciation (a contra account) has a credit balance, even though it appears in the asset section of the balance sheet.

10. T   (LO 3)

11. F   (LO 3) The Unearned Revenues account is a liability account.

12. F   (LO 3) The credit is to a liability account.

13. T   (LO 4)

14. F   (LO 3) If payment has not yet been received, the debit is to Accounts Receivable.

15. T   (LO 3)

16. T   (LO 3)

17. F   (LO 5) Income Summary does not appear on any financial statement.

18. F   (LO 5) Only nominal accounts are closed.

19. T   (LO 5)

20. F   (LO 5) The Dividends account is closed directly to Retained Earnings.

21. F   (LO 5) When there is a net loss, Income Summary is credited when closed.

22. F   (LO 5) It does not contain Dividends because that account will have a zero balance.

23. T   (LO 5)

24. F   (LO 1) Earnings management refers to the unethical manipulation of income.

Multiple Choice

1.   c   (LO 3) An adjusting entry normally contains at least one balance sheet account and at least one income statement account. Choice **c** does not, nor does it fit the description for any adjusting entry.

2.   b   (LO 3) Office supplies are not considered long-lived assets subject to periodic depreciation, as are the other items listed. Instead, they are expensed once they have been consumed (used up).

3.   b   (LO 3) Unearned Fees is used to record a firm's liability for amounts received but not yet earned. This recognition is required so that revenue amounts can be represented properly and allocated in the appropriate accounting period. As the revenues are earned, the proper amounts are transferred from liabilities to revenues. Between the time the revenues are received and the time they actually are earned, one accounting period may have ended and another accounting period may have begun.

4. a   (LO 3) Depreciation is the allocation of the cost of an asset over the asset's expected useful life. The matching rule requires the allocation of the cost while the asset is being used in a firm's revenue-generating activities.

5. c   (LO 4) Net income is the result of the calculation that nets revenues and expenses. The adjusted trial balance contains summary balances of each general ledger account after adjusting entries have been made.

6. c   (LO 5) Retained Earnings is the only account listed that would remain open after the closing procedures are complete at the end of the accounting cycle. The post-closing trial balance is a listing of such accounts, along with their account balances.

7. a   (LO 1) Estimates are involved in the preparation of account balances used to report net income. An example of this kind of estimate is the recording of depreciation expense. Although not exact, the reported net income of one accounting period can be compared with the net income of other accounting periods, providing a basis for conclusions about the firm.

8. d   (LO 3) Until Prepaid Rent is expired and is recorded as an expense through adjustments, it remains an asset on a firm's books.

9. b   (LO 3) Because of the nature of accruals and deferrals, Cash is *never* involved in the end-of-period adjustments.

10. c   (LO 4) After preparation of the trial balance, but before preparation of the adjusted trial balance, an adjusting entry is made to record office supplies consumed. This entry reduces the Office Supplies account and increases the Office Supplies Expense account.

11. a   (LO 5) Of the accounts listed, Unearned Commissions is the only one not involved in the closing process. Unearned Commissions is a permanent balance sheet account and remains open from one period to the next if it contains a balance.

12. b   (LO 5) When Income Summary has a debit balance after expenses and revenues have been closed, the account is closed by a credit entry equal to the debit balance. The corresponding debit is an entry to Retained Earnings, reducing the balance of that account by an amount equal to the net loss for the period.

13. c   (LO 5) Updating the revenue and expense accounts is the purpose of the adjusting entries. The closing entries are prepared after the adjusting entries.

14. c   (LO 5) Temporary accounts are those that are closed at the end of the period (revenues, expenses, and dividends).

15. a   (LO 5) All the components of a statement of retained earnings have been provided, except for net income or loss. A net income figure of $55,000 will correctly answer the question.

Exercises

1.   (LO 3)

Newton Transit Company
Partial Balance Sheet
December 31, 20x5

Assets

Cash		$ 5,000
Accounts receivable		3,000
Company vehicles	$24,000	
Less accumulated depreciation,		
Company vehicles	9,000	15,000
Total assets		$23,000

2.   (LO 3)

    a. $970 ($510 + $800 − $340)

    b. $1,750 [($14,000 ÷ 4 yrs.) × 1/2 yr.]

    c. $450 ($600 × 3/4)

3. (LO 3)

		General Journal		
Date*		**Description**	**Debit**	**Credit**
a.		Supplies Expense	125	
		Supplies		125
		Recorded supplies consumed during the period		
b.		Wages Expense	2,000	
		Wages Payable		2,000
		Recorded accrued wages		
c.		Unearned Revenues	600	
		Revenues from Services		600
		Recorded earned revenues		
d.		Depreciation Expense, Buildings	4,500	
		Accumulated Depreciation, Buildings		4,500
		Recorded depreciation on buildings		
e.		Advertising Expense	2,000	
		Prepaid Advertising		2,000
		Recorded advertising used during the year		
f.		Insurance Expense	250	
		Prepaid Insurance		250
		Recorded insurance expired during the year		
g.		Accounts Receivable	2,200	
		Revenues from Services		2,200
		Recorded revenues earned for which payment has not been received		
h.		Income Taxes Expense	21,700	
		Income Taxes Payable		21,700
		Recorded accrued income tax expense		

*In reality, all of the adjusting entries would be dated December 31.

4. (LO 6)

    a. $6,200 ($1,200 + $8,700 − $3,700)

    b. $35,400 ($900 + $35,000 − $500)

    c. $3,000 ($1,800 + $3,600 − $2,400)

5. (LO 5)

General Journal

Date*		Description	Debit	Credit
July	31	Revenue from Services	4,700	
		Income Summary		4,700
		To close the revenue account		
	31	Income Summary	700	
		Rent Expense		500
		Telephone Expense		50
		Utilities Expense		150
		To close the expense accounts		
	31	Income Summary	4,000	
		Retained Earnings		4,000
		To close the Income Summary Account		
	31	Retained Earnings	2,500	
		Dividends		2,500
		To close the Dividends account		

6. (LO 5)

Frank's Fix-It Services, Inc.
Statement of Retained Earnings
For the Month Ended July 31, 20xx

Retained Earnings, July 1, 20xx	$3,000
Net income	4,000
Subtotal	$7,000
Less Dividends	2,500
Retained Earnings, July 31, 20xx	$4,500

Solution to
Crossword Puzzle: Chapters 2 and 3

¹R	E	T	U	R	²N	O	N		³I	N	C	O	M	⁴E

Across / grid solution:

- ¹RETURN ON ³INCOME
- RENT (down 1)
- ⁶DEFERRAL ⁷EXP (down)
- ⁵WAGER (down)
- ⁸RE...
- ⁹P ¹⁰LEDGER ¹¹R
- ¹²JOURNALIZE (down)
- POSTCLOSING (down 9)
- ¹³SERVICE ¹⁴C
- ¹⁵VALUATION (down)
- ¹⁶TRIAL BALANCE ¹⁷ACCACCRUED
- ¹⁸DEBIT
- ¹⁹SALARY ADJUSTS
- ²⁰LOSS ²¹NOTE ²²PAYS
- ²³N
- ²⁴DOUBLE ENTRY
- EXPIRE (down 4)

SUPPLEMENT TO CHAPTER 3

Exercise

1.

Mike's Maintenance, Inc.
Work Sheet
For the Year Ended December 31, 20xx

Account Name	Trial Balance Debit	Trial Balance Credit	Adjustments Debit	Adjustments Credit	Adjusted Trial Balance Debit	Adjusted Trial Balance Credit	Income Statement Debit	Income Statement Credit	Balance Sheet Debit	Balance Sheet Credit
Cash	2,560				2,560				2,560	
Accounts Receivable	880		(e) 50		930				930	
Prepaid Rent	750			(a) 550	200				200	
Lawn Supplies	250			(c) 150	100				100	
Lawn Equipment	10,000				10,000				10,000	
Accum. Deprec., Lawn Equipment		2,000		(b) 1,500		3,500				3,500
Accounts Payable		630				630				630
Unearned Landscaping Fees		300				180				180
Common Stock		5,000				5,000				5,000
Retained Earnings		1,000				1,000				1,000
Dividends	6,050				6,050				6,050	
Grass-Cutting Fees		15,000		(e) 50		15,050		15,050		
Wages Expense	3,300		(d) 280		3,580		3,580			
Gasoline Expense	140				140		140			
	23,930	23,930								
Rent Expense			(a) 550		550		550			
Depreciation Expense, Lawn Equipment			(b) 1,500		1,500		1,500			
Lawn Supplies Expense			(c) 150		150		150			
Landscaping Fees Earned				(f) 120		120		120		
Wages Payable				(d) 280		280				280
Income Taxes Expense			(g) 1,570		1,570		1,570			
Income Taxes Payable				(g) 1,570		1,570				1,570
			4,220	4,220	27,330	27,330	7,490	15,170	19,840	12,160
Net Income							7,680			7,680
							15,170	15,170	19,840	19,840

CHAPTER 4

Self-Test

1. c   (LO 3)
2. b   (LO 1)
3. a   (LO 2)
4. c   (LO 3)
5. b   (LO 3)
6. b   (LO 3)
7. a   (LO 4)
8. c   (LO 5)
9. c   (LO 5)
10. d   (LO 3)

Matching

1. e
2. l
3. p
4. c
5. g
6. q
7. k
8. b
9. m
10. f
11. o
12. j
13. i
14. a
15. h
16. n
17. d

Short Answer

1. (LO 3)

Business Organization	Name for Equity Section
Sole proprietorship	Owner's equity
Partnership	Partners' equity
Corporation	Stockholders' equity

2. (LO 4) *Profit margin* shows net income in relation to net sales.

   Asset turnover shows how efficiently assets are used to produce sales.

   Return on assets shows net income in relation to average total assets.

   Return on equity shows net income in relation to average owner's investment.

   Debt to equity ratio shows the proportion of a business financed by creditors and the proportion financed by owners.

3. (LO 4) *Working capital* equals current assets minus current liabilities.

   Current ratio equals current assets divided by current liabilities.

4. (LO 2) *Consistency and comparability*—Applying the same accounting procedures from one period to the next

   Materiality—The relative importance of an item or event

   Cost-benefit—Ensuring that the cost of providing accounting information does not exceed the benefits gained from it

   Conservatism—Choosing the accounting procedure that will be least likely to overstate assets and income

   Full disclosure—Showing all relevant information in the financial statements or in the notes

True-False

1. F (LO 3) They are considered current assets if collection is expected within the normal operating cycle, even if that cycle is longer than one year.

2. T (LO 2)

3. T (LO 4)

4. F (LO 4) Operating expenses consist of selling expenses and general and administrative expenses only.

5. T (LO 1)

6. T (LO 5)

7. F (LO 3) Short-term investments in stock are included in the current assets section of a balance sheet.

8. F (LO 5) Liquidity is what is being defined.

9. F (LO 3) The normal operating cycle can be less than one year.

10. F   (LO 3) *Net worth* is merely another term for *owners' equity* and would rarely equal the market value of net assets.

11. T   (LO 4)

12. T   (LO 4)

13. F   (LO 5) Working capital equals current assets *minus* current liabilities.

14. T   (LO 5)

15. F   (LO 1) Reliability is what is being described.

16. F   (LO 5) Earnings per share is a measure of profitability.

17. F   (LO 2) The dividing line between material and immaterial is a judgment call and varies from company to company.

Multiple Choice

1. c   (LO 3) The conversion of inventories to cash is the basis for a firm's operations. This conversion cycle (called the *normal operating cycle*) is frequently less than one year. However, if it is longer than one year, the inventory by definition is still classified as a current asset.

2. c   (LO 4) The single-step income statement does not isolate gross margin from sales. Instead, cost of goods sold is combined with the other expenses and then subtracted from total revenues to arrive at income before income taxes.

3. b   (LO 5) The current ratio gives creditors information about a firm's liquidity—that is, its ability to pay its debts.

4. d   (LO 3) The owner's Capital account would appear on the balance sheet of a sole proprietorship or partnership only.

5. a   (LO 5) The ratio described is profit margin, which shows the relationship between net income and net sales.

6. c   (LO 4) *Operating expenses* is a broad term referring to all the expenses of running a company other than cost of goods sold and income taxes.

7. d   (LO 1) Each choice except **d** describes an objective of FASB *Statement of Financial Accounting Concepts No. 1*. The FASB statement stresses *external* use of financial information, and management consists of internal users.

8. d   (LO 5) One calculation of return on assets is profit margin times asset turnover, which in this case equals 12 percent.

9. b   (LO 4) Because a service company does not sell merchandise, it does not use a Cost of Goods Sold account. Thus, a gross margin figure could not be obtained.

Exercises

1. (LO 3)

    1. d

    2. e

    3. c

    4. g

5. a

6. c

7. a

8. b

9. f

10. e

11. d

12. a

13. *X*

14. a

15. e

2. (LO 5)

a. $40,000 ($60,000 – $20,000)

b. 3 ($60,000/$20,000)

c. 10% ($25,000/$250,000)

d. 12.5% ($25,000/$200,000)

e. 16.7% ($25,000/$150,000)

f. 1.25 times ($250,000/$200,000)

3. (LO 4)

a.

Newcastle Corporation
Income Statement (Multistep)
For the Year Ended December 31, 20xx

Net sales	$200,000
Less cost of goods sold	150,000
Gross margin	$ 50,000
Operating expenses	30,000
Income from operations	$ 20,000
Other revenues	
Interest income	2,000
Income before income taxes	$ 22,000
Income taxes	5,000
Net income	$ 17,000
Earnings per share	$4.86

b.

Newcastle Corporation
Income Statement (Single-step)
For the Year Ended December 31, 20xx

Revenues		
Net sales	$200,000	
Interest income	2,000	$202,000
Costs and expenses		
Cost of goods sold	$150,000	
Operating expenses	30,000	180,000
Income before income taxes		$ 22,000
Income taxes		5,000
Net income		$ 17,000
Earnings per share		$4.86

CHAPTER 5

Self-Test

1. a   (LO 6)
2. d   (LO 3, 4)
3. b   (LO 3, 4)
4. a   (LO 4)
5. c   (LO 2)
6. a   (LO 4)
7. d   (LO 3)
8. c   (LO 5)
9. b   (LO 5)
10. d   (LO 6)

Matching

1. h
2. e
3. q
4. b
5. l
6. k
7. c
8. g

9. i

10. d

11. m

12. a

13. f

14. p

15. n

16. r

17. j

18. o

Short Answer

1. (LO 5)

    Requiring authorization for certain transactions

    Recording all transactions

    Using well-designed documents

    Establishing physical controls over assets and records

    Making periodic independent checks of records and assets

    Separating duties

    Employing sound personnel procedures

2. (LO 6) Any six of the following would answer the question:

    Separating the authorization, recordkeeping, and custodianship of cash

    Limiting access to cash

    Designating a person to handle cash

    Maximizing the use of banking facilities and minimizing cash on hand

    Bonding employees who have access to cash

    Protecting cash on hand with safes, cash registers, and similar equipment

    Conducting surprise audits of the cash on hand

    Recording cash receipts promptly

    Depositing cash receipts promptly

    Paying by check

    Having someone who is not involved with cash transactions reconcile the Cash account

3. (LO 6) Purchase order, invoice, and receiving report

4.   (LO 4)

  Beginning merchandise inventory
+ Net cost of purchases
= Goods available for sale
− Ending merchandise inventory
= Cost of goods sold

5.   (LO 4)

  Purchases
− Purchases returns and allowances
− Purchases discounts
= Net purchases
+ Freight in
= Net cost of purchases

True-False

1. F   (LO 4) *Beginning* inventory is needed.

2. F   (LO 2) It means that payment is due ten days *after* the end of the month.

3. T   (LO 1)

4. T   (LO 1, LO 3)

5. T   (LO 2)

6. F   (LO 2) It is a contra account to *sales*.

7. T   (LO 4)

8. T   (LO 4)

9. T   (LO 1)

10. T   (LO 4)

11. F   (LO 3, LO 4) It normally has a debit balance.

12. F   (LO 4) It requires a debit to Office Supplies (office supplies are not merchandise).

13. T   (LO 3)

14. F   (LO 2) They treat it as a selling expense.

15. F   (LO 4) Both are done at the end of the period.

16. F   (LO 2) A trade discount is a percentage off the list or catalogue price; 2/10, n/30 is a sales discount, offered for early payment.

17. F   (LO 2) Title passes at the shipping point.

18. F   (LO 5) It increases the probability of accuracy but will not guarantee it.

19. T   (LO 5)

20. F   (LO 6) This procedure could easily lead to theft.

21. F   (LO 6) The company sends the supplier a purchase order.

22. F   (LO 5) Rotating employees is good internal control because it might uncover theft.

23. T   (LO 5)

Multiple Choice

1. d   (LO 2) According to the terms, Bob would be entitled to a 2 percent purchases discount of $10. In this example (after allowing for the purchase returns), the discount would be entered as a credit to balance the journal entry, which would also include a debit to Accounts Payable for the balance due ($500) and a credit to Cash for the balance due less the discount ($490).

2. c   (LO 4) Purchase Returns and Allowances is a contra account to the Purchases account. Purchases has a normal debit balance. Its corresponding contra accounts have normal credit balances.

3. b   (LO 4) Delivery Expense is a selling expense; it is not an element of cost of goods sold.

4. d   (LO 6) The purchase requisition is the initial request for materials filed by the person or department that needs them.

5. a   (LO 6) To prevent theft by employees, internal control procedures should separate recordkeeping from the handling of assets.

6. c   (LO 3) Under the perpetual inventory system, purchases of merchandise are recorded in the Merchandise Inventory account, not in a Purchases account.

7. b   (LO 1) When operating expenses are paid for has no bearing on the length of the operating cycle.

8. d   (LO 2) The entry would also include a debit to Credit Card Discount Expense for $50 and a credit to Sales for $1,000.

9. a   (LO 1) The financing period equals the number of days taken to sell inventory, plus the number of days to make collection, minus the number of days the company takes to pay its suppliers for the goods (45 + 60 − 30 = 75).

Exercises

1. (LO 4)

General Journal				
Date		**Description**	**Debit**	**Credit**
May	1	Purchases	500	
		Accounts Payable		500
		Purchased merchandise on credit, terms n/30.		
	3	Accounts Receivable	500	
		Sales		500
		Sold merchandise on credit, terms n/30.		
	4	Freight-In	42	
		Cash		42
		Paid for freight charges		
	5	Office Supplies	100	
		Accounts Payable		100
		Purchased office supplies on credit		
	6	Accounts Payable	20	
		Office Supplies		20
		Returned office supplies from May 5 purchase		
	7	Accounts Payable	50	
		Purchases Returns and Allowances		50
		Returned merchandise from May 1 purchase		
	9	Accounts Receivable	225	
		Sales		225
		Sold merchandise on credit, terms n/30		
	10	Accounts Payable	450	
		Cash		450
		Paid for purchase of May 1		
	14	Sales Returns and Allowances	25	
		Accounts Receivable		25
		Accepted return of merchandise from customer of May 9		
	22	Cash	200	
		Accounts Receivable		200
		Received payment from customer of May 9		
	26	Cash	500	
		Accounts Receivable		500
		Received payment from customer of May 3		

2.   (LO 2, 4)

Mammoth Merchandising Company **Partial Income Statement** **For the Year Ended December 31, 20xx**			
Gross sales			$100,000
Less sales discounts		$ 300	
Less sales returns and allowances		200	500
Net sales			$ 99,500
Less cost of goods sold			
Merchandise inventory, January 1		$10,000	
Purchases	$50,000		
Less purchases discounts	500		
Less purchases returns and allowances	500		
Net purchases	$49,000		
Freight-in	2,000		
Net cost of purchases		51,000	
Goods available for sale		$61,000	
Less merchandise inventory, December 31		8,000	
Cost of goods sold			53,000
Gross margin			$ 46,500

Solution to
Crossword Puzzle: Chapters 4 and 5

	¹T		²D	E	S	T	I	N	⁴A	T	I	O	⁵N
	U		E		³R				O				E
	⁶R	E	L	E	V	A	N	⁷C	E		⁸R	A	T	E
⁹O	N		I		D		L		R		E		L
N			V	¹⁰S	E	P	A	R	A	T	I	O	N
O			E	H		S		U			S
¹¹E	A	R	N	I	N	G	S	¹²G	R	O	S	S
¹³O	R		Y	P		¹⁴I	N		N		
				P		F		N		¹⁵B
¹⁶M	A	T	E	R	I	A	L	I	T	Y	¹⁷E	O	M
A				N		E		S		N
¹⁸R	I	¹⁹S	K	²⁰G	O	O	D	S	S	O	L	D
G		T	²²D				F	²³I	N
I	²⁴E	Q	U	I	P	M	E	N	T	N
N		P	E				²⁵W	A	G	E

CHAPTER 6

Self-Test
1. b   (LO 1)
2. a   (LO 2)
3. c   (LO 3)
4. b   (LO 3)
5. d   (LO 3)
6. d   (LO 1)
7. c   (LO 3)
8. d   (LO 2)
9. d   (SO 6)
10. d   (SO 6)

Matching
1. m
2. h
3. d
4. g
5. j
6. n
7. o
8. p
9. c
10. l
11. e
12. b
13. k
14. a
15. f
16. i

Short Answer
1. (LO 3) Specific identification; average-cost; first-in, first-out; last-in, first-out methods
2. (SO 6) Retail method and gross profit method

3.   (LO 3, 4) The periodic system does not keep detailed records of inventory; the perpetual system does. Under the periodic system, physical inventory taken at the end of each period determines the cost of goods sold.

4.   (LO 1) Raw materials, work in process, and finished goods

True-False

1.   T   (LO 1)

2.   T   (LO 1)

3.   T   (LO 1)

4.   T   (LO 1)

5.   F   (LO 2) They belong in the buyer's ending inventory if the buyer has title to the goods.

6.   T   (LO 3)

7.   F   (LO 3) This is not necessarily true. The actual flow of goods is not known; the flow of costs is assumed.

8.   F   (LO 3) It results in the highest income.

9.   T   (SO 6)

10.   F   (SO 6) The cost of goods sold is estimated by subtracting the gross profit percentage of sales from total sales.

11.   F   (LO 3) The average-cost method results in a higher income before income taxes.

12.   F   (LO 4) The requirement is for LIFO, not FIFO.

13.   F   (LO 2) The consignee has possession of the goods but does not have title to them.

14.   T   (LO 4)

15.   F   (LO 1) Very little money would be tied up in inventories.

Multiple Choice

1.   b   (LO 2) Because the cost of storing goods is usually too difficult to trace to specific items of inventory, it is expensed when incurred. The other costs listed are more closely related to the cost of acquiring inventory.

2.   a   (LO 4) The FIFO method matches current selling prices with the oldest, least expensive costs. In periods of rising prices, this method yields a higher income before income taxes than the other inventory costing methods.

3.   c   (LO 1) When an item in a warehouse is not included in inventory, it results in an understated ending inventory, which, in turn, produces an overstated cost of goods sold. An overstated cost of goods sold produces an understated income before income taxes and thus an understated stockholders' equity.

4.   c   (LO 3) With low-volume, high-priced goods, it is especially important to match the selling price of an item with its cost in order to avoid distortion in the financial statements. Only the specific identification method directly matches cost and selling price.

5.   b   (SO 6) In the retail method calculation, freight-in is incorporated at cost, not at retail.

6. a (LO 1) The matching rule states that a cost must be expensed in the period in which it helps to generate revenue. Thus, the cost of inventory is expensed in the period in which the inventory is sold.

7. d (LO 2) Inventory should appear on the balance sheet of the company that has title to the goods even if the company does not have possession of them.

8. d (SO 6) The gross profit method is a simple way of estimating the amount of inventory lost or destroyed by fire, theft, or other hazards. It assumes a relatively consistent gross profit ratio over time.

9. b (LO 1) Unlike the other three choices, office wages are not factory-related and thus would not be included in the cost of a manufactured item.

Exercises

1. (LO 3)

   a. $6,600; $8,800

   b. $7,200; $8,200

   c. $6,820; $8,580

2. (SO 6)

	Cost	Retail
Beginning inventory	$ 70,000	$125,000
Net purchases	48,000	75,000
Freight in	2,000	
Cost/retail	$120,000 ÷	$200,000 = 60%
Less sales		156,000
Estimated ending inventory at retail		$ 44,000
		× 60%
Estimated cost of ending inventory		$ 26,400

3. (SO 6)

Beginning inventory at cost	$150,000
Purchases at cost	120,000
Cost of goods available for sale	$270,000
Less estimated cost of goods sold ($300,000 × 80%)	240,000
Estimated cost of ending inventory	$ 30,000

4. (SO 5)

May 1	Beginning Inventory	100 units @ $10.00		$1,000.00
4	Purchase	60 units @ $12.00		720.00
8	Sale	50 units @ $12.00		(600.00)
8	Balance	100 units @ $10.00	$1,000.00	
		10 units @ $12.00	120.00	$1,120.00
17	Purchase	70 units @ $11.00		770.00
31	Sale	70 units @ $11.00	($770.00)	
		10 units @ $12.00	(120.00)	
		20 units @ $10.00	(200.00)	(1,090.00)
31	Ending Inventory	80 units @ $10.00		$ 800.00

Cost of Goods Sold = $600.00 + $1,090.00 $1,690.00

5. (SO 5)

May 1	Beginning Inventory	100 units @ $10.00	$1,000.00
4	Purchase	60 units @ $12.00	720.00
4	Balance	160 units @ $10.75	$1,720.00
8	Sale	50 units @ $10.75	537.50)
8	Balance	110 units @ $10.75	$1,182.50
17	Purchase	70 units @ $11.00	770.00
17	Balance	180 units @ 10.85*	$1,952.50
31	Sale	100 units @ $10.85	(1,085.00)
31	Ending Inventory	80 units @ $10.84*	$ 867.50

Cost of Goods Sold = $537.50 + $1,085.00 $1,622.50
*Rounded.

CHAPTER 7

Self-Test

1. b (LO 1)

2. c (LO 2)

3. a (LO 2)

4. a (LO 3)

5. c (LO 3)

6. d (LO 3)

7. c (LO 3)

8. d (LO 4)

9. d (LO 4)

10. b (LO 2)

Matching

1. j
2. g
3. f
4. m
5. p
6. e
7. r
8. l
9. i
10. t
11. c
12. o
13. s
14. h
15. d
16. n
17. q
18. a
19. b
20. k

Short Answer

1. (LO 3) Percentage of net sales method, accounts receivable aging method, and direct charge-off method

2. (LO 1) It means that the company that sold its receivables to a factor is liable for payment in the event of a customer's default, but only if the receivables were factored with recourse.

3. (LO 3) There would be a debit balance when more accounts are written off (in dollar amounts) than have been provided for in the adjusting entries for estimated uncollectible accounts.

4. (LO 1) Cash, accounts receivable, and notes receivable

True-False

1. T   (LO 3)

2. F   (LO 3) It follows the matching rule.

3. F   (LO 3) The balance must be taken into account.

4. T   (LO 3)

5.   T   (LO 1)

6.   T   (LO 1)

7.   F   (LO 4) The computation is 700 × .05 × 90/365.

8.   T   (LO 1)

9.   F   (LO 1) The payee must make good if the maker defaults.

10. F   (LO 4) It has a duration of 62 days.

11. T   (LO 1)

12. F   (LO 3) Total assets remain the same.

13. T   (LO 4)

14. F   (LO 3) The debit is to Allowance for Uncollectible Accounts.

15. T   (LO 4)

16. T   (LO 3)

17. F   (LO 2) Accounts receivable are a short-term financial asset, but not a cash equivalent.

18. F   (LO 1) Major credit cards involve factoring without recourse.

19. T   (LO 2)

20. T   (LO 1)

21. T   (LO 2)

22. F   (LO 2) It would indicate a *deduction*.

23. F   (LO 2) No entries would be made for outstanding checks.

24. F   (LO 2) It would begin with the September 30 balance.

Multiple Choice

1.   b   (LO 4) Principal × rate × time for b equals $11.84. Each of the other choices results in $5.92.

2.   c   (LO 3) Under the percentage of net sales method, the amount of the Uncollectible Accounts Expense is based on the sales during the period. Therefore, it is not netted with an existing balance in the allowance account.

3.   a   (LO 1) Because the discounting bank has the right to extract funds from a firm's account if a note is dishonored, the firm carries that liability until such time as the note is paid to the bank. Once the note is paid, the contingent liability is eliminated.

4.   b   (LO 3) Under this method, Uncollectible Accounts Expense equals the amount deemed uncollectible ($850) minus the credit balance in Allowance for Uncollectible Accounts ($300), or $550.

5.   c   (LO 3) When an allowance account is established to record anticipated uncollectible accounts, the expense is recorded at the time the adjusting entry is made. When the actual uncollectible account is known and written off, the allowance account is reduced, and Accounts Receivable is reduced by the same amount.

6.   a   (LO 4) The discount rate is used as an adjustment to the maturity value of a note to calculate the proceeds on discounting that note to the bank. A note would not show the discount rate because the rate is not known at the time the note is written. In addition, whether a note is going to be discounted or not is irrelevant in determining the note's specifications.

7.   b   (LO 3) The direct charge-off method of handling uncollectible accounts often postpones the uncollectible accounts expense of a given accounting period to subsequent accounting periods. Usually, a significant period of time elapses between a credit sale and the determination that the corresponding receivable is uncollectible.

8.   c   (LO 1) Short-term financial assets consist of cash or assets that can be converted quickly to cash to cover operating expenses and immediate cash requirements. Although a firm's ability to convert its inventory to cash is the basis of its operations, inventory is not considered a short-term financial asset.

9.   a   (LO 2) The error would cause the balance per bank to be understated. Therefore, the $900 should be added.

10. b   (LO 2) The company presumably already has recorded the deposits in transit. However, it just learned of the bank service charges, the note collected by the bank, and the interest earned when it received its bank statement, and, therefore, must adjust for those items.

Exercises

1.   (LO 4, LO 5)

General Journal				
Date		**Description**	**Debit**	**Credit**
Dec.	31	Interest Receivable	75	
		Interest Income		75
		To record accrued interest on Notes Receivable		
	31	Uncollectible Accounts Expense	24,000	
		Allowance for Uncollectible Accounts		24,000
		To record estimated bad debts		
Jan.	3	Notes Receivable	10,000	
		Accounts Receivable		10,000
		Anna Kohn substituted a 30-day, 6% note for her debt		
	8	Allowance for Uncollectible Accounts	1,000	
		Accounts Receivable		1,000
		To write off Tom O'Brien's account		

2.   (LO 4)

   a. $15.78

   b. $910.00

   c. $42.58

   d. $3.95

3. (LO 1)

    a.   5.2 times

    b.   70.2 days

4. (LO 2)

    1. d

    2. c

    3. b

    4. d

    5. a

    6. d

CHAPTER 8

Self-Test

1.   b   (LO 1)

2.   d   (LO 2)

3.   d   (LO 2)

4.   a   (LO 4)

5.   b   (LO 2)

6.   a   (LO 2)

7.   c   (LO 2)

8.   d   (LO 4)

9.   d   (LO 4)

10. c   (LO 2)

Matching

1.   b

2.   r

3.   g

4.   e

5.   o

6.   j

7.   m

8.   l

9.   f

10. k

11. i

12. n

13. a

14. h

15. q

16. d

17. p

18. c

Short Answer

1. (LO 2) Definitely determinable liabilities and estimated liabilities

2. (LO 3) Examples include pending lawsuits, tax disputes, discounted notes receivable, the guarantee of another company's debt, and failure to follow government regulations.

3. (LO 2) Examples include income taxes payable, property taxes payable, promotional liabilities, estimated warranty expense, and vacation pay.

4. (LO 2) Examples include accounts payable, bank loans and commercial paper, short-term notes payable, accrued liabilities, dividends payable, sales and excise taxes payable, the current portion of long-term debt, payroll liabilities, and unearned revenues.

5. (LO 3) Purchase agreements and leases

6. (LO 4) Future value of a single sum, future value of an ordinary annuity, present value of a single sum, and present value of an ordinary annuity

7. (LO 2) Social security taxes, Medicare taxes, federal income taxes, and state income taxes

True-False

1. F   (LO 2) Unearned revenues are a liability representing an obligation to deliver goods or services. They are shown on the balance sheet.

2. T   (LO 3)

3. T   (LO 1)

4. T   (LO 2)

5. F   (LO 2) Sales tax payable is a definitely determinable liability.

6. F   (LO 2) A warranty is an estimated liability.

7. T   (LO 4)

8. F   (LO 4) Payments associated with an ordinary annuity are made at the *end* of each period.

9. F   (LO 2) FUTA is assessed against employers only.

10. T   (LO 3)

11. F   (LO 4) The higher the interest rate, the *lower* the present value.

12. T   (LO 1)

13. F   (LO 1) It is expressed in terms of times.

14. F (LO 2) An estimate should be recorded for Product Warranty Expense in year 1, the year of the sale.

15. F (LO 4) The correct calculation is $5,000 × .1 × 90/365.

16. T (LO 2)

17. T (LO 2)

18. T (LO 1)

Multiple Choice

1. c (LO 2) Property tax bills are usually not available to a firm until months after the liability exists. Thus, to adhere to the matching rule, the accountant usually must estimate the property taxes due for the accounting period and enter that estimate in the books as a liability. When the firm receives its property tax bill, the accountant makes the necessary adjustments.

2. d (LO 2) The liability for dividends that have been declared is definitely determinable.

3. a (LO 2) The state unemployment tax is an expense borne solely by the employer.

4. d (SO 4) Withholding an employee's federal income tax creates a current liability on the employer's books, because the tax must then be remitted to the government.

5. c (LO 2) Under the matching rule, estimated liabilities for vacation pay must be recorded as an expense of the current period. Therefore, by the time the employee exercises the right to a paid vacation, the expense has been recorded in an allowance account, Estimated Liability for Vacation Pay. As the liability expires, it is reduced by a debit entry. The credit entry is to Cash for the disbursement of pay to the employee.

6. b (LO 4) When interest is calculated on a semiannual basis, the annual interest rate is cut in half, but the number of years must be doubled to arrive at the correct number of semiannual periods.

7. d (LO 2) The accumulation of interest on a note payable creates both an expense (debited) and a liability (credited). Note that the Cash and Notes Payable accounts are not included in the adjustment.

8. d (LO 4) To calculate the present value of a single sum due in the future, one must multiply the future amount by the present value of a single sum factor, using the assumed discount rate and number of periods.

9. c (LO 4) To calculate the future value of a single sum, multiply the amount invested today by the future value of a single sum factor, in this case for two periods at 12 percent.

Exercises

1. (LO 2)

General Journal				
Date		Description	Debit	Credit
Dec.	31	Product Warranty Expense	525	
		Estimated Product Warranty Liability		525
		To record estimated warranty expense for washing machines		
Apr.	9	Estimated Product Warranty Liability	48	
		Parts, Wages Payable, etc.		48
		To record the repair of a washing machine		

2. (LO 2)

General Journal				
Date		Description	Debit	Credit
May	11	Wages Expense	260.00	
		Social Security Tax Payable		16.12
		Medicare Tax Payable		3.77
		Union Dues Payable		5.00
		State Income Tax Payable		8.00
		Federal Income Tax Payable		52.00
		Wages Payable		175.11
		To record payroll liabilities and wages expense for Pat Bauer		
	11	Payroll Taxes and Benefits Expense	36.01	
		Social Security Tax Payable		16.12
		Medicare Tax Payable		3.77
		Federal Unemployment Tax Payable		2.08
		State Unemployment Tax Payable		14.04
		To record payroll taxes on Pat Bauer's earnings		

3. (LO 1)

    a.   11 times

$$(\$290{,}000 - \$15{,}000) \div \left(\frac{\$30{,}000 + \$20{,}000}{2} \right)$$

    b.   33.2 days ($365 \div 11$)

4.   (LO 5)

Present value = $2,000 × 4.494 = $8,988

The purchase should not be made because the present value of the future cash savings is less than the initial cost of the equipment.

5.   (LO 4, 5)

a. $747 ($1,000 × .747)

b. $4,122 ($1,000 × 4.122)

c. $1,126 ($1,000 × 1.126)

d. $1,745.81 ($100,000/57.28)

Solution to
Crossword Puzzle: Chapters 6, 7, and 8

	¹B			²C	O	N	³S	I	G	N	M	E	N	T			⁴P
	A			O			P										R
⁵L	C	M		⁶M	E	R	C	H	⁷A	N	D	⁸I	S	E			E
A		M					C		V			N					S
N		⁹E	S	T	I	M	A	T	E	D		T		¹⁰I	N		E
C		R					F		R								N
E		C		¹¹F	I	¹²F	O		¹³A	G	E		¹⁴L				T
		I				C		R		G			¹⁴L				
	¹⁵B	A	N	K		¹⁶I	D	L	E		¹⁷F	I	C	A			
¹⁸S		L				I			¹⁹I		N						
A		²⁰C	O	N	T	I	N	G	E	N	T		²¹T				
²²L	O	A	N	²³S		A			T				I				
E		²⁴O	P	E	R	A	T	I	N	G			M				
S			E	L		Y			M				E				
		²⁵D	R	U	E		²⁶C	R	E	D	I	T					

CHAPTER 9

Self-Test

1.	b	(LO 1)
2.	a	(LO 2)
3.	a	(LO 3)
4.	d	(LO 6)
5.	b	(LO 4)
6.	c	(LO 1)
7.	c	(LO 5)
8.	a	(LO 6)
9.	d	(LO 6)
10.	c	(LO 3)

Matching

1. e
2. f
3. n
4. s
5. l
6. t
7. r
8. h
9. v
10. j
11. b
12. o
13. u
14. c
15. k
16. m
17. g
18. a
19. i
20. d

21. p

22. q

Short Answer

1. (LO 2) Additions, such as a new building wing, expand a physical layout. Betterments, such as a new air-conditioning system, simply improve an existing layout.

2. (LO 4) When the cash received equals the carrying value of the asset sold

3. (LO 5) The cost of the well, the estimated residual value of the well, the estimated barrels to be extracted over the life of the well, and the actual barrels extracted and sold during the year

4. (LO 2) Ordinary repairs (e.g., painting or a tune-up) merely maintain an asset in good operating condition. Extraordinary repairs (e.g., a complete overhaul) increase an asset's estimated useful life or residual value.

5. (LO 1) Amortization, depreciation, and depletion

6. (LO 3) Physical deterioration and obsolescence

True-False

1.   F   (LO 1) Free cash flow is a cash-based concept. Thus, it disregards the accrual-based concept of net income or loss.

2.   T   (LO 4)

3.   T   (LO 1)

4.   F   (LO 3) Depreciation is a process of allocation, not of valuation.

5.   F   (LO 3) The physical deterioration of a machine is irrelevant in computing depreciation.

6.   T   (LO 2)

7.   T   (LO 3)

8.   T   (LO 3)

9.   F   (LO 3) Depreciation expense will be $1,000 in the second year also.

10. T   (LO 3)

11. T   (LO 4)

12. F   (LO 3) It results in more net income.

13. F   (LO 3) Depreciable cost equals cost minus residual value.

14. T   (LO 3)

15. F   (LO 6) A trademark is a name or symbol that can be used only by its owner.

16. T   (LO 2)

17. F   (LO 2) A betterment is a capital expenditure.

18. F   (LO 2) The carrying value increases because the Accumulated Depreciation account is decreased (debited).

19. F   (LO 4) The Accumulated Depreciation account always is debited when a depreciable asset is sold.

20. F   (LO 2) Capital expenditure refers to the purchase of an asset; expense refers to the expiration of asset cost through the use or depreciation of an asset.

21. T   (LO 2)

22. F   (LO 4) Depreciation expense should be brought up-to-date before the sale is recorded.

23. T   (LO 6)

24. T   (LO 3)

25. F   (LO 6) Goodwill may only be recorded when it has been purchased.

26. T   (LO 5)

27. T   (LO 1)

Multiple Choice

1. c   (LO 2) Because the relative values of the lump-sum purchase are known, a ratio can be determined and applied to the purchase price of both assets. The total appraised value of the land and building is $80,000. Of that $80,000, $20,000, or 25%, is apportioned to the land. So 25% of the purchase price for both assets, $16,500, would be allocated to land.

2. a   (LO 3) The expired cost of an asset is its total accumulated depreciation to date. Depreciation is the allocation of the cost of an asset over its useful life.

3. d   (LO 3) The declining-balance method would probably produce the greatest depreciation charge in the first year, but it is possible that the production method would. Thus, more information is needed to answer the question.

4. c   (LO 3) The change requires an adjustment to the depreciation schedule of the asset. The remaining depreciable cost would be spread over the remaining (new) estimated useful life of the machine.

5. c   (LO 6) When the fair value of goodwill drops below its carrying value, an impairment loss must be recorded.

6. b   (LO 2) Although land is not a depreciable asset, improvements to land (buildings, street lights, pavement, etc.) are. Each improvement has an estimated useful life over which the costs will be allocated.

7. d   (LO 4) To eliminate the asset from the company's accounting records, existing accounts pertaining to the asset must be removed from the books. Because the book value of the machine was $2,000 and the original cost was $9,000, accumulated depreciation must have been $7,000 (credit balance). To eliminate that account, a debit of $7,000 should be recorded to Accumulated Depreciation.

8. b   (LO 2) A new roof has an economic life of more than a year. An expenditure for a new roof is therefore a capital expenditure.

9. d   (LO 2) Understatement of net income results from expensing a capital expenditure. By definition, capital expenditures should be spread over the useful life of the acquisition (more than one period). If the entire cost is put into one period, expenses for that period will be overstated.

10. b   (LO 5) Depletion costs assigned to a given period are the result of calculations based on expected total output over the life of an asset. Total costs divided by total expected units of output equal the depletion cost per unit. If the expected units of output are overestimated, the unit cost will be underestimated.

11. a   (LO 6) Up to the point at which software is deemed technologically feasible, its costs are treated as research and development costs and are therefore expensed.

12. d   (LO 6) Research and development costs are treated as revenue expenditures and are recognized in the period in which they are incurred.

Exercises

1. (LO 3)

	Depreciation Expense for 20x5	Accumulated Depreciation as of 12/31/x5	Carrying Value as of 12/31/x5
a.	$4,800	$ 9,600	$16,400
b.	$6,240	$16,640	$ 9,360

2. (LO 3)

$$\$2,250 = \left(\frac{\$35,000 - \$5,000}{100,000 \text{ toys}} \times 7,500 \text{ toys} \right)$$

3. (LO 2)

a. C

b. R

c. R

d. C

e. C

f. R

g. C

h. C

i. R

4. (LO 1)

Acquisition cost ($22,000 × 1.000)	($22,000)
Present value of net annual cash flows ($4,000 × 4.623)	18,492
Present value of residual value ($3,000 × .630)	1,890
Net present value of equipment	($ 1,618)

The equipment should *not* be purchased because its net present value is negative.

5.   (LO 5)

<table>
<tr><th colspan="5">General Journal</th></tr>
<tr><th colspan="2">Date</th><th>Description</th><th>Debit</th><th>Credit</th></tr>
<tr><td>Dec.</td><td>31</td><td>Depletion Expense, Coal Deposits
    Accumulated Depletion, Coal Deposits
    To record depletion of coal mine for 20xx</td><td>40,000</td><td>
40,000</td></tr>
</table>

CHAPTER 10

Self-Test

1.   a   (LO 1)
2.   c   (LO 2)
3.   b   (LO 3)
4.   d   (LO 4)
5.   b   (LO 5)
6.   d   (LO 5)
7.   c   (LO 5)
8.   b   (SO 7)
9.   d   (LO 2)
10. c   (LO 1)

Matching

1.   i
2.   u
3.   q
4.   a
5.   o
6.   s
7.   j
8.   f
9.   c
10. e
11. m
12. l
13. b
14. g

15. r

16. n

17. p

18. h

19. k

20. t

21. d

Short Answer

1. (LO 2) A debenture bond is an unsecured bond; a bond indenture is a corporation's contract with bondholders.

2. (LO 3) When the face interest rate of bonds is higher than the market interest rate for similar bonds on the date of issue, a bond issue usually sells at a premium.

3. (LO 3) Interest = Principal × Rate × Time

4. (LO 4) The present value of periodic interest payments and the present value of the face value at maturity

5. (LO 1) Stockholders retain their level of control, interest is tax deductible, and stockholders' earnings may increase because of financial leverage

True-False

1. F   (LO 2) They are creditors.

2. T   (LO 1)

3. F   (LO 2) Bond interest must be paid on each interest date. It is not declared by the board of directors.

4. T   (LO 3)

5. F   (LO 5) It is less than the cash paid.

6. T   (LO 5)

7. F   (SO 7) Bond Interest Expense is credited.

8. T   (LO 5)

9. F   (LO 5) It equals interest payments *plus* the bond discount.

10. T   (LO 6)

11. F   (LO 5) The premium amortized increases each year.

12. T   (LO 5)

13. F   (LO 1) The statement describes capital leases.

14. T   (LO 1)

15. F   (LO 6) No gain or loss is recorded.

16. T   (LO 3)

17. T   (LO 1)

18. T   (LO 1)

19. F   (LO 1) It indicates a high risk of default.

20. T   (LO 1)

Multiple Choice

1. d   (SO 7) When bonds are issued between interest dates, the amount an investor pays for a bond includes the interest accrued since the last interest date. On the next interest date, the corporation pays the interest due for the entire period to all bondholders, including those who have held a bond for only a part of the period. The corporation maintains the abnormal balance in the Bond Interest Expense account until it pays the interest to the bondholders.

2. a   (LO 1) Interest expense on a mortgage is based on the unpaid balance. As the principal of a mortgage is reduced over time, the interest portion of a fixed payment decreases, while the portion applied to the unpaid balance increases.

3. d   (LO 3) Bonds issued at a premium have a carrying value above their face value. On the balance sheet, Unamortized Bond Premium is added to Bonds Payable to produce the carrying value.

4. c   (SO 7) Interest expense for an accounting period must be recorded as an adjustment at year end. In recording interest expense for bonds sold at a discount, the calculation includes a reduction in Unamortized Bond Discount, which has a normal debit balance.

5. b   (LO 5) When the effective interest method is used, the calculation of interest expense is based on the current carrying value of the bonds. As the bond discount is amortized, that value increases. As a result, the interest expense per period also increases.

6. b   (LO 1) The lease described in b is not a capital lease because its terms do not resemble those of a purchase. It is therefore an operating lease.

7. c   (LO 6) In the transaction described, the company paid $204,000 ($200,000 × 102%) for bonds outstanding that had a carrying value of $195,000. The difference between the carrying value and the amount paid—$9,000—is recorded as a loss.

8. c   (LO 6) The carrying value of the bonds is $612,000. If one-third of the bonds are converted, the carrying value of the bonds payable will be reduced by $204,000 ($612,000/3).

Exercises

1. (LO 3, LO 5)

   a. $9,000 ($600,000 − $591,000)

   b. $21,000 ($600,000 × 7% × ½)

   c. $21,450 $\left(\$21,000 + \dfrac{\$9,000}{20} \right)$

   d. $593,700 ($600,000 − $6,300)

2. (LO 3, LO 5)

   a. $550,000 ($500,000 × 110%)

   b. $17,500 ($500,000 × 7% × ½)

c. $16,500 ($550,000 × 6% × ½)

d. $1,000 ($17,500 – $16,500)

e. $549,000 ($550,000 – $1,000)

3. (LO 5)

Interest payments ($600,000 × 8% × 10)	$480,000
Premium on bonds payable ($600,000 × 6%)	36,000
Total interest cost	$444,000

Solution to
Crossword Puzzle: Chapters 9 and 10

1 PENSIONPLAN
2 ORDINARY
3 NET
4 LIFE
5 INTEREST
6 TRADEMARK
6 TANGIBLE
7 INSTALLMENT
8 ACCELERATED
9 TRADEIN
10 FRANCHISE
11 CALLS
11 CAPITAL
1 PREMIUM
12 VALUE
13 ZERO
14 BONDS
15 TERM
16 FIXED
17 ISSUE
18 LEASE
19 LONGTERMDEBT

CHAPTER 11

Self-Test

1. a   (LO 1)
2. c   (LO 1)
3. c   (LO 2)
4. b   (LO 1)
5. b   (LO 1)
6. c   (LO 3)
7. a   (LO 4)
8. b   (LO 4)
9. a   (LO 5)
10. a   (LO 1)

Matching

1. f
2. k
3. p
4. l
5. e
6. m
7. g
8. a
9. o
10. n
11. d
12. h
13. c
14. s
15. t
16. q
17. i
18. r
19. j
20. b

Short Answer

1. (LO 1) Separate legal entity, limited liability, ability to raise capital, ease of ownership transfer, lack of mutual agency, continuous existence, centralized authority and responsibility, and professional management

2. (LO 1) Government regulation, double taxation, limited liability, and separation of ownership and control

3. (LO 2) Contributed capital, retained earnings, and treasury stock

4. (LO 3) When dividends are declared and when a corporation liquidates

5. (LO 2, LO 5) When it has treasury stock—that is, stock that it has issued but reacquired so that the stock is no longer outstanding

6. (LO 5) Treasury stock is stock that a corporation has issued and bought back. Unissued stock has never been issued.

True-False

1. T (LO 1)
2. F (LO 1, LO 4) It was established to protect the creditors.
3. T (LO 1)
4. T (LO 1)
5. T (LO 2)
6. T (LO 1)
7. F (LO 3) It may be both.
8. T (LO 3)
9. F (LO 4) Par value does not necessarily relate to market value (worth).
10. T (LO 5)
11. F (LO 3) No stockholders are ever guaranteed dividends.
12. F (LO 2) Common stock is considered the residual equity of a corporation.
13. F (LO 1) The amount of compensation is measured on the date of grant.
14. F (LO 1) Total assets and total liabilities decrease.
15. F (LO 3) Dividends in arrears are not a liability until a dividend is declared. They are normally disclosed in a note to the financial statements.
16. F (LO 5) Treasury Stock is listed in the stockholders' equity section as a deduction.
17. T (LO 1)
18. F (LO 5) Paid-in Capital, Treasury Stock is credited for the excess of the sales price over the cost.
19. T (LO 1)
20. F (LO 1, LO 5) Return on equity will increase.
21. T (LO 1)

Multiple Choice

1. d   (LO 5) When a company reissues its stock, neither losses nor gains are ever recorded. What would otherwise be considered a loss is recorded as a reduction in stockholders' equity.

2. b   (LO 5) Treasury stock is issued stock that is no longer outstanding.

3. c   (LO 2) Authorized stock is the maximum number of shares a corporation is allowed to issue. Authorized shares are therefore the sum of a corporation's issued and unissued shares.

4. d   (LO 3) Because the preferred stock is noncumulative, there are no dividends in arrears. The current dividend of $40,000 will be distributed to preferred stockholders based on 7 percent of the par value of $100; thus, $7,000 will be distributed (.07 × $100 × 1,000 shares). The remaining $33,000 will be distributed, pro rata, to the common stockholders.

5. d   (LO 1) Under most circumstances, the liability of a corporation's stockholders is limited to the amount of their investments. They are not responsible for the corporation's debts.

6. d   (LO 1) The declaration of a cash dividend requires a journal entry to record the liability and to reduce retained earnings by the amount of the declared dividend. On the date of payment, a journal entry is required to record the elimination of the liability created on the date of declaration and the reduction in cash resulting from the payment. No journal entry is required on the record date, which is the date on which ownership of the stock is determined.

7. b   (LO 1) If stock is purchased after the date of record, the new owner has no rights to the dividend that has been declared but not yet distributed to stockholders.

8. d   (LO 3) The call feature on stock specifies an amount for which the corporation can buy back the stock. It is binding on the stockholder and on the issuing corporation in spite of possible differences between the call price and the market value at the time the stock is called.

Exercises

1. (LO 1, LO 4)

<table>
<tr><th colspan="5">General Journal</th></tr>
<tr><th colspan="2">Date</th><th>Description</th><th>Debit</th><th>Credit</th></tr>
<tr><td>Jan.</td><td>1</td><td>Start-Up and Organization Expense
　　Cash
　　　　Paid legal and incorporation fees</td><td>8,000</td><td>
8,000</td></tr>
<tr><td>Feb.</td><td>9</td><td>Cash
　　Common Stock
　　Additional Paid-in Capital
　　　　Issued 5,000 shares of $100 par value common stock
　　　　for $115 per share</td><td>575,000</td><td>
500,000
75,000</td></tr>
<tr><td>Apr.</td><td>12</td><td>Buildings
　　Preferred Stock
　　Additional Paid-in Capital
　　　　Issued 2,000 shares of preferred stock in exchange for
　　　　a building</td><td>240,000</td><td>
200,000
40,000</td></tr>
<tr><td>June</td><td>23</td><td>Dividends
　　Dividends Payable
　　　　Declared a cash dividend on preferred stock</td><td>8,000</td><td>
8,000</td></tr>
<tr><td>July</td><td>8</td><td>Dividends Payable
　　Cash
　　　　Paid cash dividend declared on June 23</td><td>8,000</td><td>
8,000</td></tr>
</table>

2.   (LO 5)

\multicolumn{4}{c}{General Journal}			
Date	**Description**	**Debit**	**Credit**
Jan. 12	Treasury Stock, Common	300,000	
	Cash		300,000
	Recorded purchase of treasury stock		
20	Cash	130,000	
	Treasury Stock, Common		120,000
	Paid-in Capital, Treasury Stock		10,000
	Recorded reissue of treasury stock		
27	Cash	116,000	
	Paid-in Capital, Treasury Stock	4,000	
	Treasury Stock, Common		120,000
	Recorded reissue of treasury stock		
31	Common Stock	10,000	
	Additional Paid-in Capital	40,000	
	Retained Earnings	10,000	
	Treasury Stock, Common		60,000
	Recorded retirement of treasury stock		

3.   (LO 3)

   a. $18,000 (1,000 × $100 × 6% × 3 years)

   b. $33,000 ($51,000 − $18,000)

4.   (LO 3)

   a. $6,000 (1,000 × $100 × 6%)

   b. $45,000 ($51,000 − $6,000)

CHAPTER 12

Self-Test

1.   b   (LO 5)

2.   a   (LO 6)

3.   a   (LO 6)

4.   c   (LO 2)

5.   a   (LO 5)

6.   d   (LO 7)

7.   b   (LO 1)

8.   c   (LO 2)

9.   c   (LO 5)

10.   b   (LO 4)

Matching

1.   j

2.   c

3.   e

4.   o

5.   m

6.   b

7.   n

8.   g

9.   i

10.   p

11.   f

12.   d

13.   h

14.   a

15.   k

16.   l

Short Answer

1.   (LO 5, 6) Net loss from operations, cash dividend declaration, and stock dividend declaration are the three instances discussed in this chapter. (Certain treasury stock transactions will also reduce retained earnings.)

2.   (LO 6) A stock split changes the par or stated value of the stock; a stock dividend does not. A stock dividend transfers a portion of retained earnings to contributed capital; a stock split does not.

3.   (LO 3) It must be unusual in nature, and it must occur infrequently.

4.   (LO 1, 3) Correct order: 1, 4, 5, 3, 2

5.   (LO 5) In the statement of stockholders' equity, in the income statement, or in a separate statement (of comprehensive income)

True-False

1.   F   (LO 2, 3) The net of taxes amount is less than $20,000.

2.   T   (LO 7)

3.   F   (LO 6) Each stockholder owns the same percentage as before.

4. F (LO 6) The market value of the stock is needed to calculate the dollar amount for the journal entry.

5. F (LO 6) Its main purpose is to increase marketability by lowering the market price. The decrease in par value is a by-product of a stock split.

6. F (LO 3) This type of gain is not an unusual and infrequently occurring event.

7. F (LO 3) Extraordinary items appear on the income statement.

8. F (LO 6) It would appear within stockholders' equity as a component of contributed capital.

9. T (LO 4)

10. T (LO 2)

11. T (LO 1)

12. F (LO 4) They are included in the calculation of diluted earnings per share but not of basic earnings per share.

13. T (LO 6)

14. T (LO 1)

Multiple Choice

1. a (LO 6) A stock split simply increases the number of shares outstanding and reduces the par or stated value of the stock proportionately. It has no effect on retained earnings.

2. c (LO 6) The firm distributed a stock dividend of 1,000 shares (10% × 10,000 shares). The 11,000 shares outstanding after the stock dividend were then split into 4 shares for each 1 share (11,000 × 4), resulting in total shares outstanding of 44,000.

3. c (LO 6) When a stock dividend is declared, Stock Dividends is debited, Common Stock Distributable is credited, and Additional Paid-in Capital is credited.

4. c (LO 4) The company had 60,000 shares outstanding for 9/12 of the year and 40,000 shares outstanding for 3/12 of the year: 60,000 × 9/12 = 45,000 shares; 40,000 × 3/12 = 10,000 shares; 45,000 + 10,000 shares = 55,000 weighted-average shares outstanding for the year.

5. b (LO 5) There was a $30,000 increase in Retained Earnings during the year, even after a $15,000 cash dividend. Therefore, net income for the year must have been $45,000 ($30,000 + $15,000).

6. c (LO 3, 5) Discontinued operations are shown on the income statement.

7. b (LO 7) If a corporation has just one type of stock, it would be common stock. Book value per share would be calculated by dividing total stockholders' equity (retained earnings plus contributed capital) by the number of shares issued. The current year's dividends would have already reduced total stockholders' equity. Dividend information would be irrelevant to finding book value per share.

8. c (LO 5) Retained earnings accumulate over time as a result of undistributed income. In each accounting period that earnings are not entirely distributed to stockholders through dividends, retained earnings increase. In periods in which losses occur, retained earnings decrease. Dividends declared and transfers to contributed capital are taken from retained earnings.

9. d (LO 1) The quality of earnings may be affected by the accounting methods and estimates a company uses and by the nature of nonoperating items.

Exercises

1. (LO 6)

General Journal				
Date		Description	Debit	Credit
Sept.	1	Cash	1,200,000	
		Common Stock		1,000,000
		Additional Paid-in Capital		200,000
		To record issuance of stock		
Mar.	7	Stock Dividends	65,000	
		Common Stock Distributable		50,000
		Additional Paid-in Capital		15,000
		To record declaration of stock dividend (10,000 shares × 5% × $130 = $65,000 debit)		
	30	No entry		
Apr.	13	Common Stock Distributable	50,000	
		Common Stock		50,000
		To record distribution of stock dividend		

2. (LO 2, 3)

Operating income before taxes	$100,000
Less income taxes expense	40,000
Income before extraordinary item	$60,000
Extraordinary loss (net of taxes, $12,000)	18,000
Net income	$42,000

3. (LO 2)

General Journal

Date	Description	Debit	Credit
20x3	Income Taxes Expense	24,000	
	Income Taxes Payable		16,000
	Deferred Income Taxes		8,000
	To record income taxes for 20x3		
20x4	Income Taxes Expense	12,000	
	Deferred Income Taxes	4,000	
	Income Taxes Payable		16,000
	To record income taxes for 20x4		
20x5	Income Taxes Expense	28,000	
	Deferred Income Taxes	4,000	
	Income Taxes Payable		32,000
	To record income taxes for 20x5		

4. (LO 7)

Total stockholders' equity		$680,000
Less:	$200,000	
Par value of outstanding preferred stock	28,000	
Dividends in arrears		228,000
Equity allocated to preferred shareholders		$452,000
Equity pertaining to common shareholders		

Book value per share:
Preferred stock = $228,000 ÷ 4,000 shares = $57.00 per share
Common stock = $452,000 ÷ 30,000 shares = $15.07 per share

5. (LO 4)

$$\text{Basic earnings per share} = \frac{\$50,000 - \$20,000}{10,000 \text{ shares}} = \$3.00 \text{ per share}$$

Solution to
Crossword Puzzle: Chapters 11 and 12

			I		S		U		D
A	C	O	M	P	R	E	H	E	N	S	I	V	E
G	O		O		A		E		F
E	M		A	R	R	E	A	R	S		I
N	O	P	A	R	U		E		C
C	L		T		S	S	P	L	I	T	I
Y	E	P	H		R		T
E	X	T	R	A	O	R	D	I	N	A	R	Y
R		E	R		C		S
L	F	I	S	E	G	M	E	N	T	O
T	R	A	D	E	Z	T		O
U	S	R	E	A	B	A	S	I	C
R	E	T	I	R	E	D	T	E	K
N	I	E	E	I	C	S
N	D	I	V	I	D	E	N	D

CHAPTER 13

Self-Test

1. a   (LO 1)
2. d   (LO 1)
3. c   (LO 1)
4. c   (LO 3)
5. d   (LO 4)
6. a   (LO 5)
7. c   (LO 1)
8. b   (LO 2)
9. d   (LO 3)
10. c   (LO 2)

Matching

1. f
2. j
3. i
4. g
5. e
6. a
7. h
8. c
9. d
10. b

Short Answer

1. (LO 1) Issuing capital stock to retire long-term debt and purchasing a long-term asset by incurring long-term debt

2. (LO 3) They represent noncash expenses that have been legitimately deducted in arriving at net income. Adding them back to net income effectively cancels out the deduction.

3. (LO 1) Money market accounts, commercial paper (short-term notes), and U.S. Treasury bills

True-False

1. T   (LO 1)
2. F   (LO 3) It is considered an operating activity.
3. T   (LO 4)

4.   T   (LO 3)

5.   F   (LO 1, LO 3) Depreciation, depletion, and amortization expenses appear in the operating activities section.

6.   F   (LO 4) An increase in cash flows from investing activities implies the sale of long-term assets; thus, the business would be contracting.

7.   T   (LO 5)

8.   F   (LO 3) It is added to net income.

9.   T   (LO 5)

10. T   (LO 1)

11. F   (LO 2) Dividends are deducted because in the long run they must be paid to retain stockholders' interest.

12. T   (LO 3)

13. F   (LO 5) It is disclosed in the financing activities section.

Multiple Choice

1.   a   (LO 3) Cash receipts from sales, interest, and dividends are used to calculate cash inflows from operating activities. Under the indirect method, they are simply components of the net income figure presented.

2.   b   (LO 3) Net income in the operating activities section of the statement of cash flows includes a gain on the sale of investments. That amount needs to be backed out of the operating activities section to avoid duplication of cash inflow data.

3.   a   (LO 3) An increase in accounts payable indicates an increase in cash available to the firm. To reflect the absence of that cash outflow, the amount by which the payables have increased is added to the cash flows from operating activities section.

4.   e   (LO 1) The purchase of a building by incurring a mortgage payable does not involve any cash inflow or outflow. The investing and financing activity is disclosed in the schedule of noncash investing and financing transactions.

5.   d   (LO 5) The payment of dividends is a cash outflow and would be disclosed in the financing activities section of the statement of cash flows.

6.   b   (LO 3) The increase in inventory represents a cash outflow and would be deducted from net income in the operating activities section of the statement of cash flows. The counter-entry is the adjustment for changing levels of accounts payable.

7.   c   (LO 3, LO 5) Cash receipts from the issuance of stock are a cash inflow from financing activities. No adjustment to net income is required because the sale of stock is not recorded as a revenue and is not presented on the income statement.

8.   c   (LO 2) The numerator for all three calculations is net cash flows from operating activities.

Exercises

1.   (LO 2)

     a.   2.0 times ($120,000/$60,000)

     b.   13.3% ($120,000/$900,000)

c.   15% ($120,000/$800,000)

d. $55,000 ($120,000 − $30,000 − $75,000 + $40,000)

2.   (LO 3, LO 4, LO 5)

Harding Corporation
Statement of Cash Flows
For the Year Ended December 31, 20x5

Cash flows from operating activities		
Net income		$55,000
Adjustments to reconcile net income to net cash		
flows from operating activities		
Depreciation expense	$14,000	
Loss on sale of equipment	4,000	
Changes in current assets and current liabilities		
Increase in accounts receivable	(24,000)	
Decrease in merchandise inventory	14,000	
Increase in accounts payable	4,000	
Increase in income taxes payable	700	12,700
Net cash flows from operating activities		$67,700
Cash flows from investing activities		
Sale of equipment	$11,000	
Purchase of equipment	(27,000)	
Net cash flows from investing activities		(16,000)
Cash flows from financing activities		
Repayment of notes payable	($10,000)	
Issue of notes payable	15,000	
Dividends paid	(51,700)	
Net cash flows from financing activities		(46,700)
Net increase in cash		$ 5,000
Cash at beginning of year		103,000
Cash at end of year		$108,000

Schedule of Noncash Investing and Financing Transactions

Conversion of bonds payable into common stock $15,000

CHAPTER 14

Self-Test

1.   a   (LO 1)

2.   d   (LO 1)

3.   a   (LO 1)

4.   b   (LO 3)

5. c   (LO 2)

6. d   (LO 2)

7. c   (LO 2)

8. c   (LO 3)

9. a   (LO 3)

10. c   (LO 3)

Matching

1. g

2. b

3. l

4. e

5. j

6. f

7. h

8. i

9. k

10. d

11. c

12. a

Short Answer

1. (LO 3) Profit margin, asset turnover, return on assets, and return on equity

2. (LO 2) Horizontal analysis presents absolute and percentage changes in specific financial statement items from one year to the next. Vertical analysis, on the other hand, uses percentages to show the relationship of individual items on a financial statement to a total within the statement.

3. (LO 1) Rule-of-thumb measures, analysis of past performance of the company, and comparison with industry norms

4. (LO 3) Cash flow yield, cash flows to sales, cash flows to assets, and free cash flow

True-False

1. T   (LO 2)

2. F   (LO 2) Common-size statements show relationships between items in terms of percentages, not dollars.

3. F   (LO 3) The current ratio will increase.

4. T   (LO 3)

5. F   (LO 3) It equals the cost of goods sold divided by average inventory.

6. F (LO 3) The reverse is true because the price/earnings ratio depends on the earnings per share amount.

7. F (LO 3) Interest is not added back.

8. T (LO 3)

9. F (LO 3) The higher the debt to equity ratio, the greater the risk is.

10. F (LO 3) Receivable turnover measures how many times, on average, the receivables were converted into cash during the period.

11. T (LO 3)

12. T (LO 3)

13. F (LO 3) It is a market strength ratio.

14. F (LO 2) Net sales are set at 100 percent.

15. T (LO 1)

16. T (LO 1)

17. T (LO 3)

18. F (LO 3) A higher payables turnover will produce a *shorter* average days' payable.

19. T (LO 1)

Multiple Choice

1. b (LO 3) The interest coverage ratio measures the degree of protection creditors have from a default on interest payments on loans.

2. d (LO 3) The quick ratio measures a company's ability to cover immediate cash requirements for operating expenses and short-term payables.

3. c (LO 3) Asset turnover is calculated using net sales as the numerator and average total assets as the denominator. It is a measure of how efficiently a company uses its assets to produce sales.

4. a (LO 3) A high price/earnings ratio indicates that investors are optimistic about a company's future earnings and growth.

5. a (LO 2) Index numbers are calculated to reflect percentage changes over several consecutive years. The base year is assigned the value of 100 percent; changes from that base are then assigned a percentage so that subsequent amounts can be compared with base amounts. This method, which is used to identify trends, eliminates differences resulting from universal changes, such as inflation.

6. b (LO 1) Of the choices given, only managers are internal users of financial statements. In setting financial performance objectives for a company and in seeing that those objectives are achieved, top managers rely on the information presented in the financial statements.

7. d (LO 1) All the factors listed in a through c contribute to the complexity of comparing a company's performance with the performance of other companies in the same industry.

8. c (LO 3) The turnover of receivables is the number of times receivables are collected in relation to sales in an accounting period. A low number suggests that average accounts receivable balances are high and that credit policy is weak.

9.   b   (LO 2)   Net income is given a percentage in relation to net sales, as are all other components of the common-size income statement. Net sales are set at 100 percent.

10.   c   (LO 3)   Free cash flow is the cash that remains from operating activities after deducting the funds a company must commit to dividends and net capital expenditures.

Exercises

1.   (LO 2)

	20x6	20x5	Increase (Decrease) Amount	Percentage
Sales	$250,000	$200,000	$ 50,000	25.0
Cost of goods sold	144,000	120,000	24,000	20.0
Gross margin	$106,000	$ 80,000	$ 26,000	32.5
Operating expenses	62,000	50,000	12,000	24.0
Income before income taxes	$ 44,000	$ 30,000	$ 14,000	46.7
Income taxes	16,000	8,000	8,000	100.0
Net income	$ 28,000	$ 22,000	$ 6,000	27.3

2.   (LO 3)

a.   2.0 times ($500,000 ÷ $250,000)

b.   1.3 times $\left(\dfrac{\$500,000 - \$180,000}{\$250,000} \right)$

c.   1.9 times ($350,000 ÷ $180,000)

d.   192.1 days (365 ÷ 1.9)

e.   12.0% ($106,000 ÷ $880,000)

f.   22.1% ($106,000 ÷ $480,000)

g.   6.0 times ($600,000 ÷ $100,000)

h.   60.8 days (365 ÷ 6.0)

i.   17.7% ($106,000 ÷ $600,000)

j.   .7 times ($75,000 ÷ $106,000)

k.   12.5% ($75,000 ÷ $600,000)

l.   8.5% ($75,000 ÷ $880,000)

m.   .7 times ($600,000 ÷ $880,000)

n.   8 times $\left(\dfrac{\$40}{\$106,000 ÷ \$21,200} \right)$

CHAPTER 15

Self-Test

1.   b   (LO 2)
2.   a   (LO 5)
3.   c   (LO 4)
4.   b   (LO 4)
5.   d   (LO 1)
6.   c   (LO 3)
7.   c   (LO 4)
8.   d   (LO 1)
9.   c   (SO 1)
10. d   (LO 5)

Matching

1.   b
2.   f
3.   h
4.   g
5.   i
6.   d
7.   j
8.   n
9.   k
10. l
11. o
12. e
13. a
14. c
15. p
16. m

Short Answer

1.   (LO 1) Noninfluential and noncontrolling (less than 20%); influential but noncontrolling (20–50%); controlling (greater than 50%)

2.   (LO 1) Trading securities: debt or equity securities expected to be held for only a short period of time; held-to-maturity securities: debt securities expected to be held until their maturity date; available-for-sale securities: debt or equity securities that do not qualify as either trading securities or held-to-maturity securities

3.   (LO 3) Under the cost-adjusted-to-market method, Dividend Income is credited when dividends are received. Under the equity method, the Investment account is credited (reduced).

4.   (LO 4) When the cost exceeds the book value of the net assets purchased, any excess that is not assigned to specific assets and liabilities should be recorded as goodwill.

5.   (LO 4) Intercompany items are eliminated to avoid double-counting, as well as the presentation of misleading consolidated financial statements. For example, if intercompany receivables and payables were (incorrectly) included in consolidated financial statements, that portion would represent the amount that the combined companies owed themselves.

True-False

1.   T   (LO 3)

2.   F   (LO 3) The investor would do that under the equity method.

3.   F   (LO 4) Over 50 percent is the requirement for consolidated financial statements.

4.   T   (LO 4)

5.   T   (LO 2)

6.   F   (LO 3) The credit would be to the Investment account.

7.   F   (LO 4) Minority interest should be reported either in stockholders' equity or between long-term liabilities and stockholders' equity.

8.   T   (LO 4)

9.   F   (LO 4) Purchases of goods and services from outside parties should *not* be eliminated.

10. T   (LO 4)

11. F   (LO 5) They should be accounted for at amortized cost (cost adjusted for the effects of interest).

12. T   (LO 3)

13. F   (LO 1) It is legal in many countries.

14. T   (LO 2)

15. F   (LO 4) The correct elimination consists of a debit to Sales and a credit to Cost of Goods Sold.

Multiple Choice

1. b (LO 3) Under the cost-adjusted-to-market method of accounting for investments, dividends received are recorded as a source of income. The dividends are not used to adjust the value of the investment.

2. a (LO 4) The investment in the subsidiary company will be credited in making eliminations to prepare consolidated financial statements of the parent and subsidiary companies.

3. b (LO 4) Goodwill is used as a balancing figure on the consolidation of the parent and subsidiary companies. It does not appear on the unconsolidated financial statements of either company.

4. d (LO 4) Profit on goods sold by the subsidiary to outside parties is an income item that is part of the total income of the parent and subsidiary upon consolidation. It would not be eliminated during consolidation.

5. d (LO 3) The adjustment required to recognize a loss on long-term investments includes a debit to Unrealized Loss on Long-Term Investments and a credit to Allowance to Adjust Long-Term Investments to Market. Since the market value of the investment is $35,000 below the cost, and the allowance account has a credit balance of $10,000 (prior to adjustment), the adjustment for the current period will be for an additional $25,000.

6. a (LO 1) Trading securities are, by definition, expected to be sold in the short-run.

7. b (LO 3) Under the equity method, the Investment account is debited and the Investment Income account is credited to recognize the investor's portion of the investee's earnings.

8. c (LO 5) The proper entry debits the Investment account and credits Interest Income.

Exercises

1. (LO 4)

Date	Description	Debit	Credit
	General Journal		
	Common Stock (Day)	60,000	
	Retained Earnings (Day)	90,000	
	Building	10,000	
	Goodwill	35,000	
	Investment in Day Corporation		165,000
	Minority Interest		30,000
	Elimination that would appear on the consolidating work sheet		

2. (LO 3)

		General Journal		
Date		**Description**	**Debit**	**Credit**
		Cash	12,000	
		Dividend Income		12,000
		To record cash dividend from Ray* ($80,000 × 15%)		
		Cash	15,000	
		Investment in Marsh Company		15,000
		To record cash dividend from Marsh ($50,000 × 30%)		
		Investment in Marsh Company	19,500	
		Income, Marsh Company Investment		19,500
		To recognize 30% of income reported by Marsh Company ($65,000 × 30%)		

*Ray's earnings of $110,000 are irrelevant, since Bryant is using the cost-adjusted-to-market method to account for the investment.

3. (LO 2)

		General Journal		
Date		**Description**	**Debit**	**Credit**
Nov	17	Short-Term Investments	60,000	
		Cash		60,000
		Purchased Welu stock for trading		
Dec	31	Unrealized Loss on Investments	4,000	
		Allowance to Adjust Short-Term Investments to Market		4,000
Jan	12	Cash	66,000	
		Short-Term Investments		60,000
		Realized Gain on Investments		6,000
		To recognize sale of Welu stock		

Solution to
Crossword Puzzle: Chapters 13, 14, and 15